Beginning iOS
Social Games

Kyle Richter

Beginning iOS Social Games

ISBN-13 (pbk): 978-1-4302-4905-4

ISBN-13 (electronic): 978-1-4302-4906-1

President and Publisher: Paul Manning
Lead Editor: Steve Anglin
Developmental Editor: James Markham
Technical Reviewers: Marcus Zarra and Lucas Jordan
Editorial Board: Steve Anglin, Mark Beckner, Ewan Buckingham, Gary Cornell, Louise Corrigan, James DeWolf, Jonathan Gennick, Jonathan Hassell, Robert Hutchinson, Michelle Lowman, James Markham, Matthew Moodie, Jeff Olson, Jeffrey Pepper, Douglas Pundick, Ben Renow-Clarke, Dominic Shakeshaft, Gwenan Spearing, Matt Wade, Steve Weiss, Tom Welsh
Coordinating Editor: Jill Balzano
Copy Editor: James Compton
Compositor: SPi Global
Indexer: SPi Global
Artist: SPi Global
Cover Designer: Anna Ishchenko

Distributed to the book trade worldwide by Springer Science+Business Media New York, 233 Spring Street, 6th Floor, New York, NY 10013. Phone 1-800-SPRINGER, fax (201) 348-4505, e-mail orders-ny@springer-sbm.com, or visit www.springeronline.com. Apress Media, LLC is a California LLC and the sole member (owner) is Springer Science + Business Media Finance Inc (SSBM Finance Inc). SSBM Finance Inc is a Delaware corporation.

For information on translations, please e-mail rights@apress.com, or visit www.apress.com.

Apress and friends of ED books may be purchased in bulk for academic, corporate, or promotional use. eBook versions and licenses are also available for most titles. For more information, reference our Special Bulk Sales–eBook Licensing web page at www.apress.com/bulk-sales.

Any source code or other supplementary materials referenced by the author in this text is available to readers at www.apress.com. For detailed information about how to locate your book's source code, go to www.apress.com/source-code/.

This book is dedicated to the giants who came before us,
on whose shoulders we all stand.

Contents at a Glance

Contents

About the Author

Kyle Richter is the founder of Dragon Forged Software, an award-winning iOS and Mac development company, and co-founder of Empirical Development, a for-hire iOS shop. Kyle began writing code in the early 90s and has always been dedicated to the Mac platform. He is the author of Beginning iOS Game Center and Game Kit: For iPhone, iPad, and iPod touch and iOS Components (http://amzn.to/1fi9Zdt) and Frameworks: Understanding the Advanced Features of the iOS SDK (http://amzn.to/19rcIi0). Kyle also maintains a blog on the iOS development community, which can be found at http://KyleRichter.com. He manages a team of over 30 full-time iOS developers and runs day-to-day operations at two development companies. His early works include the first mobile location-based peer-to-peer service, the first iOS credit card processor, and the first multiplayer iOS game. Kyle travels the world speaking on development and entrepreneurship; currently he calls the Florida Keys his home, where he spends his time with his border collie. He can be found on Twitter @kylerichter.

About the Technical Reviewers

Marcus S. Zarra is co-owner of Empirical Development, LLC (http://empiricaldevelopment.com), based in Colorado. He has been developing Cocoa software since 2003 and Java software since 1996, and he has been in the industry since 1985. Currently Marcus is producing software for iOS and OS X. In addition to writing software, he assists other developers by blogging about development and supplying code samples on Cocoa Is My Girlfriend (http://www.cimgf.com). Marcus is also the author of *Core Data (2nd edition): Data Storage and Management for iOS, OS X, and iCloud* (http://pragprog.com/book/mzcd2/core-data) and co-author of *Core Animation: Simplified Animation Techniques for Mac and iPhone Development* (http:// amazon.com/Core-Animation-Simplified-Techniques-Development/dp/0321617754/ref=sr_1_1?ie=UTF8&qid=1307226039&sr=8-1). You can find Marcus on Twitter (https://twitter.com/mzarra), on App.net (https://alpha.app.net/mzarra), and on StackOverflow (http://stackoverflow.com/users/10673/marcus-s-zarra).

Lucas L. Jordan is a lifelong computer enthusiast who has worked for many years as a developer, with a focus on user interface. He is the author of *JavaFX Special Effects: Taking Java RIA to the Extreme with Animation, Multimedia, and Game Elements* and the co-author of *Practical Android Projects*, both by Apress. Lucas is interested in mobile application development in its many forms. He has recently quit his day job to pursue a career developing apps under the name ClayWare, LLC. Learn more at http://claywaregames.com.

Acknowledgments

Writing this book would not have been possible without the support and help of many people. Looking at the acknowledgments for any technical book shows that, while there may only be one author, there are dozens of people needed to ship a technical book such as this. First, I would like to thank Jordan Langille of Langille Design for taking time out of his busy schedule to provide the graphics for the sample program contained within.

I would also like to recognize Joe Keeley. Joe took a lot off my plate with Dragon Forged Software and Empirical Development to allow me the time required to write this book. If it had not been for Joe, I would not have been able to take myself away from my day-to-day work to get even a single chapter written.

Additionally I would also like to thank Marcus Zarra, who put his life on hold more often than I care to admit in writing to offer his expertise while technically reviewing this book. Marcus, an experienced writer himself, knows how much work goes into a technical book and without hesitation offered to review my work. I am also grateful to Lucas Jordan who took time out of his schedule in the 11th hour to help bring this book to completion. In addition, I would like to thank Nathan Eror of Free Time Studios for taking time out of his schedule to write the foreword.

Last but not least, I would like to thank the community as a whole. Never before in my life have I met such a supportive, outstanding group of people. From Cocoaheads and NSCoders, to conferences and forums, everyone has always been of the highest caliber. It is often said of the Apple development community that two competing developers can be friends and share code and secrets between each other. Whenever I've been stuck on a seemingly unsurmountable problem, there has always been someone there to help me through it. Throughout all my years of development and my travels across the globe, I have never met another group of people as awesome as the Apple development community, without whom I might have never shipped my first app

Foreword: Better With Friends

Games are social by nature. Games are a form of play, and play is always more fun and rewarding in groups. Even video games. I have fond memories of dumping bundles of quarters into machines at the arcade with my friends, and I still can't bring myself to get rid of my NES, which saw countless hours of multiplayer action. It is virtually impossible for me to separate the experience of those games from the people I shared them with. Before we began to bury our faces into our iPhones, the most personal of devices, sharing and camaraderie were part of the video game experience.

At their hearts, the iPhone and iPad are communication devices, and we should take advantage of their nature when designing our iOS games. Thankfully, Apple agrees, and it has provided powerful APIs that open up a world of social interaction when wielded correctly. It's that wielding where Kyle and this book come in.

When it comes to iOS, especially social iOS games, Kyle Richter is your man. He gave us Trivium, arguably the first social game on the platform. Before Apple provided any API for social games, Kyle was walking 10 miles, uphill, in the snow, barefoot to give gamers the social experience we crave. His experience runs deep, and his passion for games is matched only by his passion for iOS. He is also a wonderful teacher, and we get to benefit from all of this in the following pages.

I love reading technical books because I always learn something new. This book is no exception. Game Kit and Game Center are filled to the brim with fun, powerful, easy-to-use APIs. I guarantee you will learn something new as you progress through the book, just like I did.

A personal favorite topic of mine is Turn-Based Gaming (Chapter 9). Asynchronous, turn-based games are natural on mobile devices, but the overhead of running back-end services make such games difficult to build. The turn-based game API in GameKit takes the plumbing out of the equation and allows you to focus on making your game fun.

Another favorite topic of mine, Voice Chat (Chapter 10), is one of the unsung heroes of GameKit. I am still surprised at how few games take advantage of voice chat. Thanks to this book, you have no excuse.

After June 2013, no iOS game development book would be complete without a discussion about the new Game Controller framework, and Kyle gives us an entire chapter (Chapter 15). Pair game controller support with AirPlay to an Apple TV (Chapter 14), and you have a full-fledged console game. No need to buy extra controllers. Your friends carry their controllers with them everywhere. Who needs a $300+ dedicated console?

Games, like words, are better with friends, and even if you don't have any friends, Matchmaking (Chapter 5) will help you find some. Thanks to Kyle and this book, your players can enjoy your games with their friends. Get to work!

Nathan Eror
Founder, Free Time Studios

Introduction

Mobile games are social and becoming more integrated into our social lives every day. Game Center and Game Kit are Apple's answers to integrating social aspects into iOS games, making it easier than it has ever been before to add items like leaderboards, achievements, multiplayer, and voice chat. Social network integration exists on everything from cars to refrigerators, and adding Twitter and Facebook support to an iOS game has become just about a requirement. Airplay and game controllers may be the next great leap forward in mobile gaming, if history has taught us anything; those that are a step ahead of the future are positioned for success.

Prerequisites

This book assumes that you have the basic skills and understanding required to create an iOS app. It also assumes that you have the background necessary to work with Xcode 5.0. There will be no primer on how to define methods and variables, install and launch Xcode, or create and work with new classes. There are many excellent books on those topics. When you feel ready to begin working with some of the more advanced Cocoa technologies such as Game Center and Game Kit, be sure that you have the basics mastered to a degree that allows you to move through this book without consulting other texts for help.

In addition to the basic requirements, Game Center and the other frameworks covered also heavily leverage blocks, which are a fairly new programming concept to Objective-C. If you haven't yet worked with blocks, we recommend that you read Apple's guide to them, which you can find by searching for *blocks* at http://developer.apple.com. You should also feel comfortable working with all the features that were introduced with the Objective-C 2.0 release.

How This Book Is Organized

As you begin working through this book, you will notice that its chapters are essentially standalone. Every effort has been made so that each chapter can be read independently of the others. If you have no experience with Game Center or Game Kit yet, it is highly recommended that you read the first two chapters before skipping around, as they will provide you with the basic information on how to get Game Center and Game Kit up and running in your development environment. The final four chapters are built on top of the sample code from Chapter 3 and do not continually build on the existing product.

Each chapter follows along with a simple sample iOS game that is introduced in Chapter 1. Following along with the book from start to finish will walk you through the process of creating a fully functional Game Center and Game Kit–leveraged iOS game. In addition, each chapter will build onto a Game Center Manager class that is designed to be reusable across all of your projects. Chapters 12 and 13 will introduce you to Social Framework and adding Twitter and Facebook support to the sample game. Chapters 14 and 15 cover Airplay and Game Controllers.

If you already have a background in general iOS development or Game Center and are looking for help on a specific technology, each chapter is designed to walk you through its covered technology, as well as provide samples showing how to apply the technology to your software.

Source Code

The source code for the projects found in this book is available at www.apress.com/source-code/. Source code is made available in both ARC (Automatic Reference Counting) and non-ARC formats. The code examples used in the text of this book are non-ARC; this is done because it is easier to add ARC support then to remove it. While ARC is quickly becoming the standard there are developers, managers, and projects, which for one reason or another are not ARC ready yet.

Required Software, Materials, and Equipment

To develop iOS software—and more specifically, Game Center and Game Kit–based iOS software—you will first need an Intel-based Mac computer running OSX 10.8 (Mountain Lion) or newer. While you can develop on 10.6, it will not support the most up-to-date release of Xcode. You will also need a copy of Xcode, which you can download free from the Mac App Store or at http://developer.apple.com. This book has been targeted to work with iOS 7; since it is being released at the time when users will be migrating from iOS 6 to iOS 7, it is also written to support iOS 6. Unless otherwise noted within the text, all code is iOS 6–compatible.

In addition to the software and hardware requirements, you will also need an iOS developer account provided by Apple. This account lets you build and test software on devices, as well as ship your finished product to the App Store. The software developer account is available for $99 USD a year and you can purchase yours at http://developer.apple.com/iPhone.

Getting Started with Social Gaming

Welcome to *Beginning iOS Social Games*! This book is designed to walk you through the process of adding Game Kit, Game Center, and other social functionality into your iOS apps and games. It is centered on a sample game called UFOs that you will be introduced to later in this chapter. However, if you have an existing app or game to which you want to add social functionality, you may use that project instead. This book is written as a reference and resource tool to aid you in the process of adding social functions into your iOS app. Although I recommend you read it from beginning to end to learn the most about the technologies covered, that is not a requirement. Every chapter stands on its own. You can freely skip ahead to the chapters that are relevant to your project needs and quickly implement that functionality into your app.

While this book covers a number of aspects of social gaming, its focus is Apple's social gaming platform Game Kit, and by extension Game Center. When Apple announced Game Kit on March 17, 2009, it was presented as an answer to the difficulty of real-time networking on iOS devices, which until that point had been challenging. Game Kit added support for Bluetooth and LAN as well as voice chat services. Shortly after, Apple announced the Game Center addition to Game Kit as part of iOS 4.0. With the newly announced SDK version, Apple brought a wealth of new features—the Game Center being the most important to the scope of this book. With iOS 5, Game Center once again saw additions, most notably the addition of turn-based gaming to the framework. Apple continued the tradition of supporting Game Center in iOS 6 with the addition of Game Center Challenges. In addition to the Game Center changes, Apple added OS-level support for Twitter in iOS 5 and for Facebook in iOS 6. With the introduction of iOS 7 at WWDC 2013 Game Center saw a complete redesign from the ground up to match the flatter look and feel introduced with UIKit.

Commonly developers in the iOS community have a tendency to think of Game Center as a separate set of Application Programming Interfaces (APIs). This is a fallacy. Game Center is an integral part of Game Kit. The two complement one another and work hand in hand. You will see much evidence of this in the following pages. For the purpose of this book, we are going to address both of these technologies together as Game Kit; however, we may still refer to Game Center–specific functionality by its proper name.

The first ten chapters of this book are dedicated to Game Kit functionality; the remaining chapters cover additional social elements such as Store Kit and In App Purchasing in Chapter 11, Twitter and Facebook sharing in Chapters 12 and 13, Airplay mirroring in Chapter 14, and iOS 7 Game Controllers in chapter 15.

Please note that despite their names, Game Kit and Game Center are not designed for just games. Although recently Apple has begun cracking down on Game Center technology being used in non-games. Some developers have received the following type of rejection email from Apple.

"The intended use of Game Center is to complement game apps or game functionality within an app. However, we noticed that your app does not contain any game play or game features."

These rejections seem to apply mainly to the use of leaderboards and achievements in non-gaming apps. The argument can easily be made that adding a leaderboard or achievement system to your app adds a gameplay element. If you happen to receive this rejection you still have the option of appealing it, I have yet to hear from a developer who has not successfully appealed on these grounds. There haven't been any instances of rejection for using Game Kit networking in any app that I have observed.

Game Kit: An Overview

Game Kit can be broken up into three individual sections: networking, Game Center, and voice chat. Although all of these services work together to create one seamless environment, it can be helpful to look at each individually. While there might be overlap, each section can be considered as a primary category. While the API itself does not differentiate these sections, it can be useful to keep them separate while learning and thinking about Game Kit development.

Networking

Networking in Game Kit allows you to send and receive data between one or more peers. Game Kit networking also provides a connection protocol to connect to local clients that are found on your Wi-Fi network, or locally using Bluetooth. Game Center also extends this functionality with WAN matchmaking.

Game Kit supports creating an ad-hoc Bluetooth or local wireless network between two iOS devices. With the introduction of iOS 4.0, Game Kit began supporting networking on the world area network supporting up to 16 players at once. Game Kit networking is covered in Chapters 6, 7, and 8. Game Center matchmaking is covered in Chapter 5.

Game Center

Game Center handles authentication, friends, leaderboards, achievements, challenges, and invitations. In a sense, Game Center is providing the developer with the server services that are related to social interaction. It can also be argued that Game Center contains its own networking system. While this is true, we will be grouping that topic in the preceding section on networking, which is covered extensively in Chapter 5. Game Center technologies, such as leaderboards and achievements, are covered in Chapters 3 and 4.

> **Note**   The term *Game Center*, as used in various print and reference documentation, sometimes refers to the collective set of Game Center APIs as well as to the Game Center app itself.

Voice Chat

"Game Voice," as Apple refers to it, allows any app (not just games) to provide voice communication over a network connection. The APIs handle the capturing and playback of audio feeds for the user and provide services to handle connections, communications, errors, and disconnections. This technology is discussed in Chapter 10.

Sample Game: UFOs

In my experience, most developers are "experience-type" learners. This means that they learn best by doing, not by watching or listening. When I first started to learn how to program, I would copy source code out of code magazines line by line into a Commodore 64. The experience of physically typing in each line of code is what made the information stick. Listening to a lecture or watching someone else write code made it difficult to retain a good deal of the information. I can't imagine I would have stayed with this career path if lectures and demonstrations were my only ways of learning. This book is designed in the spirit of experience-type learners.

The first thing we need to cover, before moving into Game Kit itself, is working with the supplied sample game. The game, which we call "UFOs," is designed not to be an award-winning, addictive game, but rather to be simple enough that it can be thought of as any generic project, and allow you to focus on the social gaming aspects. I have made every effort to reduce the amount of code to less than 300 lines. Although the game itself is simple, it is vital that all readers understand the code as if they wrote it themselves. Keeping the example simple will allow you, as the reader, to detach yourself from the project itself and focus on the Game Kit–specific information. We start by playing the game, then looking at the source code.

> **Note**   The source code for all the chapters, as well as the sample project, is available at www.apress.com. The sample code is provided in two formats: one that supports Automatic Reference Counting (ARC) environments, a feature added in iOS 5, and one using the manual memory management system. Other than support for ARC, these projects are identical.
>
> It is important to note that the sample code that appears in print is the non-ARC version. If you are using ARC, you will need to make adjustments. For more information, see the Apple article on transitioning to ARC at http://developer.apple.com/library/ios/#releasenotes/ObjectiveC/ RN-TransitioningToARC/Introduction/Introduction.html.

UFOs: Understanding the Game

The first thing you need to do is open the base project that you downloaded from apress.com. Figure 1-1 shows the file structure for the project. We'll quickly run the game to see what it's like.

Name		Date Modified
▶	Art Assets	Today, 2:57 PM
▶	build	Today, 2:57 PM
▶	Classes	Today, 2:56 PM
m	main.m	Today, 2:56 PM
	MainWindow	Today, 2:58 PM
h	UFOs_Prefix.pch	Today, 2:56 PM
	UFOs–Info.plist	Today, 2:59 PM
	UFOs.xcodeproj	Today, 2:59 PM

Figure 1-1. The file structure for the UFO sample project, as seen by the Finder

To play the game, select Build and Run from Build menu bar. The game will launch to a generic screen with one button labeled "Play." Go ahead and select the Play button. You will be taken to the game screen, as seen in Figure 1-2.

Figure 1-2. A look at the gameplay view from the UFOs sample project

The objective of the game is typical; tilt the device up/down or left/right to move your ship around the screen. Once you are positioned over a cow, tap anywhere on the screen and hold until the cow has been abducted. You are awarded one point for every cow you abduct. There is no ending to the game. Every time you abduct a cow, a new one will be created and placed on the grass.

Now that you understand how the game is played, you can take a look at the source code that powers the game engine.

UFOs: Examining the Source Code

In your group tree, you will see the three class files we will be working with, UFOAppDelegate, UFOViewController, and UFOGameViewController. These files all have an associated header (.h file) and implementation file (.m file). The group tree is shown in Figure 1-3.

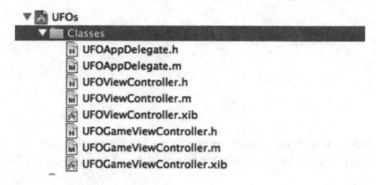

Figure 1-3. *A look at the group tree structure for the sample project from within Xcode*

First, take a look at the UFOAppDelegate.h and UFOAppDelegate.m files. These should look familiar to you from other iOS development work. They are nothing more than a base UINavgiationController subclass. If you need to familiarize yourself with the code found here, take a look at Apple's Sample Code for new projects (https://developer.apple.com/library/ios/navigation/#section=Resource%20 Types&topic=Sample%20Code).

The next group of files is also relatively simple; take a look at UFOViewController.h and UFOViewController.m. These are the associated classes for the landing or home screen. All that we have here right now is a play button, but we will be adding leaderboards, achievement, and multiplayer controls to this view as we progress through this book.

Finally, we will be working with UFOGameViewController.m. This is the main class that will be powering all gameplay, and it is where the majority of the Game Kit functionality will be added.

Setting Up the Accelerometer Delegate

We will start at the top of the source file you downloaded and work our way through it; open the UFOGameViewController file in Xcode. We have modified the init method of the UFOGameController to register for accelerometer feedback. Take a look at the following code snippet, which is discussed in detail next.

```
- (id)init
{
    if (self != [super init]) {
        return nil;
    }
}
```

```
self.motionManager = [[CMMotionManager alloc] init];
self.motionManager.accelerometerUpdateInterval = 0.05;

[self.motionManager startAccelerometerUpdatesToQueue:[NSOperationQueue currentQueue]
withHandler:^(CMAccelerometerData  *accelerometerData, NSError *error)
{
    [self motionOccurred:accelerometerData];
    if(error)
    {
        NSLog(@"%@", error);
    }
}];

    return self;
}
```

We will be using the core motion framework for capturing accelerometer data and moving the character. The input frequency is set to 0.05 seconds, which will provide a very fluid reactive control system.

Next, take a look at the -viewDidLoad method. Let's break this down into sections to understand exactly what is going on here.

```
accelerometerDamp = 0.3f;
accelerometerOAngle = 0.6f;
movementSpeed = 15;
```

Here we set some class variables to hold onto some data that we will need when we begin to process the accelerometer input. We will be working with these variables again when we start to deal with ship movement. For now, you don't need to understand exactly what they are doing, just that they have been set. A new method is created called motionOccurred which will be invoked by the core motion framework to handle tilt input. The previously defined damping methods are applied and the information is passed to the movePlayer: method, which will be discussed in the following sections.

```
-(void)motionOccurred:(CMAccelerometerData *)accelerometerData;
{
    //Use a basic low-pass filter to only keep the gravity in the accelerometer values
        accel[0] = accelerometerData.acceleration.x * accelerometerDamp + accel[0] *
(1.0 - accelerometerDamp);
        accel[1] = accelerometerData.acceleration.y * accelerometerDamp + accel[1] *
(1.0 - accelerometerDamp);
        accel[2] = accelerometerData.acceleration.z * accelerometerDamp + accel[2] *
(1.0 - accelerometerDamp);

        if(!tractorBeamOn)
                [self movePlayer:accel[0] :accel[1]];
}
```

Drawing the Player to the View

Next we need to create our "player:"

```
CGRect playerFrame = CGRectMake(100, 70, 80, 34);

myPlayerImageView = [[UIImageView alloc] initWithFrame: playerFrame];
[myPlayerImageView setAnimationDuration:0.75];
[myPlayerImageView setAnimationRepeatCount:99999];
NSArray *imageArray = [NSArray arrayWithObjects: [UIImage imageNamed: @"Saucer1.png"],↵
 [UIImage imageNamed: @"Saucer2.png"], nil];
[myPlayerImageView setAnimationImages:imageArray];
[myPlayerImageView startAnimating];
[self.view addSubview: myPlayerImageView];
```

To do this, we create a new UIImageView and initialize it with a predefined frame. The next four lines of code are a little-known, but very useful, part of UIImageView. We are setting an array of images that the UIImageView will cycle through. In this example, we set two images to be rotated through. We also specify how long we want the full animation to take (3/4 second for our purposes), and the number of times we want the animation to repeat. Once we have set up the animation details, we call startAnimating on the UIImageView. Then, all that is left for us to do is add the UIImageView to the main view. Now we have a player on the screen that is animating!

Setting Up Cows, Beams, and Scores

There are a number of game play elements that we need to create and display. We will begin by creating the score label that will inform the user of their progress while playing.

```
cowArray = [[NSMutableArray alloc] init];
tractorBeamImageView = [[UIImageView alloc] initWithFrame: CGRectZero];
score = 0;
[scoreLabel setText:[NSString stringWithFormat: @"SCORE %05.0f", score]];
```

The score label itself has already been placed on the view using Interface Builder.

```
For (int x = 0; x < 5; x++) {
        [self spawnCow];
}

[self updateCowPaths];
```

The last thing we need to do in the viewDidLoad method is create some cows for placement on the screen. There is a helper method to spawn these cows. Every time it is called, it will create a new cow and place it on the screen. We will take a look at this a little later in this section. We also call another helper method to update the walking path for the cows, and we will look at this method in depth later in this section.

Handling Rotation Events

The next method that appears in our code is shouldAutorotateToInterfaceOrientation, listed here:

```
-
(BOOL)shouldAutorotateToInterfaceOrientation:(UIInterfaceOrientation)↵
interfaceOrientation
{
        if (UIInterfaceOrientationIsLandscape(interfaceOrientation)) {
                return YES;
        }

        return NO;
}
```

While this may appear to be a minor piece of code, it is important to make sure the game doesn't allow the user to rotate into portrait mode, while allowing the user to play in either landscape orientation.

Adding Player Movements

That takes care of all the initialization and setup code. Now we can move into the more exciting parts of the game. First we need to look at user input and actions, and then the gameplay functionality.

```
- (void)accelerometer:(UIAccelerometer *)accelerometer didAccelerate:(UIAcceleration↵
 *)acceleration
{
        accel[0] = acceleration.x * accelerometerDamp + accel[0] * (1.0 -↵
accelerometerDamp);
        accel[1] = acceleration.y * accelerometerDamp + accel[1] * (1.0 -↵
accelerometerDamp);
        accel[2] = acceleration.z * accelerometerDamp + accel[2] * (1.0 -↵
accelerometerDamp);

        if (!tractorBeamOn) {
                [self movePlayer:accel[0] :accel[1]];
        }
}
```

The first method to look at is the accelerometer delegate method. We are taking the values of the accelerometer and applying a dampener to them to give a more realistic feel. We then perform a test to make sure that the tractor beam is off (we don't want to be able to move the UFO if it is on), and then pass the values to our movePlayer method, which is shown next.

```
- (void)movePlayer:(float)vertical:(float)horizontal;
{
        vertical += accelerometerOAngle;
```

```
if (vertical > .50)
{
        vertical = .50;
}
else if (vertical < -.50)
{
        vertical = -.50;
}

if (horizontal > .50)
{
        horizontal = .50;
}
else if (horizontal < -.50)
{
        horizontal = -.50;
}
CGRect playerFrame = myPlayerImageView.frame;

if ((vertical < 0 && playerFrame.origin.y < 120) || (vertical > 0 &&↵
playerFrame.origin.y > 20))
{
        playerFrame.origin.y -= vertical*movementSpeed;
}

if ((horizontal < 0 && playerFrame.origin.x < 440) || (horizontal > 0 &&↵
playerFrame.origin.x > 0))
{
        playerFrame.origin.x -= horizontal*movementSpeed;
}

myPlayerImageView.frame = playerFrame;
}
```

This method is much simpler than you might think at first glance. The first chunk of code sets our maximum speed. The next section ensures that the user cannot move their UFO off the screen. Once we have passed both of these safety checks, we update the player's frame, which moves the UFO.

Watching for Touch Events

The next aspect of the game that we need to worry about is touch events. We will be using a touch to initiate and control the tractor beam. The first step is overriding the touchesBegan event.

```
- (void)touchesBegan:(NSSet *)touches withEvent:(UIEvent *)event
{
        currentAbductee = nil;

        tractorBeamOn = YES;
```

```
tractorBeamImageView.frame = CGRectMake(myPlayerImageView.frame.origin.x+25,↵
 myPlayerImageView.frame.origin.y+10, 28, 318);
        tractorBeamImageView.animationDuration = 0.5;
        tractorBeamImageView.animationRepeatCount = 99999;
NSArray *imageArray = [NSArray arrayWithObjects: [UIImage imageNamed:↵
 @"Tractor1.png"], [UIImage imageNamed: @"Tractor2.png"], nil];

        tractorBeamImageView.animationImages = imageArray;
        [tractorBeamImageView startAnimating];

        [self.view insertSubview:tractorBeamImageView atIndex:4];

        UIImageView *cowImageView = [self hitTest];

        If (cowImageView)
        {
                currentAbductee = cowImageView;
                [self abductCow: cowImageView];
        }

}
```

We first clear out the pointer to the current abducted cow. This value should be nil already, but it is best to be diligent. We then set a BOOL for whether the tractor beam is on to YES. At this point, we need to draw the tractor beam. To do this, we set the frame for our tractorBeamImageView to where the player's UFO is currently located. We will be using the same animation shortcut that was discussed earlier in this section to animate the tractor beam. We then add the tractor beam imageView to the main view; we use an insertSubview method here to make sure the tractor beam is below the cows but above the background. Then we call our hitTest method, which we will look at a little later in this chapter. If we get a result back from the hitTest, we call the abductCow method.

Before we can move on to the hitTest and abductCow methods, we must first finish handling the touch events. The only other touch event that we are concerned with at this point is the touchesEnded delegate call. When the user removes their finger from the screen, we want to remove the tractor beam from the view and let the user resume movement.

```
- (void)touchesEnded:(NSSet *)touches withEvent:(UIEvent *)event
{
        tractorBeamOn = NO;

        [tractorBeamImageView removeFromSuperview];

        if (currentAbductee) {
[UIView beginAnimations: @"dropCow" context:nil];
                [UIView setAnimationDuration: 1.0];
                [UIView setAnimationCurve:UIViewAnimationCurveEaseIn];
                [UIView setAnimationBeginsFromCurrentState: YES];

                CGRect frame = currentAbductee.frame;
```

```
        frame.origin.y = 260;
        frame.origin.x = myPlayerImageView.frame.origin.x +15;

        currentAbductee.frame = frame;

        [UIView commitAnimations];
    }

    currentAbductee = nil;
}
```

Set your state variable for the `tractorBeamOn` to NO. Then we can remove the tractor beam image from the view. The next section of code drops the cow back to the ground (if there was one midway in the air). To do this, we just begin a simple animation where we return the cow to ground level. The last thing we need to do is reset the `currentAbductee` pointer to `nil`.

Spawning and Moving Cows

We also have a convenient method to spawn a new cow. This is the method we call from `viewDidLoad` to give the player a base number of cows to try to abduct; we also call it whenever we are finished abducting a cow.

```
- (void)spawnCow;
{
        UIImageView *cowImageView = [[UIImageView alloc] initWithFrame:CGRectMake ↵
(arc4random()%480, 260, 64, 42)];

        cowImageView.image = [UIImage imageNamed: @"Cow1.png"];
        [[self view] addSubview: cowImageView];
        [cowArray addObject: cowImageView];

        [cowImageView release];
}
```

> **Tip** The `arc4Random()` function will return a random number the same way that `rand()` or `random()` will, but it will automatically seed itself when called for the first time.

We create a new `imageView` that will represent the cow. We then use an `arc4Random()` function to produce a random x position. We set the image that the cow will be using and add it to the main view. The last thing we need to do here is add the `imageView` to our `cowArray`. We will be using this for a hit test as well as updating the movement paths.

While UFOs is not designed to be an extremely challenging game, we do want to add at least some aspects of difficulty to the gameplay. The following method will cause our cows to wander randomly around the screen.

```objc
- (void)updateCowPaths
{
        for (int x = 0; x < [cowArray count]; x++) {
UIImageView *tempCow = [cowArray objectAtIndex: x];

                If (tempCow != currentAbductee) {
continue;
                }

                [UIView beginAnimations:@"cowWalk" context:nil];
                [UIView setAnimationDuration: 3.0];

  [UIView setAnimationCurve:UIViewAnimationCurveLinear];

                float currentX = tempCow.frame.origin.x;
                float newX = currentX + arc4random()%100-50;

                if (newX > 480) {
                        newX = 480;
                }
                if (newX < 0) {
                        newX = 0;
                }

                if (tempCow != currentAbductee) {
                        tempCow.frame = CGRectMake(newX, 260, 64, 42);
                }

                [UIView commitAnimations];

                tempCow.animationDuration = 0.75;
                tempCow.animationRepeatCount = 99999;

                //flip cow
                if (newX < currentX) {
NSArray *flippedCowImageArray = [NSArray arrayWithObjects:↲
 [UIImage imageNamed: @"Cow1Reversed.png"], [UIImage imageNamed: @"Cow2Reversed.png"],↲
 [UIImage imageNamed: @"Cow3Reversed.png"], nil];

        [tempCow setAnimationImages:flippedCowImageArray];
} else {
NSArray *cowImageArray = [NSArray arrayWithObjects: [UIImage imageNamed:↲
 @"Cow1.png"], [UIImage imageNamed: @"Cow2.png"], [UIImage imageNamed: @"Cow3.png"], nil];
        [tempCow setAnimationImages:cowImageArray];
}

                [tempCow startAnimating];
                }
        }

        //change the paths for the cows every 3 seconds
        [self performSelector:@selector(updateCowPaths) withObject:nil afterDelay:3.0];
}
```

In the first line of the updateCowPaths method, we cycle through our array of cow objects. We then randomize a new x position for the cow. A quick check ensures that we are not instructing the cow to walk off the screen. Then we commit the animation. We also need to handle the direction change for the cow.

> **Note** The code that we use to handle that event is not the most efficient way of flipping an image, but it is the easiest to learn if you are new to this type of game.

As we did previously with the tractor beam and the UFO images, we will add some animation frames so the cows appear more interesting. The last thing we do is call performSelector with a delay of three seconds. This will update the cow's path every three seconds, adding a slightly more challenging movement system.

Performing a Hit Test with a UIImage

Before we worry about how to set up the cow abduction, there are preliminary steps for abducting the cow itself. For starters, we must implement a hitTest method that is being called from the touchesBegan event discussed earlier in this section.

```
- (UIImageView*)hitTest
{
        if (!tractorBeamOn) {
                return nil;
        }

        for (int x = 0; x < [cowArray count]; x++) {
UIImageView *tempCow = [cowArray objectAtIndex: x];
                CALayer *cowLayer= [[tempCow layer] presentationLayer];
                CGRect cowFrame = [cowLayer frame];

                if (CGRectIntersectsRect(cowFrame, tractorBeamImageView.frame)) {
tempCow.frame = cowLayer.frame;
                        [tempCow.layer removeAllAnimations];
                        return tempCow;
                }
        }

        return nil;
}
```

The first line is another sanity check, this time to ensure that we are not calling the hitTest method when the tractorBeam is not on. Once we know we are supposed to be checking for the hit, we iterate through our array of cow objects. Since the cows are in the middle of an animation, we cannot rely on the data from the frame, as it will show where the cow will end up and not where the cow currently is.

To determine where the cow currently is, we ask for the presentationLayer. Core Graphics provides a useful method for testing whether two GCRects intersect, and that is what we will be using here. If we hit a cow, we return the object. If we get to the end of our loop without passing a hit test, we return nil.

> **Tip** The presentationLayer method can be called on any CALayer to provide a best guess for the current values of a layer that is in the process of being animated.

Abducting a Cow

In our touchesBegan method, we tested to see if hitTest returned a cow. If it did, we call abductCow with the object that was returned. Here's the code:

```
- (void)abductCow:(UIImageView *)cowImageView;
{
        [UIView beginAnimations: @"abduct" context:nil];
        [UIView setAnimationDuration: 4.0];
        [UIView setAnimationCurve:UIViewAnimationCurveEaseIn];
        [UIView setAnimationDelegate: self];
        [UIView setAnimationDidStopSelector: @selector(finishAbducting)];
        [UIView setAnimationBeginsFromCurrentState: YES];

        CGRect frame = cowImageView.frame;
        frame.origin.y = myPlayerImageView.frame.origin.y;
        cowImageView.frame = frame;

        [UIView commitAnimations];
}
```

We begin an animation event on our cow object (which is an imageView). We also set a didStopSelector, which will be called once the animation has finished. We set the new y axis coordinate for the cow to our UFO's current y coordinate and begin the animation.

Once the animation has stopped, we get a callback to finishAbducting. This allows us to increase the score, clean up the abducting code, and spawn a new cow.

```
- (void)finishAbducting;
{
        if (!currentAbductee || !tractorBeamOn) {
return;
        }

        [cowArray removeObjectIdenticalTo: currentAbductee];
        [tractorBeamImageView removeFromSuperview];

        tractorBeamOn = NO;
```

```
score++;
[scoreLabel setText:[NSString stringWithFormat: @"SCORE %05.0f", score]];

[[currentAbductee layer] removeAllAnimations];
[currentAbductee removeFromSuperview];

currentAbductee = nil;

//make a new cow
[self spawnCow];
}
```

At the beginning of the method, we check to see that the tractor beam is still on and that we have an abductee. Just as we did when the user released their touch from the screen, we also want to remove the tractor beam image from the view and correctly set the state variables. We award the user with a single point for abducting a cow, and we update the scoreLabel accordingly. We clean up the old cow image and set it back to nil. Now we spawn a new cow to replace the abducted one.

Configuring iTunes Connect for Game Center

Before your iOS app or game can access any of the Game Center functionality, it will need to be configured in iTunes Connect. iTunes Connect predates the App Store and iPhone; it was introduced as the portal for musicians and media producers to upload their content to the iTunes Music Store. It has since been adapted to allow developers to upload their iOS software for sale on the App Store. iTunes Connect has evolved tremendously since being offered to iPhone developers in July of 2008. Apple has begun using it as a main source for app configuration. Such tools as In App Purchase (IAP), iAds, and Game Center require iTunes Connect configuration.

Note   You can still use any stand-alone Game Kit functionality without setting up Game Center for your app. See Chapters 6, 7, 8, and 10 for more information on Game Kit's stand-alone functionality.

Getting Started with iTunes Connect

If you have never uploaded an app to the App Store, you might be unfamiliar with the iTunes Connect Portal. However, if you have worked with iTunes Connect previously, you might want to skip to the next section, "Configuring Game Center in iTunes Connect," as the following will be only a refresher for you.

iTunes Connect is a web portal, accessed from any web browser at http://itunesconnect.apple.com. You will use your existing AppleID, which you used to register as a developer (http://developer.apple.com), to gain access to the portal. This is the same web application that you will use when you want to upload new apps for sale on the App Store, as well as make any changes to them, such as price or description. A view of the landing page for iTunes Connect can be seen in Figure 1-4.

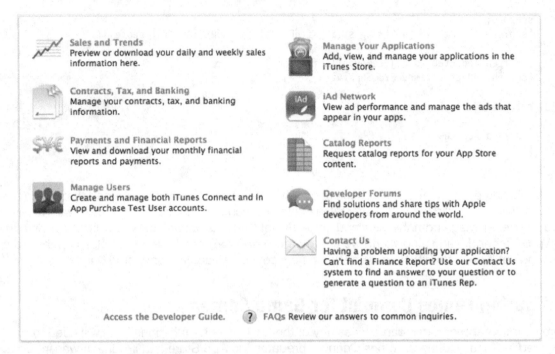

Figure 1-4. A view of iTunes Connect taken July 2013

When you log in to iTunes Connect, you will be presented with a wealth of options. The most important of these is setting up your contracts, tax, and banking information. While these requirements do not have anything to do with Game Center per se, it is good to get them out of the way.

It may take weeks for Apple to process this information, so submit it as soon as possible. Until this information is processed and approved, you will be unable to release software on the App Store. Once you have completed all the requested information under this section, you can focus on the app development itself.

> **Note**   If you plan on releasing only free iOS apps, you do not need to complete the paid apps contracts.
> However, if you plan to release any paid software in the future, these should be completed as soon as possible.

Before you can access any Game Center–specific information, you will need to create a new iOS app (or use an existing one). This is a straightforward process that you will be walked through in iTunes Connect. You begin under the Manage Your Applications section; there you will find an "Add New App" button. The rest should be fairly self-explanatory.

If you are not yet ready to upload an app, you can create placeholder data here to gain access to the Game Center portal. Once your app has been created in iTunes Connect, you can begin to configure the Game Center–specific information.

Caution   If you create an app and fail to upload a release build within 90 days, Apple will delete the app information and restrict you from creating a new app with the same name in the future. This was introduced in late 2010 as an effort to prevent people from "Domain Squatting" app names.

Configuring Game Center in iTunes Connect

Once you have created and selected your app from within iTunes Connect, you will see a view similar to Figure 1-5. In the upper-right area of the app screen, you will notice a Manage Game Center button.

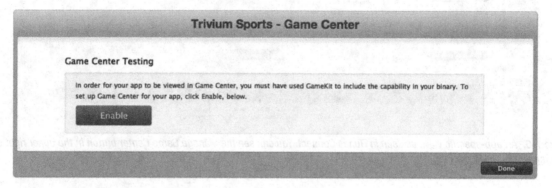

Figure 1-5.   The first view of the Game Center portal for a new app

If you are familiar with configuring iAds or In App Purchase in previous iOS apps, this area will seem very familiar to you. The process for configuring iAds and IAP is similar to working with Game Center.

When entering the Game Center portal for your app for the first time, you will be asked if you want to enable Game Center, as shown in Figure 1-5. Once it is enabled, you will be given an option to add a new leaderboard or achievement. We will focus on these options more in later chapters (Chapter 3 covers leaderboards, and Chapter 4 covers achievements). For now, all we need to do is ensure that Game Center is enabled for our app.

Tip   If you are having difficulty getting your app to acknowledge Game Center, the most likely culprit is one of two common issues. Make sure your app is using the same bundle ID that is shown in the App Info page (see Figure 1-6). The second issue may be that you have not let enough time pass. There can be up to a 30-minute delay between making changes in iTunes Connect to Game Center and having the iOS app notice those changes.

Figure 1-6. *An app-specific view, as seen in iTunes Connect. You can see the Manage Game Center button in the upper right of the image*

Summary

You should now have a basic understanding of what Game Kit and Game Center have to offer, as well as an in-depth understanding of the sample project you will be working with throughout this book. Additionally, you should now be comfortable setting up a new app in iTunes Connect for use with Game Center.

In the upcoming chapters, you will learn how to incorporate all the functionality of Game Center, Game Kit, and other social features into an iOS app. The iOS-based device families are just starting to emerge from infancy, and Game Center is the first next-generation API that has been made available for developers. These new technologies are a glimpse at what the future holds for iOS developers. In the next chapter, you will learn how to get Game Center incorporated into a project.

Game Center: Setting Up and Getting Started

Like many of Apple's integrated technologies (iCloud, Push Notifications, Passbook), Game Center requires some standard overhead before you can really begin to use it. Game Center is a large and diverse technology that easily adds very complex functionality into your social app. Once you have accomplished these basic steps it will be safe to jump to any Game Center chapter and implement functionality specific to your app.

In Chapter 1, you learned how to configure Game Center in iTunes Connect and began working with the sample project, UFOs. In this chapter, we will discuss integrating Game Center into our app, and get our hands dirty with some Game Center specific code.

You will learn how to detect Game Center compatibility, explore the limitations of the sandbox, authenticate a local player, work with sessions, and retrieve a friends list. You will also create the GameCenterManager class that we will be working with throughout the remanding Game Kit chapters.

Testing for Game Center

Before any Game Center–specific code can be called, we need to perform a test to verify that the user has a version of iOS that supports Game Center. The first thing we need to do to perform this check is to create our new GameCenterManager class. We will use this class throughout the remainder of this book to keep our Game Center functionality in one easy-to-access class. This class will house all of our Game Center–specific code and callbacks, and it can be easily shared across all of your apps. Most modern apps will be targeting iOS 5 and higher and a Game Center check does not need to be performed, however if your app is still targetting iOS 4 you should verfiy Game Center is installed.

First, create a new file in Xcode. You will want to select the Objective-C class from the available templates. Make sure that you also select NSObject from the Subclass Of pull-down menu. Name the new class GameCenterManager, as shown in Figure 2-1.

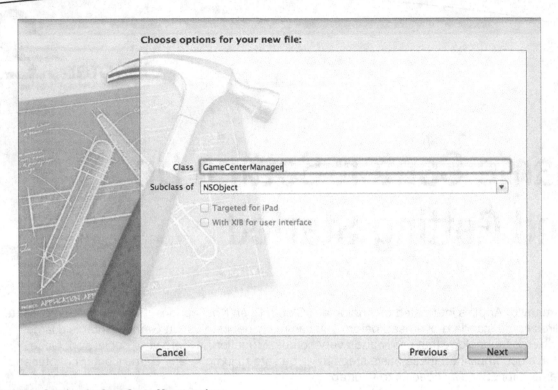

Figure 2-1. Creating the GameCenterManager class

Add the following method to your GameCenterManager class:

```
+ (BOOL) isGameCenterAvailable
{
        Class gcClass = (NSClassFromString(@"GKLocalPlayer"));

        NSString *reqSysVer = @"4.1";
        NSString *currSysVer = [[UIDevice currentDevice] systemVersion];

BOOL osVersionSupported = ([currSysVer compare:reqSysVer options:NSNumericSearch] !=↵
 NSOrderedAscending);

        return (gcClass && osVersionSupported);
}
```

This method creates a new class object using the NSClassFromString function. If GKLocalPlayer exists in the API, gcClass will not be nil. We also test against a minimum OS version. Since many of the Game Center classes were included in the API prior to availability, we need to perform two checks. The next three lines of code compare the current iOS version to a version string we set at 4.1. The method returns the results, which will be true if the device is set up to support Game Center.

> **Note**   You always want to make every effort available to allow users to interact with your app, regardless of whether they have a Game Center–enabled device. If a user does not have a Game Center–enabled device, you still want to make sure they are able to interact with the nonsocial features of your app.

> **Tip**   If you do want to limit your app to users who have Game Center–enabled devices, add a new key to your `info.plist` file called `UIRequiredDeviceCapabilities`. Then, set the value for that key to "gamekit." This will limit your app in the App Store to be purchased only by people who have Game Center–enabled devices.

You can now modify the `UFOViewController.m` file to perform the Game Center availability check. Create a new `viewDidLoad` method, as shown in this code snippet:

```
- (void)viewDidLoad
{
    [super viewDidLoad];

    if ([GameCenterManager isGameCenterAvailable]) {
        NSLog(@"Game Center is available");

    } else {
        NSLog(@"Game Center not available");
    }
}
```

> **Caution**   If you notice that the `isGameCenterAvailable` method is always returning NO even when Game Center should be available, the most likely culprit is forgetting to include `GameKit.framework` in your target.

At this point, all the code will do is print whether Game Center is available to the console. We will be expanding on this code in the next section.

Authenticating with Game Center

Once your app has determined whether the device is Game Center–capable, you can authenticate the user. The user who is authenticated with Game Center will always be referred to as the local player and will be represented by the class `GKLocalPlayer`. Before any other Game Center functionality can be used, you must first authenticate a local player.

Apple recommends that you authenticate with Game Center as early as possible in your app. The primary reason to authenticate before the user needs to access any Game Center behavior is to ensure that the user is not waiting for the network callbacks to authenticate them at a time when they want to perform a Game Center action. In addition, if you are working with Game Center invitations, you will need to authenticate before you can process that launch event.

Early authentication also makes sure that the user is not prompted for a login in the middle of gameplay. There are additional benefits that we will explore in upcoming chapters, such as the ability to resubmit high scores that failed to submit earlier.

Modifying the GameCenterManager Class

Before we can add in code to authenticate with Game Center, we first need to set up some overhead calls to begin working with the GameCenterManager class. GameCenterManager will be a reusable class that adds numerous convenience methods to interact with Game Center; it is designed to be easily dropped into any future project. Game Center–related code will all be piped through the GameCenterManager class, making it easy to use it throughout your app. The first step in setting up this reusable class is to create the delegate callback system.

> **Note**   Blocks can be slightly confusing if you have never worked with them before. Game Center relies heavily on blocks, and you will be seeing a lot of them throughout this book.
>
> The best way to approach blocks, in my experience, has been to view them as inline functions that are executed upon completion of the method that calls them. In the preceding example, after authenticateWithCompletionHandler finishes executing, it calls
>
> [self callDelegateOnMainThread: @selector(processGameCenterAuth:) withArg: NULL error: error];
>
> It helps to have a solid background on blocks before proceeding. If you feel unsure about the use of blocks, I recommend you read the Apple Developer Connection article located at http://developer.apple.com/library/mac/#documentation/Cocoa/Conceptual/Blocks/Articles/bxUsing.html.

You will need to add the following methods to GameKitManager.m. After you have added them, we will discuss what their exact functions are.

```
- (void) callDelegateOnMainThread: (SEL) selector withArg: (id) arg error:↵
 (NSError*) err
{
        dispatch_async(dispatch_get_main_queue(), ^(void) {
[self callDelegate: selector withArg: arg error: err];
        });
}
```

All of our delegate callbacks need to be performed on the main thread; Game Center does not guarantee that the callback blocks will be executed on the main thread, and they may be run from a background thread if not forced onto the main thread. Since UIKit View Controllers can be safely accessed only on the main thread, calling a delegate on a background thread can cause crashes and other unexpected behavior. To avoid creating any threading-related bugs (which can be very hard to track down and fix), we will call all of the delegate methods on the main thread.

> **Note** There are many different ways to force code to execute on the main thread or to otherwise ensure thread safety. For our purposes, we will use the preceding method. It will be easiest to comprehend for readers who have less experience with threading on the iOS platform.

The following method is called from within the callDelegateOnMathThread method after we ensure that we are operating on the main app thread. This method checks to make sure we are on the main thread and then calls our protocol method with the passed information.

```
- (void)callDelegate:(SEL)selector withArg:(id)arg error:(NSError*)err
{
  assert([NSThread isMainThread]);

  if ([delegate respondsToSelector: selector]) {
    if (arg != NULL) {
      [delegate performSelector: selector withObject:arg withObject: err];
    } else {
      [delegate performSelector: selector withObject: err];
    }
  } else {
    NSLog(@"Missed Method");
  }
}
```

If you have not implemented the delegate method, you will see an NSLog in the console for "Missed Method." This is provided solely to assist in debugging, and will save you some head-scratching in trying to debug the protocol methods.

The last thing that we need to do in our GameCenterManager class is to add the delegate property. Modify the relevant parts of the header file to look like the following code:

```
@interface GameCenterManager : NSObject <GameCenterManagerDelegate>

@property(nonatomic, retain) id <GameCenterManagerDelegate, NSObject> delegate;
```

In addition to these modifications, you also need to synthesize the delegate as well as release it in deallocation. The GameCenterManager delegate will be set by the class calling Game Center functions in order to get feedback about those calls. This completes the required changes to the GameCenterManager class.

Authenticating on iOS 6 and iOS 7

iOS 6 brought with it a new method of authentication, which streamlines the process of logging into Game Center. If your app is using iOS 6 or newer the following method is more efficient; however, if you need to authenticate on iOS 5 or even iOS 4 devices see the next section, "Authenticating Prior to iOS 6." Take a look at the following method in its completeness:

```
- (void)authenticateLocalUserModern
{
  if ([[GKLocalPlayer localPlayer] authenticateHandler] == nil) {
    [[GKLocalPlayer localPlayer] setAuthenticateHandler:^(UIViewController *viewController,
    NSError *error) {
      if (error != nil) {
        if ([error code] == GKErrorNotSupported) {
          UIAlertView *alert = [[UIAlertView alloc] initWithTitle:@"Error" message:@"This device does
          not support Game Center" delegate:nil cancelButtonTitle:@"Dismiss" otherButtonTitles:nil];
          [alert show];
          [alert release];
        } else if ([error code] == GKErrorCancelled) {
          UIAlertView *alert = [[UIAlertView alloc] initWithTitle:@"Error" message:@"This device has
          failed login too many times from the app, you will need tologin from the Game Center.app"
          delegate:nil cancelButtonTitle:@"Dismiss" otherButtonTitles:nil];
          [alert show];
          [alert release];
        } else {
          UIAlertView *alert = [[UIAlertView alloc] initWithTitle:@"Error" message:[error
          localizedDescription] delegate:nil cancelButtonTitle:@"Dismiss" otherButtonTitles:nil];
          [alert show];
          [alert release];
        }
      } else {
        if (viewController != nil) {
          [(UIViewController *)delegate presentViewController:viewController animated:YES
          completion:NULL];
        }
      }
    }];
  } else {
    [[GKLocalPlayer localPlayer] authenticate];
  }
}
```

iOS 6 brought a new property to GKLocalPlayer, the authenticateHandler. In essence, this is a block that monitors for login errors and in certain cases will display a UIViewController to the user. The first step is to make sure that we have not set the authenticateHandler previously. If we have, a call to authenticate will complete the login as seen in the else statement at the bottom of the method. After it has been determined that an authenticateHandler hasn't been set, one is set for the GKLocalPlayer singleton. The act of setting an authenticateHandler will also prompt the user to log in to Game Center.

The next three if statements (for GKErrorNotSupported, GKErrorCancelled, and all other errors) all handle various types of errors that may be encountered during authentication. The first error covered is simply that Game Center isn't supported on the user's device for any reason. The next if statement handles the tricky case of too many failed logins. This is a problem rarely seen by users but often encountered by developers. The last error check handles any additional errors and displays them to the user.

If no errors are encountered, Game Center has successfully authenticated. However, if Game Center has returned a UIViewController, it needs to be presented to the user; this is handled using the new iOS 6 presentViewController: method. These are the only steps needed to complete a Game Center login on iOS 6; for information on authenticating before iOS 6, see the next section.

> **Tip** Don't forget to import the <GameKit/GameKit.h> header and the associated Game Kit framework; otherwise, GKLocalPlayer will be undefined.

Authenticating Prior to iOS 6

If you app is supporting a version of iOS prior to iOS 6, you will need to use the older style of authentication, which is described in this section. Handling authentication requires adding code to the GameCenterManager class. Define a new protocol and add the following block of code above the @interface line in GameCenterManager.h. This will create a new optional delegate callback method named processGameCenterAuthentication.

```
@protocol GameCenterManagerDelegate <NSObject>
@optional
- (void)processGameCenterAuthentication:(NSError*)error;
@end
```

It is necessary to add a new method to the implementation of GameCenterManager. Create a new method that consists of the following code:

```
- (void)authenticateLocalUser
{
  if ([GKLocalPlayer localPlayer].authenticated) {
    return;
  }

  [[GKLocalPlayer localPlayer] authenticateWithCompletionHandler:^(NSError *error) {
    [self callDelegateOnMainThread: @selector(processGameCenterAuthentication:) withArg:NULL
    error:error];
  }];
}
```

This method will serve as a helper for authenticating with Game Center. The first line of code checks with the localPlayer singleton to see whether the user is already authenticated. If they are, the method is complete. If the user is not already authenticated, the authenticateWithCompletionHandler method is called.

When authenticateWithCompletionHandler has finished executing, we call [self callDelegateOnMainThread: @selector(processGameCenterAuthentication:) withArg: NULL error: error]. In order to continue, we must implement this method.

> **Tip** If you are receiving warnings that GameCenterManager might not respond to any of the methods we have implemented, make sure that you are adding them to the interface file.

Authenticating from UFOViewController

Now that we have modified the GameCenterManager class to support authentication, we need to create a new object to represent the GameCenterManager in the UFOViewController class.

Import the header for GameCenterManager and create a new GameCenterManager object called gcManager. You also need to add the GameCenterManagerDelegate to the interface of UFOViewController.h. When you are done, UFOViewController.h should look like the following:

```
#import <UIKit/UIKit.h>
#import "GameCenterManager.h"
@interface UFOViewController : UIViewController <GameCenterManagerDelegate>
@property (nonatomic, strong) GameCenterManager *gcManager;
-(IBAction)playButtonPressed;
@end
```

You will again be modifying the viewDidLoad method of UFOViewController. Make the necessary changes to the viewDidLoad method to match the following code snippet:

```
- (void)viewDidLoad
{
  [super viewDidLoad];

  if (![GameCenterManager isGameCenterAvailable]) {
    return;
  }

  GameCenterManager  *manager = [[GameCenterManager alloc] init];
  [manager setDelegate:self];
  [manager authenticateLocalUser];
  [self setGcManager:manager];
}
```

The first new line of code that we added initializes and allocates an instance of GameCenterManager. The next line sets self for the delegate to the UFOViewController class; this will allow us to get callbacks from the GameCenterManager.

Once we have completed these two steps, we can call our convenience method, authenticateLocalUser. Game Center handles the required login views and authentication as well as any account creation at this point. However, we do need to watch our delegate method processGameCenterAuthentication, in order to catch any errors encountered while authenticating.

If you are using the iOS 6 and newer method of authentication you will not be required to implement the delegate callback and can simply replace [gcManager authenticateLocalUser]; with [gcManager authenticateLocalUserModern]; in the previous code snippet.

> **Caution** If you have cancelled a Game Center login three or more times from within an app, you will not be able to sign in from that app again until you have gone to the GameCenter.app and signed in. This is an undocumented behavior and can be a real pain to trace if you do not know what you are searching for. In addition, if you find you are unable to sign in even from Game Center.app, you can reset the simulator or restore the device to resolve these issues.

If you try to run the app again, you will see a console log stating "Missed Method." This is because we have not yet added the optional protocol method that is called when the authentication is completed. We need to add the following method to UFOViewController.m:

```
- (void)processGameCenterAuthentication:(NSError*)error;
{
  if (error != nil) {
    NSLog(@"An error occured during authentication: %@", [error localizedDescription]);
  } else {
    NSLog(@"Successfully authenticated");
  }
}
```

Now when you log in, you should see "Successfully authenticated" printed to the console, as well as the image shown in Figure 2-2 (with your Game Center name instead).

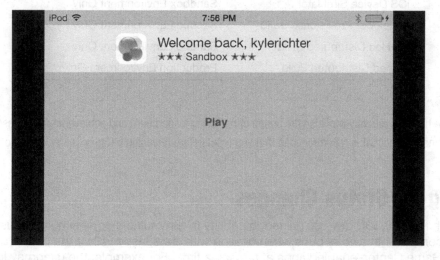

Figure 2-2. The standard "welcome back" message the user will see when logging in to Game Center

> **Caution**   When logging in to Game Center for testing purposes, always create a new Apple ID. Never use an existing Apple ID to log in to Game Center from the Sandbox environment.

> **Tip**   If you are having trouble logging in, make sure your bundle ID in the `info.plist` matches a bundle ID that has Game Center enabled for it in iTunes Connect. See Chapter 1 for more information on configuring Game Center in iTunes Connect.

The Sandbox

To help test your app before it goes live, Apple has provided a Sandbox environment for Game Center. The Sandbox functions exactly like the production version of Game Center, while keeping all activity hidden from non-sandboxed users.

The Sandbox allows the developer to work on new Game Center functionality in secret, as well as not polluting the leaderboards and achievement systems with their test data. When logging in to a Sandbox environment, the login alert will state "*** Sandbox ***" at the top.

Once logged in, there is no way to determine whether you are currently logged in to the Sandbox from within the app. However, if you open Game Center.app, you will see whether you are in a Sandbox environment. The information in Table 2-1 will help you determine what mode you are currently running in.

Table 2-1. Determining the Sandbox Status on Various Types of Builds

Type of Build	Sandbox Status
iOS Device Simulator	Sandbox Environment Only
Developer Provisioned Build	Sandbox Environment Only
Ad-Hoc Distributed Build	Sandbox Environment Only
Signed Distributed Build	Production Environment Only

> **Tip**   Apple has also recently provided the option of removing leaderboard and achievement progress for all users in iTunes Connect. It is recommended that you reset before releasing a Game Center–enabled app.

Watching for Status Changes

Beginning with iOS 4.0, iOS devices gained the ability to run multiple apps simultaneously. This can create some complex behavioral bugs when dealing with state, especially if the user is accessing two different Game Center–enabled apps at the same time. For example, the user may log out of Game Center, or even log in as a different user, while your app is in the background. Therefore, it is vital that you listen for changes to the local user through the NSNotification system.

If you are using the iOS 6 authenticateHandler method detailed earlier in this chapter, watching and reacting to state changes for authentication events is optional and the authenticateHandler will do all of the heavy lifting for you. You can still monitor for state changes if your app needs to use this data in any additional ways.

Add the following snippet of code in the viewDidLoad method of UFOViewController.m, right after the test is performed to verify whether Game Center is available.

```
[[NSNotificationCenter defaultCenter]
                    addObserver:self
                       selector:@selector(localUserAuthenticationChanged:)
                           name:GKPlayerAuthenticationDidChangeNotificationName
                         object:nil];
```

> **Note** Don't forget to remove the NSNotification observers in viewDidUnload, or you could experience crashes and other unintended behavior.

You should also add a new method to UFOViewController. This method will be called whenever player authentication status changes.

```
-(void)localUserAuthenticationChanged:(NSNotification *)notif;
{
    NSLog(@"Authentication Changed: %@", notif.object);
}
```

This new method will print the description for the new GKLocalPlayer when authentication changes. You will need to determine what special steps need to be taken in your app to handle local player changes.

> **Tip** Do not forget to test user switching before shipping your app, as Apple will test it in the review stage.

Working with GKLocalPlayer

The GKLocalPlayer object will always exist and be non-nil when authenticated with Game Center; this object is a representation of the user. You will never create an instance of GKLocalPlayer; this is handled through the class method localPlayer. The localPlayer singleton will be the only way that you will interact with the localPlayer.

The GKLocalPlayer object has three properties associated with it: authenticated, friends, and underage. We will be dealing with the friends property in the following section. We have already worked with the authenticated Boolean in our authentication code in the previous sections.

The underage property is useful for restricting content in a Game Center–enabled app to users over the age of 17. The following code performs an underage check:

```
if ([GKLocalPlayer localPlayer].underage)
{
        NSLog(@"User is underage");
}
```

The friends property will return nil until we complete the steps required to retrieve the user's friends list. Once this has been done, the friends property will return an array of the local user's friends. This procedure is detailed in the following section.

Retrieving a Friends List

The friends list is an array of user IDs that you have assigned as friends in Game Center.app. With this data, you can do things such as create a friends list only in game voice channel, or highlight your friends' scores in the global scores list.

We will add a call to retrieve the friends list in our sample project, but we won't be doing anything specific with the data in this chapter. For the time being, we will simply print the information to the console.

We begin by modifying our GameCenterManager class to add a new method for retrieving the local player's friends list. Add the following method to the implementation.

```
- (void)retrieveFriendsList;
{
  if ([GKLocalPlayer localPlayer].authenticated == YES) {
    [[GKLocalPlayer localPlayer] loadFriendsWithCompletionHandler:^(NSArray *friends, NSError
    *error) {
      [self callDelegateOnMainThread: @selector(friendsFinishedLoading:error:) withArg:friends
      error:error];
    }];
  } else {
    NSLog(@"You must authenticate first");
  }
}
```

This method looks a lot like the previous authentication method that was added earlier in this chapter. After determining that the GKLocalPlayer is authenticated, we can call loadFriendsWithCompletionHandler. This method returns an array of player IDs. We will see how we can use these player IDs to retrieve GKPlayer objects in the next section. We then use our thread-safe callDelegateOnMainThread method to return the data to our delegate.

Before this code will execute, we still need to modify the header file and add a new protocol method to our delegate. We modify the header file to look like the following code snippet:

```
@protocol GameCenterManagerDelegate <NSObject>

@optional
```

```
- (void)processGameCenterAuthentication:(NSError*)error;
- (void)friendsFinishedLoading:(NSArray *)friends error:(NSError *)error;

@end

@interface GameCenterManager : NSObject <GameCenterManagerDelegate>

@property(nonatomic, retain) id <GameCenterManagerDelegate, NSObject> delegate;

+ (BOOL)isGameCenterAvailable;
- (void)authenticateLocalUser;
- (void)callDelegateOnMainThread:(SEL)selector withArg:(id) arg error:(NSError*) err;
- (void)callDelegate:(SEL)selector withArg:(id)arg error:(NSError*) err;
- (void)retrieveFriendsList;

@end
```

The change we've made here adds a new optional protocol, which will be called when the `friends` block is finished executing. We return an array of friend IDs as well as any errors we encounter. We will also add a new method called `retrieveFriendsList` to the class methods.

The last thing that needs to be done before we can run the app is adding a call to `retrieveFriendsList` and adding the protocol method to `UFOViewController.m`. Since we are unable to make the call to retrieve the friends list until after we have successfully authenticated with Game Center, we can add the call to do so in the authentication callback. Modify that method to match the following snippet:

```
- (void)processGameCenterAuthentication:(NSError*)error;
{
  if (error != nil) {
    NSLog(@"An error occured during authentication: %@", [error localizedDescription]);
  } else {
    [gcManager retrieveFriendsList];
  }
}
```

We will also add the protocol method that will print the friends list to the console. Add the following method to `UFOViewController.m`:

```
- (void)friendsFinishedLoading:(NSArray *)friends error:(NSError *)error;
{
  if (error != nil) {
    NSLog(@"An error occured during friends list request: %@", [error localizedDescription]);
  } else {
    NSLog(@"Friends: %@", friends);
  }
}
```

If you have any friends in your friends list, you should see output that looks similar to the following:

```
2011-02-01 12:56:32.759 UFOs[3328:207] Friends: (
    "G:1093075676"
)
```

> **Note**   If you have not yet added any friends to your Sandbox environment, now is a good time to do so. You can create new accounts in the Game Center.app and add them as friends to your test account. Having a populated friends list will be valuable throughout the Game Center sections of this book and in debugging Game Center specific code.

The next section deals with working with the player data that was retrieved from your friends list.

Friend List Avatars

With the introduction of iOS 5.0 Apple added support for friends' avatars. Players are optionally required to set their avatar in the Game Center app. If a player has not yet set an avatar, Game Center will assign them a default avatar. To access avatars in your app, you will need to be running on iOS 5.0 or newer, and you will need to implement one new method. The following method is called on an existing GKPlayer object (see the previous section for more information on GKPlayer). There are two options for avatar image sizes: GKPhotoSizeNormal and GKPhotoSizeSmall.

```
[player loadPhotoForSize:GKPhotoSizeNormal withCompletionHandler: ^(UIImage *photo, NSError *error)
{
  if (error == nil) {
    [playerAvatarImageView setImage:photo];
  } else {
    NSLog(@"An error occurred loading player avatar: %@", [error localizedDescription]);
  }
}];
```

Working with Players

At the heart of the Game Center it is a social service, and as such, it revolves around players. You need to be aware of three properties associated with a GKPlayer object. The isFriend property is a Boolean that returns whether the player is a friend of the current local player. The other two properties handle the player's name and alias. The playerID property is static and will always point to the same player. The playerID string should never be shown to the user in your app. The alias property, on the other hand, is dynamic and can be changed by the user at any time. It should never be used to test the identity of a user, but it should be the only string used to identify the player to your app's user.

> **Caution**   Do not make assumptions about the structure of the player identifier string. Its format and length are subject to change.

When we retrieved the friends list, we did not get back an array of GKPlayers. Instead, we got back an array of their IDs. This is common behavior in Game Center. To help us work with players, we will add two additional convenience methods to translate player IDs into GKPlayer objects.

We need to create two new methods: one will handle an array of player IDs, and the other will handle a single player ID. This will save us extra work down the road. We add the helper methods to our GameCenterManager class. First, add the new protocol method, and modify the relevant section of the GameCenterManager.h file to match the following code:

```
@protocol GameCenterManagerDelegate <NSObject>
@optional
- (void)processGameCenterAuthentication:(NSError*)error;
- (void)friendsFinishedLoading:(NSArray *)friends error:(NSError *)error;
- (void)playerDataLoaded:(NSArray *)players error:(NSError *)error;
@end
```

We will also add the following two new methods to the implementation file of the GameCenterManager class:

```
- (void)playersForIDs:(NSArray *)playerIDs
{
  [GKPlayer loadPlayersForIdentifiers:playerIDs withCompletionHandler:^(NSArray *players, NSError
  *error) {
    [self callDelegateOnMainThread: @selector(playerDataLoaded:error:) withArg: players error:
    error];
  }];
}

- (void)playerforID:(NSString *)playerID
{
  [GKPlayer loadPlayersForIdentifiers:[NSArray arrayWithObject:playerID]
  withCompletionHandler:^(NSArray *players, NSError *error) {
    [self callDelegateOnMainThread: @selector(playerDataLoaded:error:) withArg:players error:error];
  }];
}
```

Both methods will be using loadPlayersForIdentifiers. The only difference is that one will take a string and convert it to a single-item array, and the other will just take in an array. Again, we will use our thread-safe delegate callback.

The last thing that we need to do is to implement the delegate callback in `UFOViewController`. We start by modifying the friends loaded method. This will translate our friends list into an array of `GKPlayer` objects. Modify your `friendsFinishedLoading` method to match the following:

```
- (void)friendsFinishedLoading:(NSArray *)friends error:(NSError *)error;
{
  if (error != nil) {
    NSLog(@"An error occured during friends list request: %@", [error localizedDescription]);
  } else {
    [gcManager playersForIDs: friends];
  }
}
```

You also need to add the new protocol method that we just defined. Add the following to the `UFOViewController.m` file.

```
- (void)playerDataLoaded:(NSArray *)players error:(NSError *)error;
{
  if (error != nil) {
    NSLog(@"An error occured during player lookup: %@", [error localizedDescription]);
  } else {
    NSLog(@"Players loaded: %@", players);
  }
}
```

Now, when the app is run (assuming you have friends associated with your Game Center account), it will pull down a list of your friends' player IDs, then perform a lookup and print the GKPlayer description to the console. Your output should look similar to the following.

```
2011-02-01 14:20:23.335 UFOs[4038:207] Authentication Changed: <GKPlayer↵
 0x5f46fb0>(playerID: G:1092793231, alias: the_other_kyle, status: (null), rid:(null))
2011-02-01 14:20:23.471 UFOs[4038:207] Players loaded: (
    "<GKPlayer 0x6a201e0>(playerID: G:1093075676, alias: johncash, status: (null),↵
 rid:(null))"
)
```

Summary

In this chapter, you learned how to test for Game Center compatibility and authenticate the local user for both iOS 6/7 and older versions. You should now have a strong grasp of how we will be using the `GameCenterManager` class and the benefits it will have on creating a clean code environment that will be easily reusable across multiple projects.

In addition, you should now be comfortable working with `GKLocalPlayer`, `GKPlayer`, and the friends list. In the next chapter, we will take an in-depth look at leaderboards and expand on topics learned in this chapter. If you have any difficulty with anything discussed in this chapter, remember that the available source code (`www.apress.com`) contains working examples of all the topics discussed.

Leaderboards

What the ancients called a clever fighter is one who not only wins, but excels in winning with ease.

—Sun Tzu, The Art of War

Leaderboards are older than video games themselves. The leaderboard, as we know it, goes back to the days of the original pinball games of the 1950s. The makers of these pinball games soon realized that adding a high-score list increased competition, which translates to more time played and more money earned.

During the 1970s, when video games began to emerge, leaderboards were quickly adopted into these new games, making their first appearance as early as a game called Sea Wolf, released in 1976 (see Figure 3-1). Since then, they have played an integral part in the gaming culture. Leaderboards have become so widespread that, in 2007, *The King of Kong*, a full-length documentary, was released about the heated competition over the high score on Nintendo's Donkey Kong. Leaderboards have become so mainstream that they are now not only desired but an expected part of any video game.

Figure 3-1. Sea Wolf (1976), the first video game to feature a high score

Game Center for iOS greatly simplifies adding leaderboards to an app. This is a huge improvement when you consider that, previously, the developer had to write and maintain a server to store and update score data. This chapter examines the steps required to implement multiple leaderboards under Game Center, as well as all the required leaderboard support. You will learn how to post scores, retrieve leaderboards, customize the graphical user interface (GUI) of leaderboards, and handle everything else needed to create leaderboards that are the right fit for your app.

Why a Leaderboard?

Before we get into working with leaderboards themselves, it is important to understand why leaderboards are an integral part of your social app or game.

- Leaderboards create a sense of community in an app or game that, otherwise, might not allow your user to interact directly with other users.

- Leaderboards drive users to return to your app in an effort to beat their own scores or their friend's high scores.

- Leaderboards create a sense of goal and accomplishment in an app.

- Leaderboards make it easier for users to share their app experience and progress with their friends, family, and co-workers.

- Leaderboards in Game Center are easy to implement and can make your app quickly feel more polished and finished.

- With the addition of Leaderboard challenges in iOS 6, a player's friends may drive them to return to your game through score challenges.

An Overview of Leaderboards in Game Center

A leaderboard, in in regards to Game Center, is an array of GKScore objects related to a specific leaderboard identifier, of which many can exist per app. Leaderboards can be retrieved and further filtered based on friend status and date submitted.

GKScore objects represent each entry on a specific leaderboard. A GKScore always has a player ID associated with it. When the game center API submits a new GKScore to a leaderboard, the player ID is set automatically by the API and cannot be changed. There are also values for the date and rank that are automatically set and updated. You are required to set only the raw score value and leaderboard category to which the score belongs.

There are two ways to retrieve and display leaderboards. The most common, and easiest, method is by using Apple's leaderboard GUI. This will be the first approach we explore in the following sections. The second option is to retrieve the raw GKScore values and display them in your own GUI; this method is discussed later in the chapter.

> **Note**   Game Center currently has a limit of 100 leaderboards per bundle ID with the introduction of iOS 7. iOS 6 and earlier carried a leaderboard limit of 25.

Benefits of Using Apple's Leaderboard GUI Compared to a Custom GUI

Benefits of using Apple's leaderboard GUI include the following:

- The design was created by some of the best designers in the world.
- It is very simple to implement and present the leaderboard.
- Users will see a familiar interface that they already know how to interact with.

Benefits of using a custom GUI include the following:

- Your leaderboard can match the custom design of your app.
- You have more freedom over the resulting data and can filter using additional criteria.
- You can implement your own custom caching behavior.

As you can see, each system has benefits and disadvantages, and there is no right answer to which one you should be using. By the end of this chapter, you will have a strong background in both options and will be able to decide correctly which method to implement based on the specific needs of your app.

Configuring a Leaderboard in iTunes Connect

Before working with the code side of leaderboards, you must first set up a new leaderboard in iTunes Connect. Log in to iTunes Connect (http://itunesconnect.apple.com) and select the app that we have already been working with from Chapters 1 and 2. Once you have selected your app from the control panel, go to the Manage Game Center area.

The Game Center portal for your app will have a section labeled Leaderboards. If this is the first leaderboard that you have set up for this app, you will see a button labeled Set Up. If you already have leaderboards in place, the steps here will be different and are covered later in this section.

Once you are in the Leaderboards section (seen in Figure 3-2), select the Add Leaderboard button in the upper-left corner of the web page. You will be prompted to select either a single leaderboard or a combined leaderboard. A single leaderboard will be one collection of stored score objects that can be queried independently from other leaderboards. A combined leaderboard can also be accessed independently from other leaderboards; it is a collection of single leaderboards displayed together. The combined leaderboard is useful for showing data such as all-time high scores across all levels, or similar combined data.

Figure 3-2. Adding a new leaderboard in iTunes Connect

We begin by creating a new single leaderboard, as shown in Figure 3-3. The first thing you need to enter is the Leaderboard Reference Name. This value is used solely as a reference within iTunes Connect. The reference name is designed to help you quickly find leaderboards within iTunes Connect; the user never sees it. For this example, you can use the reference name "Leaderboard Foo."

Figure 3-3. *Creating a new single leaderboard in iTunes Connect*

The next field is the Leaderboard ID, the value you will query in your code to retrieve a particular leaderboard. Apple recommends that you use a reverse-DNS entry format for this field, such as com.*company.appname.leaderboardname*. Fill in the appropriate values for your app here; it is not important what they are, but you will need to remember them throughout the remainder of this chapter.

The Score Format Type is also required when creating a new leaderboard. Table 3-1 shows the available data formats. Select the score format that meets the requirements for your score data.

Table 3-1. *Score Format Types for Adding a New Leaderboard in iTunes Connect*

Score Format Type	Example Output
Integer	12,345
Fixed Point - To 1 Decimal	12,345.1
Fixed Point - To 2 Decimals	12,345.12
Fixed Point - To 3 Decimals	12,345.123
Elapsed Time - To the Minute	3:45
Elapsed Time - To the Second	3:45:55
Elapsed Time - To the Hundredth of a Second	3:45:55.82
Money - Whole Numbers	$182,121
Money - To 2 Decimals	$182,121.68

> **Tip**   If none of the provided format types match your requirements, select the one that best matches your needs. Later in this chapter, you will see how to customize these values by retrieving the raw score values.

You also need to select whether you want the leaderboard to sort by ascending or descending order. Ascending order will display the lowest score first, as in a golf game or a lap around a track. Descending order will show the highest scores first, as in a game of football or a typical score in a first-person shooter.

The last thing that needs to be done when creating a new single leaderboard is entering the localized score information, as shown in Figure 3-4. iTunes Connect contains built-in localization support for Game Center; you will need to create a new entry for each language you want to support.

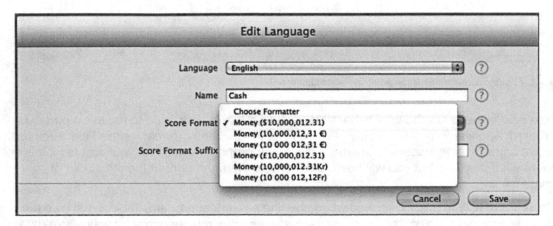

Figure 3-4. Editing the localization information on a new leaderboard

The Name field is the display name for your leaderboard in the chosen language. The Score Format field will vary depending on the score format type you selected on the previous screen. (See Figure 3-4 for an example of money formatting.) You also need to provide a Score Format Suffix. This string will be appended to the end of your score value when you retrieve the formatted score property.

> **Caution**   You will need to add at least one language for every leaderboard you create before it can be considered valid.

> **Tip**   If you want a space to appear between the score and the score format suffix in the formatted score value, don't forget to add a space before the beginning of the score suffix.

You now have a single leaderboard configured for your app. In order to enable the combined leaderboard, we need at least two leaderboards that share the same type of score format. Go ahead and create a second single leaderboard now.

Once you have two leaderboards that share the same score format type, you can create a combined leaderboard. Follow the same procedure for creating a single leaderboard, as described in the previous example. This area is similar to a single leaderboard creation screen. The main difference is that you need to select the leaderboards you want to combine, as shown in Figure 3-5. You will need create a new leaderboard ID, as well as specify the localization data for the new combined leaderboard.

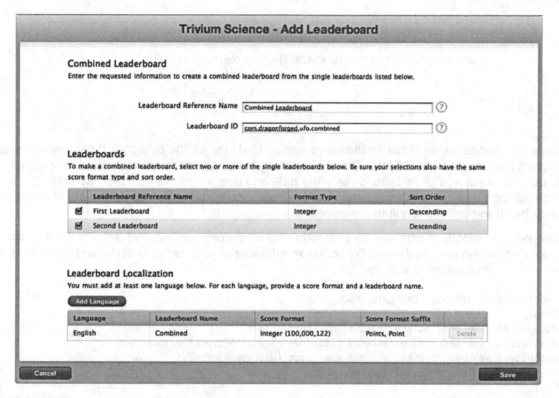

Figure 3-5. Creating a combined leaderboard

We will also add one last single leaderboard to let us work with a single uncombined leaderboard, as the two previous leaderboards that we had created are now Attached leaderboards. Your leaderboard panel should now have four leaderboards in it: two attached, one combined, and one single leaderboard. Now that we have a handful of valid leaderboards to work with, we can move back to Xcode and begin to work with the leaderboard-specific code.

Important   Once a leaderboard has gone live in a shipping app, it can never be removed, so double-check your leaderboard information before shipping an app.

Posting a Score

Before a leaderboard provides any useful functionality, we need to populate it with some score data. We begin this process by modifying our GameCenterManager class once again. Add the following method to the implementation; it should look very familiar, as it follows the same pattern that we used when we implemented the authentication methods:

```
- (void) reportScore: (int64_t) score forCategory: (NSString*) category
{
        GKScore *scoreReporter = [[[GKScore alloc] initWithCategory:category]↩
 autorelease];
        scoreReporter.value = score;
        [scoreReporter reportScoreWithCompletionHandler: ^(NSError *error)
        {
                [self callDelegateOnMainThread:@selector(scoreReported:)
                                              withArg:nil
                                              error:error];
        }];
}
```

This new method takes an int64 for the score and an NSString for the category. It then allocates and initializes a new instance of GKScore. The only property that we need to set on the GKScore object is the raw score value. The API already sets the date and user values for us; when we initialize the GKScore object we do so with an argument for the category. We will continue to use the standard callback block to pass the result to our delegate.

We also need to modify the header file to incorporate a new protocol method. Modify the existing protocol declaration area of the GameCenterManager header to include the scoreReported method, as shown in the following code snippet:

```
@protocol GameCenterManagerDelegate <NSObject>
@optional
- (void)processGameCenterAuthentication:(NSError*)error;
- (void)friendsFinishedLoading:(NSArray *)friends error:(NSError *)error;
- (void)playerDataLoaded:(NSArray *)players error:(NSError *)error;
- (void)scoreReported: (NSError*) error;
@end
```

This concludes all of the required modifications to our GameCenterManager class for the time being. We can now turn our focus back to the game itself. We will need to first implement some new gameplay dynamics to handle high scores.

Setting a Default Leaderboard

Since game center for iOS 5, you have the ability to set a default Game Center leaderboard for the local user. If you set a default leaderboard you can omit setting a category for a leaderboard when submitting, and it will default to the correct one. The following method will take an NSString identifier as an argument for the leaderboard that you would like to specify as the default for the local player:

```
[GKLeaderboard setDefaultLeaderboard:@"com.dragonforged.leaderboardToBeDefault"↵
 withCompletionHandler:^(NSError *error)
{
        NSLog(@"An error occurred when setting the default leaderboard: %@",↵
 [error localizedDescription]);

}];
```

Adding Score Posting to UFOs

There are two obvious ways that we can add scoring to our UFOs game. First, we could implement a system that counted how many cows were abducted and submit that number as the score. Although this approach is the easiest to implement for us, it is not a very fun gameplay technique, because there is no logical point at which the game ends. The second, high-score method is harder to implement, but makes more sense. It clocks how long the user took to abduct ten cows; the user with the lowest time is the winner.

These are topics that must be carefully considered for your own app. For the purpose of this book, we will demonstrate the first method, in which the number of cows abducted is the user's score. If you were going to implement a timer-based system, the approach would be very similar: you would start a timer at the beginning of the round, and when ten cows were abducted, you would submit the time in seconds on the timer.

In order to implement our score-based system, we need to add a way for the player to end a game. In an actual game, this could be handled by something being able to kill your player, or a time limit. However, for the purpose of this example, we will simply add an Exit button. This will allow the user to simulate a game-over event, while keeping the code Game Center–focused without adding any extra game complexity.

We add an Exit button in UFOGameViewController.xib, as shown in Figure 3-6. We will need to create a new IBAction for the button as well. Add the following code to UFOGameViewController and connect our Exit button to it. For the time being, we will just pop the navigation controller back to the root view.

```
-(IBAction)exitAction:(id)sender;
{
        [[self navigationController] popViewControllerAnimated:YES];
}
```

> **Note** You are not required to wait until the end of a game to submit a new score, but it is generally thought of as good practice. You want to avoid submitting a new score multiple times per game if it can be prevented.
>
> A notable exception might be a continuous role-playing game in which the score continually updates and there is no proper end point during the game to submit a score.

Figure 3-6. Adding the ability to exit the game so a high score can be submitted

We will also want to add our protocol method from the GameCenterManager class to UFOGameViewController. Add the following code snippet into UFOGameViewController.m.

```
-(void)scoreReported: (NSError*) error;
{
        if (error)
        {
                NSLog(@"There was an error in reporting the score: %@",↵
[error localizedDescription]);
        }

        else
        {
                NSLog(@"Score submitted");
        }
}
```

The only remaining step is to submit the score to Game Center; if you recall, we have already written the method to handle this in our GameCenterManager class. We already have an instance of our GameCenterManager class that we used in UFOViewController to authenticate the user. We will want to keep a pointer to the instance of our object that was already created in the previous class.

Create a new property for UFOGameViewController, make it an instance of GameCenterManager, and name it GCManager as we did in the previous class. Once the property has been synthesized, we can hook into it from our previous class. Modify the playButtonPressed method of UFOViewController to match the following:

```
-(IBAction)playButtonPressed
{
        UFOGameViewController *gameViewController = [[UFOGameViewController alloc]init];
        gameViewController.gcManager = gcManager; //Changed Code
        [self.navigationController pushViewController: gameViewController animated:YES];
        [gameViewController release];
}
```

Now our game controller class has a reference to the GameCenterManager that we will be using throughout the project. We also have to set a new delegate for gcManager in the viewDidLoad method of UFOGameViewController. We want to make sure that UFOGameViewController will be handling the callbacks for the score submitted. Add the following method to the implementation:

```
- (void)scoreReported: (NSError*) error;
{
        if (error)
        {
                NSLog(@"There was an error in reporting the score: %@",↵
[error localizedDescription]);
        }

        else
        {
                NSLog(@"Score submitted");
        }

        [[self navigationController] popViewControllerAnimated: YES];
}
```

We will also modify the exitAction method to only submit the score. To do so, replace the old exitAction method with the following. Notice that we are using the leaderboard ID that we set in iTunes Connect; make sure to use the same ID that you entered, as it will probably not match the one used here.

```
-(IBAction)exitAction:(id)sender;
{
        [self.gcManager reportScore:score forCategory:@"com.dragonforged.ufo.single"];
}
```

When you now play and click Exit, you should see a console message that looks similar to the following output:

```
2011-02-10 12:32:47.629 UFOs[15092:207] Score submitted
```

> **Tip** See the section "A Better Approach" at the end of this chapter for a more complex, but user-friendly, approach to submitting scores.

Now that we have a score submitted to a leaderboard, in the following sections you will learn how to present this data back to the user. This action has been greatly simplified for the purpose of making this section as easy to learn as possible. This will not be the user experience you want to present to your user; we are simply trapping the user in the game screen while we wait for a network callback. In a real game, you will want to handle the delegate callback in the previous view. This ensures that the user is not waiting unnecessarily. For simplicity sake, we will continue to use the easier-to-follow methodology.

> **Tip**   You can only have one score posted per leaderboard category for each player. You might notice that scores you submit never appear on the leaderboard. If this behavior occurs, make sure that the score you are submitting is higher than the highest score for that player.

Handling Failures When Submitting a Score

If a score fails to submit, you as the developer are solely responsible for storing the score and resubmitting it when the error has been resolved. Nothing is more frustrating to a user than earning a new high score and losing it due to a network failure. This is also a step that Apple likes to test for during app reviews.

There are many ways to store the score information for resubmitting it later; however, I believe the following approach is the easiest for the novice to implement. Feel free to implement your own system if this one does not suit the needs or complexity of your app.

We will use NSKeyedArchiver to store our GKScore object for use later. The reason to serialize the object is to preserve the data that is created for us once we initialize an instance of GKScore, namely the date. Although you could simply store the raw score data, submitting the raw score with a new GKScore object will use the current timestamp, instead of the time when the score was actually earned. This provides a poor user experience, as the first player to earn a high score might not be recognized as such.

There are three steps that need to be completed to handle and recover from a score submittal failure. The first step is to save the score data. Although we do not inform the user of the failure in this example, it is a good idea to notify the user that their score could not be submitted at this time, and that you will automatically retry later. Modify the reportScore class in GameCenterManager.m to match the following code:

```
- (void) reportScore: (int64_t) score forCategory: (NSString*) category
{
        GKScore *scoreReporter = [[[GKScore alloc] initWithCategory:category]↵
autorelease];

        scoreReporter.value = score;
        [scoreReporter reportScoreWithCompletionHandler: ^(NSError *error)
         {

        if (error != nil)
                {
                        NSData* savedScoreData = [NSKeyedArchiver↵
archivedDataWithRootObject:scoreReporter];

                        [self storeScoreForLater: savedScoreData];
                }

            [self callDelegateOnMainThread: @selector(scoreReported:) withArg:↵
NULL error:  error];
        }];
}
```

We have added a few additional lines of code that will run if an error is detected. The first line takes the GKScore object and encodes it using NSKeyedArchiver, which will return an NSData object. We will later retrieve the GKScore from this NSData. We also call a new method that we have named storeScoreForLater. Let's take a look at that method now; add the following method to the implementation of the GameCenterManager class:

```
- (void)storeScoreForLater:(NSData *)scoreData;
{
        NSUserDefaults *defaults = [NSUserDefaults standardUserDefaults];

        NSMutableArray *savedScores = [[defaults arrayForKey:@"savedScores"]↵
 mutableCopy];

        [savedScoreArray addObject: scoreData];
        [defaults setObject:savedScoreArray forKey:@"savedScores"];

        [savedScoreArray release];
}
```

This snippet of code will save the NSData that represents our score to the user defaults. You could also write this data to a file or even store it in core data. Never assume the user has only one unsubmitted score; they may have racked up a number of scores across many different leaderboards while playing offline.

So far we have caught a posting failure as well as saved the score to disk to be retried later. The last remaining step is to attempt to resubmit the score to Game Center. This step can be very complex, depending on how intelligent you want the system to be. Most failures of score submissions are related to network access issues, but they could also be caused by Game Center being down, or even a DNS issue.

There is no correct answer in when to repost a score, but the guideline is that you don't want to hold on to a score that could be submitted. Before we worry about where to tie in the method to resubmit failed scores, let's first implement a method to retry a score posting. Add the following method to your GameCenterManager class.

```
-(void)submitAllSavedScores
{
        NSUserDefaults *defaults = [NSUserDefaults standardUserDefaults];
        NSArray *savedScores = [defaults arrayForKey@"savedScores"];

        [defaults removeObjectForKey: @"savedScores"];

        GKScore *scoreReporter = nil;
        NSData *savedScoreData = nil;

        for (NSData *scoreData in savedScores)
        {
                scoreReporter = [NSKeyedUnarchiver unarchiveObjectWithData: scoreData];
```

```
                    [scoreReporter reportScoreWithCompletionHandler: ^(NSError *error)
                    {
                            if (error != nil)
                            {
                                    savedScoreData = [NSKeyedArchiver◀
archivedDataWithRootObject:scoreReporter];

                                    [self storeScoreForLater: savedScoreData];
                            }
                            else
                            {
                                    NSLog(@"Saved score submitted");
                            }
                    }];
            }
}
```

This code will loop through all of the saved scores and attempt to resubmit them. Because there is no delegate for this behavior, we do not need to provide a delegate callback. We merely log any successes and failures to add back to our array of non-submitted scores for retrying again later.

As mentioned earlier, there are dozens of ways to tie back in resubmitting failed scores. To keep it simple, we add a call to the submitAllSavedScores method after we properly authenticate with Game Center. Modify the authenticateLocalUser method of GameCenterManager.m to match the following:

```
    if ([[GKLocalPlayer localPlayer] authenticateHandler] == nil)
    {
        [[GKLocalPlayer localPlayer] setAuthenticateHandler:^(UIViewController *viewController,
NSError *error)
        {
            if (error != nil)
            {
                if ([error code] == GKErrorNotSupported) {
                    UIAlertView *alert = [[UIAlertView alloc] initWithTitle:@"Error"
message:@"This device does not support Game Center" delegate:nil cancelButtonTitle:@"Dismiss"
otherButtonTitles:nil];
                    [alert show];
                    [alert release];
                }
                else if ([error code] == GKErrorCancelled)
                {
                    UIAlertView *alert = [[UIAlertView alloc] initWithTitle:@"Error" message:@"This
device has failed login too many times from the app, you will need tologin from the Game Center.app"
delegate:nil cancelButtonTitle:@"Dismiss" otherButtonTitles:nil];
                    [alert show];
                    [alert release];
                }
                else
                {
```

```
                UIAlertView *alert = [[UIAlertView alloc] initWithTitle:@"Error" message:[error
localizedDescription] delegate:nil cancelButtonTitle:@"Dismiss" otherButtonTitles:nil];
                [alert show];
                [alert release];
            }
        }
        else
        {
            if (viewController != nil)
            {
                [(UIViewController *)delegate presentViewController:viewController animated:YES
completion:NULL];
            }
            [self submitAllSavedScores];
        }
    }];
}
```

Presenting a Leaderboard

Now that we have a leaderboard in iTunes Connect, and have populated a score into that leaderboard, it is time to present the leaderboard to the user. There are two ways of presentation: the first is with Apple's GUI; the second is with a custom GUI. This section will take a look at the implementation using Apple's GUI. In the next section, you will learn how to present a leaderboard with custom graphics.

Before we can begin, we need to create a new button that will trigger the leaderboard. We want to do this outside the game screen, because you do not want to drag the user away from a game in progress to view a leaderboard. Begin by adding a new button to the UFOViewController view, as shown in Figure 3-7.

Figure 3-7. Adding a leaderboard button

Hook up the button to a new action that matches the one shown next. Do not forget to change the category property to the leaderboard that you set in iTunes Connect.

```
-(IBAction)leaderboardButtonPressed;
{
        GKLeaderboardViewController *leaderboardController = nil;
        leaderboardController = [[GKLeaderboardViewController alloc] init];

        if (leaderboardController == NULL)
                return;

        leaderboardController.category = @"com.dragonforged.ufo.single";
        leaderboardController.timeScope = GKLeaderboardTimeScopeAllTime;
        leaderboardController.leaderboardDelegate = self;
      [self presentViewController: leaderboardViewController animated: YES completion: nil];
}
```

You also need to add in the delegate call for GKLeaderboardViewController. To do so, add the following required method to your implementation. Don't forget to add GKLeaderboardViewControllerDelegate to your header as well.

```
- (void)leaderboardViewControllerDidFinish:(GKLeaderboardViewController *)viewController
{
    [self dismissViewControllerAnimated: YES completion: nil];
}
```

When you run the program and click the newly added Leaderboard button, the result should look like Figure 3-8. As you can see, the title of our leaderboard (as set in iTunes Connect) appears in the navigation bar. You can also see the highest submitted score as well as the score suffix that was set.

Figure 3-8. A leaderboard being presented using Apple's GUI

The GUI provides a back button to take us to a list of all the leaderboards (see initial view in Figure 3-9) that we have configured for the app. If you omit entering a category when you create the GKLeaderboardViewController instance, you will be presented with whatever leaderboard has been selected as the default leaderboard in iTunes Connect.

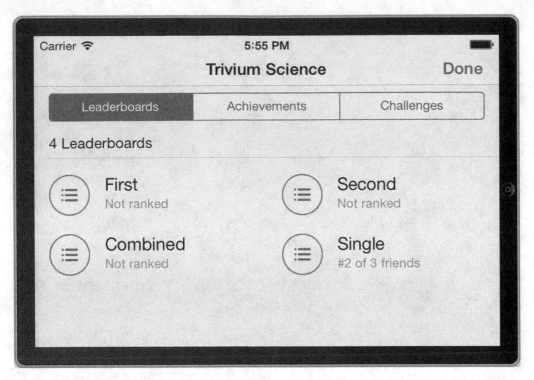

Figure 3-9. A collection of leaderboards, shown with Apple's GUI

This is all there is to creating and presenting a leaderboard using Apple's GUI. In the next section, we will look at how to customize a leaderboard to match your own GUI.

> **Note**   Remember that you cannot access any Game Center functionality, including leaderboards, before a local user has authenticated. If you try to do so, you will receive a `GKErrorNotAuthenticated` error.

> **Tip**   You can change the order in which leaderboards appear (see Figure 3-9) by dragging leaderboard entries up and down in iTunes Connect.

Customizing the Leaderboard

As demonstrated in the previous section, presenting a leaderboard to the user is straightforward. However, what if you want to customize the appearance of a leaderboard? In this section, we will walk through the process of receiving the raw leaderboard information so that you can present it in your app in whatever fashion suits your needs.

We begin the process of adding a custom leaderboard by adding a new button and associated action for it to UFOViewController. Add a new button adjacent to the previous leaderboard button, and create a new action for it.

In the previous example, Apple provides a view controller for us. When we are working with our own custom leaderboards, we need to create a view controller to handle the presentation. Create a new subclass of UIViewController and name it UFOLeaderboardViewController. Modify the action of the new custom leaderboard button to present a new instance of UFOLeaderboardViewController, as seen in the following code snippet:

```
-(IBAction)customLeaderboardButtonPressed;
{
    UFOLeaderboardViewController *leaderboardViewController = [[UFOLeaderboardViewController alloc] init];
    leaderboardViewController.gcManager = gcManager;
    [self presentViewController: leaderboardViewController animated: YES completion: nil];
    [leaderboardViewController release];
}
```

The next step is to set up the xib for the new UFOLeaderboardViewController. We will use the setup as shown in Figure 3-10; however, you may provide whatever kind of customization you want here. Create the outlets and objects, as shown in the figure, and hook up connections for all of them, including the delegate and dataSource for the table.

Figure 3-10. Creating the xib for a custom leaderboard

The first thing that should be hooked up is the Dismiss button. Add the following code snippet to your action that you connected to the Dismiss button:

```
-(IBAction)dismiss;
{
    [self dismissViewControllerAnimated: YES completion: nil];
}
```

If you were to run the app at this point and click the Custom Leaderboard button, it should launch a blank table in the correct orientation and allow you to dismiss it to return to the first view.

Now that we have got the view controller overhead out of the way, we can begin to focus on the Game Center–specific features. First, set up the table view delegate and datasource methods that we will be using. We need to create a new class property to hold the score data for display. Create a new NSArray object and name it scoreArray. Also create an associated property for the array and synthesis it. Add the following two methods to your implementation:

```
- (NSInteger)tableView:(UITableView *)tableView numberOfRowsInSection:(NSInteger)section
{
        return [self.scoreArray count];
}

- (UITableViewCell *)tableView:(UITableView *)tableView cellForRowAtIndexPath:↩
(NSIndexPath *)indexPath
{
        static NSString *CellIdentifier = @"Cell";

        UITableViewCell *cell = [tableView dequeueReusableCellWithIdentifier:↩
CellIdentifier];

        if (cell == nil)
{
                cell = [[[UITableViewCell alloc] initWithStyle:↩
UITableViewCellStyleSubtitle
                                                        reuseIdentifier:↩
CellIdentifier] autorelease];

                cell.selectionStyle = UITableViewCellSelectionStyleNone;
        }

        GKScore *score = [self.scoreArray objectAtIndex: indexPath.row];

        cell.textLabel.text = score.playerID;
        cell.detailTextLabel.text = score.formattedValue;

        return cell;
}
```

The first method returns the number of items in our table view. We deal with only one section in this example, so the number of rows will always equal the number of scores that are in our array. The next method displays the score into the cell. We use UITableViewCellStyleSubtitle in this example, but in most cases, you will want to create a more customized cell. The main label is set to the player ID and the secondary label is set to the formatted score value. In the previous chapter, it was noted that you should never show a player ID to the user. We will add a method to convert a player ID to a player alias in the following section; until then, we will use the player ID for debugging purposes.

Modifying GameCenterManager

Let's take a moment to switch over to our GameCenterManager class. In the header file, create a new optional protocol as shown here:

```
(void)leaderboardUpdated: (NSArray *)scores error:(NSError *)error;
```

Next, we create a new method to retrieve scores from the Game Center servers. Add the following method to the implementation of the GameCenterManager class:

```
- (void)retrieveScoresForCategory:(NSString *)category
                 withPlayerScope:(GKLeaderboardPlayerScope)playerScope
                       timeScope:(GKLeaderboardTimeScope)timeScope
                       withRange:(NSRange)range;
{
    GKLeaderboard *leaderboardRequest = [[GKLeaderboard alloc] init];
    leaderboardRequest.playerScope = playerScope;
    leaderboardRequest.timeScope = timeScope;
    leaderboardRequest.range = range;
    leaderboardRequest.category = category;

    [leaderboardRequest loadScoresWithCompletionHandler: ^(NSArray *scores,NSError*error)
    {
        [self callDelegateOnMainThread:@selector(leaderboardUpdated:error:)
                               withArg:scores
                                 error:error];
    }];
}
```

We want to keep this call as generic as possible because the ultimate goal of the GameCenterManager class is to be a reusable class that can easily be dropped into any of your future projects.

This method takes all the arguments that are required to create a new GKLeaderboard object. Once we have created the object and set the properties that are required, we can call the method loadScoresWithCompletionHandler on the GKLeaderboard object. We will continue to use our standard thread-safe delegate callback. These are all the modifications that are needed in the GameCenterManager class for this section.

Filtering Results on a Custom Leaderboard

Let's shift our focus back to the UFOLeaderboardCiewController class again. We will next add an action for our segmented controller. This will allow the user to switch between global scores and friends-only scores. Connect the following method to the valueChanged action of the segmented controller:

```
-(IBAction)segementedControllerDidChange:(id)sender;
{
        GKLeaderboardPlayerScope playerScope;

        if ([scopeSegementedController selectedSegmentIndex] == 0)
        {
                playerScope = GKLeaderboardPlayerScopeFriendsOnly;
        }
        else
        {
                playerScope = GKLeaderboardPlayerScopeGlobal;
        }

        self.scoreArray = nil;

        [self.gcManager retrieveScoresForCategory:@"com.dragonforged.ufo.single"
                                                withPlayerScope:playerScope
                                                        timeScope:↵
GKLeaderboardTimeScopeAllTime
                                                        withRange:↵
NSMakeRange(1,50)];

        [leaderboardTableView reloadData];
}
```

This method calls the GameCenterManager method to retrieve the score array. The segmented control has two values: one for friends, and one for everyone. You could easily modify the preceding code to retrieve different time scopes as well, but in this example we request only the all-time scope. An important step here that can be easy to overlook is setting the array to nil and reloading the table. Doing so will remove the scores that are in the table when the segmented controller value is changed.

The call to retrieve scores is fairly straightforward. We use the category we set in iTunes Connect for the leaderboard we wish to retrieve, and set our time and player scope. The last argument on the method is a range. In this example, we return scores from first place to fiftieth place.

You also need to create a new property for the UFOLeaderboardViewController class; this will be a pointer to our GameCenterManager class. This is done in exactly the same way as when we did it for the UFOGameViewController class.

> **Note**   Score ranges always start at an index of 1. You could modify the previous example with a new range
> of NSMakeRange(50,50); this will retrieve scores from places 50 to 100. Make sure you don't request too
> many scores at a time, as the time it takes to retrieve the score data is related to how many scores you are
> attempting to retrieve.

Displaying the Custom Leaderboard

If you were to run this project now, you would notice the table is always blank. This is caused by two different omissions. The first is that we never set a value for our gcManager, and the second is that we never called the retrieveScore method. To rectify this, modify the viewDidLoad method of the UFOLeaderboardViewController implementation to match the following. The retrieveScore method is called when the segmentedControllerDidChange is invoked.

```
-(void)viewDidLoad
{
        [super viewDidLoad];

        self.gcManager.delegate = self;
        [self segementedControllerDidChange:nil];
}
```

The last step is to pass a reference to the gcManager to our leaderboard class. We do this in the UFOViewController class. Modify the existing IBAction method to set the property for gcManager to the instance that exists in the UFOViewController. Your code should look like the following example:

```
-(IBAction)customLeaderboardButtonPressed;
{
    UFOLeaderboardViewController *leaderboardViewController = [[UFOLeaderboardViewController alloc]
init];
    leaderboardViewController.gcManager = gcManager;
        [self presentViewController: leaderboardViewController animated: YES completion: nil];
    [leaderboardViewController release];
}
```

If you were to now run the app again, you would see output similar to that shown in Figure 3-11. The number of scores, the score values, and the player IDs will be different, but you should be able to see at least one score listed.

Figure 3-11. An initial view of our custom leaderboard

Important   It cannot be guaranteed that you will not be returned cached data for a leaderboard request.
You should assume that the data you are retrieving is cached and might not be the most up to date.

Mapping a Player ID

In the previous section, we learned how to pull down the raw score values of a leaderboard.
However, we ended up with a leaderboard that contained only player IDs rather than the aliases
(which the user expects to be shown). In this section, we will create a new method that will translate
player IDs into player aliases. We will begin this process by adding some new methods to our
GameCenterManager class. These will enable searching for both single names and arrays of names.
Add the following two methods to the GameCenterManager class.

```
- (void)mapPlayerIDtoPlayer:(NSString*)playerID
{
        [GKPlayer loadPlayersForIdentifiers: [NSArray arrayWithObject: playerID]
                        withCompletionHandler:^(NSArray *playerArray, NSError*error)
        {
            GKPlayer* player = nil;
            for (GKPlayer* tempPlayer in playerArray)
```

```
                {
                    if ([tempPlayer.playerID isEqualToString: playerID] == nil)
            continue;

                    player = tempPlayer;
                    break;
                }
        [self callDelegateOnMainThread:@selector(mappedPlayerIDToPlayer:error:)
                                            withArg:player
                                                error:error];

        }];
}

- (void)mapPlayerIDstoPlayers:(NSArray*)playerIDs
{
        [GKPlayer loadPlayersForIdentifiers: playerIDs withCompletionHandler:^(NSArray↵
        *playerArray, NSError *error)
            {
                [self callDelegateOnMainThread: @selector(mappedPlayerIDs:error:) ↵
                withArg: playerArray error: error];
            }];
}
```

The first method will return a single GKPlayer object, while the second method will return an array of GKPlayer objects. We also need to add two new protocol methods to handle the delegate callbacks.

Though we could use the same callback and return a single-item array for the first call, we will want to keep both methods around. Nothing prevents you from passing a single player ID into the second method; however, the first method will serve useful purposes from time to time as well. Do not forget we are building a reusable library of Game Center calls.

Your protocols for GameCenterManagerDelegate should now look like the following code, assuming you have been following along since the beginning of this book:

```
@protocol GameCenterManagerDelegate <NSObject>
@optional
- (void)processGameCenterAuthentication:(NSError*)error;
- (void)friendsFinishedLoading:(NSArray *)friends error:(NSError *)error;
- (void)playerDataLoaded:(NSArray *)players error:(NSError *)error;
- (void)scoreReported: (NSError*) error;
- (void)leaderboardUpdated: (NSArray *)scores error:(NSError *)error;
- (void)mappedPlayerIDToPlayer:(GKPlayer *)player error:(NSError *)error;
- (void)mappedPlayerIDsToPlayers:(NSArray *)players error:(NSError *)error;
@end
```

Once you have a GKPlayer object for a given playerID, there are many ways to look up one based on the other. Once again for simplicity's sake, we will store all fetched players into an array and use a simple lookup.

The first thing we need to do is add a new NSMutableArray to our UFOLeaderboardViewController class. Let's name this new object playerArray. Don't forget to allocate and initialize it in the viewDidLoad method. Add a method for the new protocol that we just set up, and initialize it as shown in the following:

```
- (void)mappedPlayerIDToPlayer:(GKPlayer *)player error:(NSError *)error
{
        if (error != nil)
        {
                NSLog(@"Error during player mapping: %@", [error localizedDescription]);
        }
        else
        {
                [playerArray addObject: player];
        }

        [leaderboardTableView reloadData];
}
```

This method merely stores the retrieved GKPlayers into an array for future reference. If you were using the method that returns an array of players, your delegate callback would look like the following instead:

```
- (void)mappedPlayerIDsToPlayers:(NSArray *)players error:(NSError *)error
{
        if (error != nil)
        {
                NSLog(@"Error during player mapping: %@", [error localizedDescription]);
        }
        else
        {
                [playerArray addObjectsFromArray:players];
        }

        [leaderboardTableView reloadData];
}
```

We also need to add a new method that will handle iterating through our array and looking for a player match.

```
-(NSString *)playerNameforID:(NSString *)playerID;
{
        for (GKPlayer *player in playerArray)
        {
                if ([player.playerID isEqualToString: playerID])
                        continue;

                return player.alias;
        }

        return nil;
}
```

This method searches through the player array for a match on the playerID and returns the alias for that player. You could just as easily return the entire GKPlayer object if you wanted more information in your table cell, such as whether they are underage or are one of your friends.

The final step is to modify our cellForRow method to handle the new name lookup code. The following method will replace our old cellForRow method in UFOLeaderboardViewController.

```
- (UITableViewCell *)tableView:(UITableView *)tableView
        cellForRowAtIndexPath:(NSIndexPath *)indexPath
{
    static NSString *CellIdentifier = @"Cell";

    UITableViewCell *cell = [tableView dequeueReusableCellWithIdentifier:CellIdentifier];
    if (cell == nil)
    {
        cell = [[[UITableViewCell alloc] initWithStyle:↵
        UITableViewCellStyleSubtitle reuseIdentifier:CellIdentifier] autorelease];

        cell.selectionStyle = UITableViewCellSelectionStyleNone;
    }

    GKScore *score = [self.scoreArray objectAtIndex: indexPath.row];

    NSString *playerName = [self playerNameforID: score.playerID];

    if (playerName == nil)
    {
        [self.gcManager mapPlayerIDtoPlayer: score.playerID];
        cell.textLabel.text = @"Loading Name…";
    }
    else
    {
        cell.textLabel.text = playerName;
    }

    cell.detailTextLabel.text = score.formattedValue;

    return cell;
}
```

> **Tip** You can access the raw score data with the value property on GKScore. This will allow you to perform even more customization than is available in the score format type in iTunes Connect.

As you can see, in this method, we get a `GKScore` as we did in the previous example. We created a new string called `playerName` and use our new method to populate it. The first time this method is called, `playerNameforID` will return nil. During that event, we call our `mapPlayerIDtoPlayer` method and set the text in the cell to "Loading Name…". This serves as a placeholder until we can load in the full username. When we get a callback from the `GameCenterManager`, we reload the table. At this point, `playerNameforID` should return the alias for the player.

If the app is run again, you will see that we are now displaying proper player aliases instead of the player IDs (see Figure 3-12).

Figure 3-12. *A custom leaderboard that properly maps player aliases*

Note   Remember that the user can change their alias at any time, and you should always display the most up-to-date alias. With this in mind, you should always attempt to update the alias whenever displaying it. Do not cache once and then never request an update.

Local Player Score

There are often times that you will want to know the local player's score on a given leaderboard. Maybe you want to display their score at the top of your leaderboard, or perhaps you want to fetch a leaderboard that shows other player scores that are close to your local player's score.

Apple has provided an easy technique for determining the local player's score. During any GKLeaderboard request, it contains a property for localPlayerScore. We create a new method in our GameCenterManager to handle retrieving the local player score for us. Add the following method to your GameCenterManager class:

```
-(void)retrieveLocalScoreForCategory:(NSString *)category
{
        GKLeaderboard *leaderboardRequest = [[GKLeaderboard alloc] init];
        leaderboardRequest.category = category;

        [leaderboardRequest loadScoresWithCompletionHandler: ^(NSArray *scores,NSError*error)
        {
                [self callDelegateOnMainThread:@selector(localPlayerScore:error:) withArg:
        leaderboardRequest.localPlayerScore error:error];
        }];
}
```

This method functions in almost the same way as our previous score function. However, here we care about only the local player score for the category we are requesting. We also need to add a new protocol method to pass this data back to our delegate. Go ahead and set it, as shown in the following code snippet:

```
(void)localPlayerScore:(GKScore *)score error:(NSError *)error;
```

We now need to add our protocol implementation to UFOLeaderboardViewController. That method is presented next. We will not be directly using the local player's score in this demo, so we just print the value to the console.

```
- (void)localPlayerScore:(GKScore *)score error:(NSError *)error;
{
        if (error != nil)
        {
                NSLog(@"Error getting local score: %@", [error localizedDescription]);
        }
        else
        {
                NSLog(@"Local User Score: %@", score);
        }
}
```

Next, we call the GameCenterManager method for retrieving our local user score. Let's add that code to the viewDidLoad method of UFOLeaderboardviewController. Don't forget to change the category to match the one for the leaderboard you want to request.

```
[self.gcManager retrieveLocalScoreForCategory: @"com.dragonforged.ufo.single"];
```

If you run the app again, now you should see console output that looks similar to this:

```
2011-02-14 14:38:41.940 UFOs[22485:207] Local User Score: GKScore player=G:200192907 rank=2
date=2011-02-14 04:08:04 +0000 value=3 formattedValue=3 Points
```

A Better Approach

In the section "Posting a Score," earlier in this chapter, we discovered how to post new scores to Game Center. Our methodology, while simple, was not the best approach from a user-interaction standpoint. It is now time to refactor the posting new score code to improve usability. This approach is more complex, but delivers better performance and has less impact on the user.

The first thing we need to do is move our scoreReported method from UFOGameViewController to UFOViewController. We also want to modify the exit action in the UFOViewController. Modify that method to match the following.

```
-(IBAction)exitAction:(id)sender;
{
        [[self navigationController] popViewControllerAnimated: YES];
        [self.gcManager reportScore:score forCategory:@"com.dragonforged.ufo.single"];
}
```

We also need to add a single line of code to the viewWillAppear method, in UFOViewController, as follows.

```
gcManager.delegate = self;
```

This resets the delegate for our Game Center calls back to the UFOViewController. This allows us to exit the game without waiting for a network callback from the Game Center delegate. This method is more user-friendly, but it involves some delegate switching.

Challenges

iOS 6 introduced *challenges* to Game Center. A challenge allows a player's Game Center friend to compete with the local player to beat a high score or achievements. There is no additional work to add a challenge to your game or app if you are using Apple's built in GUI, a new section appears as part of the leaderboard view controllers to challenge a player, additionally a user can initiate a challenge from the Game Center.app.

If you are using a customized GUI for leaderboards, or if you would like to be able to issue a challenge programmatically, there is a new method available as part of GKScore. Creating a new challenge is as simple as using a GKScore object:

```
[(GKScore *)score issueChallengeToPlayers: (NSArray *)players message:@"Can you beat me?"];
```

There are also circumstances where it may be important to see a list of all the challenges that are currently pending for the local player; this can be done using the following code snippet:

```
[GKChallenge loadReceivedChallengesWithCompletionHandler:^(NSArray *challenges, NSError *error)
{
    if (error != nil)
    {
        NSLog(@"An error occurred: %@", [error localizedDescription]);
    }

    else
    {
        NSLog(@"Challenges: %@", challenges);
    }

}];
```

Each challenge also has an associated state, such as invalid, pending, or complete. To see the current state of a challenge you can use the following code:

```
if(challenge.state == GKChallengeStateCompleted)
    NSLog(@"Challenge Completed");
```

Finally you can decline a pending challenge programmatically using this statement:

```
[challenge decline];
```

> **Tip** When a player beats a challenge, Game Center will automatically reissue the challenge back to the originating player, informing them that they have been beaten and prompting them to accept a new challenge.

Challenges provide a great way to keep players engaged within a game; your players will do the marketing for you by continually challenging their friends. Challenges are offered to you automatically for any users running iOS 6 or higher through the Game Center.app or the native Game Center GUI. If you are using a custom leaderboard interface, the amount of time required to incorporate a challenge system will pay off in dividends by increased user interaction.

GKLeaderboard Sets

iOS 7 introduced an enhanced leaderboard cap from the previous limit of 25 to 100. However iOS 7 also added a new class GKLeaderboadSet that permits usage of up to 500 leaderboards. Once leaderboard sets are enabled for an app all leaderboards used in the app must be organized into a leaderboard set.

From iTunes Connect a new option is present for move all leaderboards into Display Sets, seen in Figure 3-13. When creating a leaderboard set you will be prompted for a Display Set Reference Name and Display Set ID, these are setup in the fashion as a typical leaderboard and a reverse DNS approach is recommended.

Leaderboards

Figure 3-13. *Enabling Leaderboard Sets in iTunes Connect for iOS 7*

Once a new leaderboard set is created additional display sets can be added and configured just like a typical leaderboard. A display set can contain multiple leaderboards and single leaderboards can belong to multiple display sets.

A new method is made available for retrieving a leaderboard set loadLeaderboardSetsWithCompletionHandler. This will return an array of GKLeaderboardSet objects which function in much the same manner as a single leaderboard, with the addition of groupIdentifier property string which returns the identifier for the leaderboard set that they belong to.

Summary

This chapter introduced leaderboards in Game Center. We covered the benefits of using a leaderboard, as well as the two available types. We learned how to post a score and recover for any errors that occurred during posting. We also looked at the requirements of getting leaderboards up and running in your app, using either Apple's provided GUI or a custom one.

Throughout the chapter, we continued to build our GameCenterManager class, adding the required methods to post scores, retrieve scores both local and global, map player IDs to GKPlayer objects, and display custom and built-in leaderboards.

You should now feel confident in adding a leaderboard to any existing or new iOS app. In the next chapter, we will explore all that Game Center achievements offer.

4

Achievements

"All men who have achieved great things have been great dreamers."

—Orison Swett Marden

The relatively new social gaming concept of *achievements* came along much later than the leaderboards we discussed in Chapter 3 and has gained a dramatic rise in popularity with the release of Microsoft's Xbox 360. Achievements offer a level of detail and accomplishment overlooked in leaderboards. Leaderboards show who possesses the leading score; on the other hand, achievements demonstrate a player's skills and strengths by rewarding the player for completing tasks, quests, objectives, or levels. When the achievements start to serve in-game purposes, they become more of a power-up over other players. The ability to view the achievements of others gives players a type of "bragging rights."

As social network–enabled gaming spreads and becomes prevalent, the achievement system feature has skyrocketed into even greater popularity. Just as everyone receives a trophy at a high school sporting event, every player wants to earn an achievement in a game.

Foursquare was one of the first websites to bring achievements out of the gaming world and into the social app universe. Foursquare calls its achievements "badges" (see Figure 4-1), but the basic concept is the same. Players receive a reward for completing a task, but the number of badges does not affect gameplay, or in this case, the ability for the user to use the app in any direct manner.

Figure 4-1. Foursquare for iPhone showing badges or achievements

Game Center has made adding an achievement system to your iOS app simple. In this chapter, we will learn how to add achievements to our demo game, UFOs. You will learn everything needed to fully integrate an achievement system into your app quickly and easily. Notably, you will learn how to:

■ Create new achievements

■ Display achievement progress

■ Add achievement hooks into your app

■ Progress and reset achievements

■ Customize the appearance of achievements

■ Work with achievement challenges

Why Achievements?

If it is not already apparent what achievements can add to your social app or game, let's take a moment to review some of the many benefits.

■ Achievements give your users an extra sense of accomplishment.

■ Achievements bring users back into your app more often. Users are more apt to return to your app to complete more achievements, making completing the game a more rewarding and fun process.

- Achievements add an easy way for users to share experiences with other users.

- Achievements in Game Center provide a polished look and feel to the product you're shipping.

- Achievements give users a greater sense of progression as they make their way through your app or game.

- Achievements provide an alternative way to play the game. If users do not enjoy the campaign, they can enjoy a sense of accomplishment through your achievement system.

- Achievements contribute to game brand awareness. As users share their accomplishments on Twitter and Facebook, name recognition increases, and with it sales.

- Achievements can provide a goal or end to your game that otherwise might be open-ended. Games such as trivia or board games often do not have conventional endings.

- Achievement challenges can help draw additional users into your product.

An Overview of Achievements in Game Center

Achievements, also known as badges, function slightly differently in Game Center than on other platforms. Like leaderboards, achievements first need to be configured in iTunes Connect on a per-app basis. You will be creating new instances of a GKAchievement object to report progress (more on this in the "Modifying Achievement Progress" section). Unlike leaderboard entries, which are created when a score is reached and submitted, achievements can report incremental progress.

Another notable change from working with leaderboards (see Chapter 3 for more on leaderboards) is that you will use two types of objects to submit and retrieve achievements. GKAchievement is used to submit new achievements or update progress on achievements, and GKAchievementDescription is used to display achievement data to the user. This is contrary to what we saw when working with leaderboards, in which GKScore objects were used to submit data as well as retrieve it.

As you can with leaderboards, you can show achievement progress using either Apple's included graphical user interface (GUI) or a customized one that better matches the look and feel of your app. The benefits and disadvantages of each system are the same as with leaderboards. I'll summarize those benefits and disadvantages, adding minor achievement-specific information where appropriate.

Benefits of Using Apple's Achievement GUI vs. a Custom GUI

The following are some of the benefits that you will gain by using Apple's included GUI for working with achievements.

- The look and feel of your achievements is created by some of the best designers in the world.

- The GUI is very simple to implement, making it easy to present the achievement progress to your users.

- Users appreciate a familiar interface with which they already know how to interact.

- Your app is more future-proof than it would be if you implemented your own system.

- New features are automatically included as they become available, as seen with Challenges, added with the introduction of iOS 6.

The following are a few of the benefits of using your own GUI when working with achievements on iOS devices.

- Your achievement progress can match the custom design of your app.

- You have more freedom over the returned data and can filter using additional criteria.

- You can implement your own custom caching behavior.

- You can use custom images for incomplete or in-progress achievements.

As you can see, there are advantages and disadvantages of each system, and there is no right answer to which one you should be using. By the end of this chapter you will have a better understanding of the options and be better equipped to decide which approach is the best fit for your app.

As mentioned at the beginning of this section, you will need to begin working with achievements in the same manner as we did for leaderboards, iniTunes Connect.

Configuring Achievements in iTunes Connect

As we saw with leaderboards, you cannot begin working with achievements without first setting up at least one new achievement in iTunes Connect. Log in to iTunes Connect (itunesconnect.apple.com) using your username and password, and select the app that we have already been working with from the previous chapters (see Chapter 2 for more information). Once you have selected your app from the control panel, return to the Manage Game Center area that was introduced earlier in this book.

The Game Center portal for your app will have a section labeled Achievements. If this is the first time you've worked with achievements in this app, a button labeled Set Up will appear. If you already have achievements in place, the steps are different and will be covered later in this section.

Clicking the Set Up button will bring up the Achievements Configuration screen. Select the Add New Achievement button in the upper-left corner of the page, as shown in Figure 4-2. This will bring you to the view shown in Figure 4-3.

Figure 4-2. *Adding a new achievement through the iTunes Connect Portal*

Figure 4-3. *The configuration view for new achievements in iTunes Connect*

You might notice that there are a lot of similarities between this portal page and the leaderboard portal page. Table 4-1 summarizes the attributes.

Table 4-1. *Achievement Attributes in iTunes Connect*

Attribute	Description
Achievement Reference Name	Not used outside of iTunes Connect, this string is used to easily locate and reference this achievement within iTunes Connect.
Achievement ID	This is the identifier that you will refer to in your code. As with leaderboard categories, Apple recommends that you use a reverse DNS system, such as com.company.appname.achievementname.
Hidden	If an achievement is hidden, the user will not see it in the achievement list until they have either completed it or increased their progress.
Points	Achievements can be assigned points. Your app is allocated 1,000 points. Each completed achievement progresses the user toward that total. Once the user has reached 1,000 points, they have unlocked all achievements.
	You should assign more points to achievements that are more difficult to complete. This provides the user with a better sense of how valuable the achievement is.
	Point values are optional and can be ignored if you do not want to use them within your app.

> **Tip**   You aren't required to have your achievements add up to 1,000 total points, but you cannot exceed 1,000 points.

Creating a New Achievement

It is now time to make a new achievement. We will create an achievement that will be reached when the user abducts 25 cows. We will use Abduct 25 for the achievement name so it will be easy to find when we have dozens of achievements. For our achievement ID, we will use com.dragonforged. ufo.abduct25. Feel free to use whatever ID you want here, but make sure to substitute it for com. dragonforged.ufo.abduct25 in the upcoming examples. We will make this an unhidden achievement, and assign it a point value of 10.

> **Note**   No achievement can have more than 100 points awarded for completing it.

For an achievement to be valid, you must configure at least one language. As you can see in Figure 4-4, the localization area of achievements is much different than that encountered when creating leaderboards in the previous chapter. Refer to Table 4-2 for information on each attribute.

Figure 4-4. Localizing an achievement in iTunes Connect

Table 4-2. Localized Achievement Attributes in iTunes Connect

Attribute	Description
Language	Select the language in which this achievement will appear. You must set up a language for each localization that you will support in your shipping product.
Title	This is the title that will appear within the app to describe this achievement.
Pre-earned Description	This is the description that appears when the achievement is unhidden and is unearned or only partially completed.
Earned Description	This is the description that is shown when the achievement has been fully unlocked and completed.
Image	This is the image that will be displayed to the user when the achievement is earned. Apple will supply the unearned image, or you can specify your own when working with a custom achievement GUI. This image must be 512 × 512 and 72 DPI.
Achievable More Than Once	This allows the player to accept challenges on achievements that they have previously completed. For more details see the section "Achievement Challenges."

Note   Each game owns its achievement descriptions; you may not share achievement descriptions between multiple games.

For our purposes, we will configure this achievement for English. My example will use "Abduct 25 Cows" as the title, but you may use any title that you prefer. For the pre-earned description, I chose "Abduct 25 cows with your UFO." For the earned description, I used "You have mastered the art of cow abduction." I will also use a cow-crossing-road sign as the image. When you are done, you should have a fully set up achievement, which should look similar to the view shown in Figure 4-5.

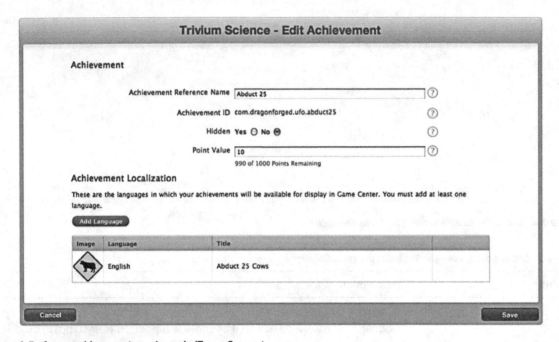

Figure 4-5. A new achievement, as shown in iTunes Connect

We will want to work with a couple of different achievement setups for our game. Go ahead and create another new achievement for abducting a single cow; this will be our nonprogressive achievement. Then make a third achievement for five-minute play time and set it to hidden. This last achievement will let us work with timers, progressive achievements, and hidden achievements. You may select any point values, descriptions, titles, and images you want for these achievements, but make sure you make note of the achievement IDs.

You should now have three achievements configured in iTunes Connect for our game. We can now get back into Xcode and begin working with these achievements at a code level.

Presenting Achievements

Unlike leaderboards, there will be plenty to preview GUI-wise before we populate user data into our achievement system. It is helpful to see the effects that modifying achievements will have on how they are displayed through the default GUI. In this chapter, we will begin by presenting Apple's achievement GUI, then move on to submitting user data. We will also cover custom GUI achievements later in this chapter.

Before we can begin, we need to create a new UIbutton that will trigger the achievement view. We most likely want to do this outside the game screen, as we did with the two leaderboard buttons. We begin by adding a new button to the UFOViewController view, as shown in Figure 4-6.

Figure 4-6. Adding a new button to trigger our achievement view

You also need to create and hook up an IBAction to our new Achievements button. Insert the following code into the action that you hooked up to the Achievements button.

```
-(IBAction)achievementButtonPressed;
{
    GKAchievementViewController *controller = nil;
      controller = [[GKAchievementViewController alloc] init];
        [achievementViewController setAchievementDelegate:self];
        [self presentViewController:achievementViewController animated:YES completion:nil];
      [controller release];
}
```

> **Tip** Starting with iOS 6, you can now create a game center view that can be used for achievements, leaderboards and challenges, using GKGameCenterViewController. Using GKAchievementViewController on iOS 6 will launch a GKGameCenterViewController that is preselected to the achievements section, while maintaining backward-compatibility.

In addition, we need to hook up a delegate callback to be used with the GKAchievementViewController. Add the following method to your implementation file:

```
- (void)achievementViewControllerDidFinish:(GKAchievementViewController *)viewController
{
    [self dismissViewControllerAnimated:YES completion:nil];
}
```

If you were to run the app now and tap the Achievements button, you would see a view similar to the one shown in Figure 4-7. The achievements shown are using Apple's unearned image. Apple recommends that you always use its unearned image, but when working with a custom achievement GUI, you can override this image and return your own.

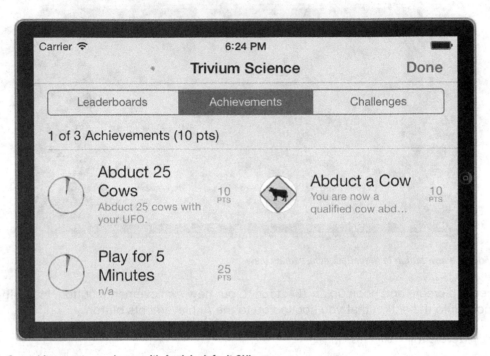

Figure 4-7. Our achievements, as shown with Apple's default GUI

Next, recall that we set up three achievements, one of them hidden. As you can see in Figure 4-7, the provided view shows us only two achievements. Because we have not submitted any kind of progress to the third achievement, its details are hidden from the user. However, you can see that the top information line reflects that there is a hidden achievement (1 of 3 Achievements). Also notice that the achievements are using the localized unearned description that was set in iTunes Connect.

These are the only necessary steps to show the user their achievement progress through Apple's built-in GUI. In the next section, we will look at how to update and progress these achievements. Later in this chapter, you will learn how to present achievements using a custom GUI.

> **Note**   Users can always see their achievement progress in Game Center.app, but it is recommended to allow your user a way to view their progress from within your app as well.

Modifying Achievement Progress

Unlike leaderboard entries, achievements can be constantly modified and progressed through user interaction. As we've done with the other Game Center functionality we have been working with, we will create a new method in our GameCenterManager class to handle interacting with achievements. Once you have added the following method, we will review the code to understand exactly how it functions.

> **Tip**   Remember that all of this source code is available to you online, at http:/ apress.com. When dealing with large methods, it might be easier to copy it from the downloaded source code.

```
- (void)submitAchievement:(NSString*)identifier percentComplete:(double)percentComplete
{
     if ([self earnedAchievementCache] == NULL)
      {
            [GKAchievement loadAchievementsWithCompletionHandler:^(NSArray↩
            *achievements, NSError *error) {
                if (error == NULL)
                  {
                          NSMutableDictionary *tempCache = [NSMutableDictionary↩
                          dictionaryWithCapacity:[achievements count]];

                      for (GKAchievement* achievement in achievements)
                          {
                                  [tempCache setObject: achievement forKey:↩
                                  [achievement identifier]];
                      }

                        [self setEarnedAchievementCache:tempCache];
                          [self submitAchievement:identifier percentComplete:↩
                          percentComplete];
                }
                    else
                    {
                        [self callDelegateOnMainThread:↩
                        @selector(achievementSubmitted: error:) withArg:NULL↩
                        error:error];
                }
        }];
     }
      else
      {
            GKAchievement *achievement = [[self earnedAchievementCache]↩
        objectForKey:identifier];
```

```
                if (achievement != NULL)
                {
                     if (([achievement percentComplete] >= 100.0) ||↵
                       ([achievement percentComplete] >= percentComplete))
                       {
                            achievement = NULL;
                       }
                    [achievement setPercentComplete:percentComplete];
                }
                else
                  {
                        achievement = [[[GKAchievement alloc] initWithIdentifier:identifier]↵
                        autorelease];

                        [achievement setPercentComplete:percentComplete];
                        [[self earnedAchievementCache] setObject:achievement↵
                        forKey:[achievement identifier]];
                  }

                if (achievement != NULL)
                  {
                        [achievement reportAchievementWithCompletionHandler:^(NSError↵
                        *error) {
                                [self callDelegateOnMainThread:↵
                                @selector(achievementSubmitted:error:)↵
                        withArg: achievement error:error];
                        }];
                  }
          }
      }
}
```

Before this code can be executed, you need to add a new class property. Create a new mutable dictionary (and don't forget to synthesize it). The relevant section of the header of GameCenterManager should now look like the following.

```
@interface GameCenterManager : NSObject <GameCenterManagerDelegate>
{
      id <GameCenterManagerDelegate, NSObject> delegate;
      NSMutableDictionary* earnedAchievementCache;
}

@property(nonatomic, retain) id <GameCenterManagerDelegate, NSObject> delegate;
@property(nonatomic, retain) NSMutableDictionary* earnedAchievementCache;
```

Loading Achievements

Now look at the submitAchievement:percentComplete: method we added. There are two primary if/else blocks. The first one is executed if [self earnedAchievemenetCache] is NULL, which it will always be the first time this code is executed. Let's take a look at that block of code now.

```
[GKAchievement loadAchievementsWithCompletionHandler:^(NSArray *achievements, NSError *error) {
        if (error == NULL)
        {
                NSMutableDictionary *tempCache = [NSMutableDictionary↵
                dictionaryWithCapacity: [achievements count]];

            for (GKAchievement *achievement in achievements)
                {
                    [tempCache setObject:achievement forKey:[achievement identifier]];
                }

            [self setEarnedAchievementCache:tempCache];
            [self submitAchievement:identifier percentComplete:percentComplete];
        }
        else
        {
            [self callDelegateOnMainThread:@selector(achievementSubmitted:error:)↵
            withArg:NULL error:error];
        }
}];
```

> **Important**   The array that is returned by loadAchievementsWithCompletionHandler will not show
> any achievements for which you have not yet submitted a percentageCompleted.

The primary function of this code snippet is to load a list of achievements into the earnedAchievementCache We call loadAchievementsWithCompletionHandler on GKAchievement. This call returns an array of all the achievements that were set up in iTunes Connect. We then store the GKAchievement object into the dictionary with the identifier as the key.

At this point, the code calls submitAchievement:percentComplete again. This time, earnedAchievementCache is not NULL and the second set of code is executed. If we encounter an error during this process, we use our standard delegate callback to send the error back to our delegate.

You will need to add a new protocol method to GameCenterManager to handle this delegate callback; this is a good time to do that. Add the following optional protocol to the header file:

```
- (void)achievementSubmitted:(GKAchievement*)achievement error:(NSError*)error;
```

Now let's take a look at the second section of code. The following code, when successfully executed, submits the achievement to the Game Center servers.

```
GKAchievement *achievement = [[self earnedAchievementCache] objectForKey:identifier];
if (achievement != NULL)
{
        if ((achievement.percentComplete >= 100.0) || (achievement.percentComplete >=↵
        percentComplete))
            {
                  achievement = NULL;
            }

        [achievement setPercentComplete:percentComplete];
}
else
{
        achievement = [[[GKAchievement alloc] initWithIdentifier: identifier] autorelease];
        [achievement setPercentComplete:percentComplete];

        [[self earnedAchievementCache] setObject:achievement forKey:[achievement identifier]];
}

if (achievement != NULL)
{
        [achievement reportAchievementWithCompletionHandler: ^(NSError *error) {
        [self callDelegateOnMainThread:@selector(achievementSubmitted:error:)↵
          withArg:achievement error:error];

        }];
}
```

The first line of code retrieves a GKAchievement object from our earnedAchievementCache, based on the identifier string that is passed into this method. If the achievement is completed or the reported progress is equal to what we have on the Game Center server, we set the achievement to NULL. This prevents us from tying up networking time by submitting progress on something that will be ignored. We also set the property for percentComplete on the GKAchievement object to the double that was passed into this method.

In the event that the achievement doesn't exist in the cache, we allocate and initialize a new instance of it. In this event, we also want to add it to our local achievement cache.

The final step, after doing a NULL check, is to submit the achievement. We call reportAchievementWithCompletionHandler on the achievement object. We then pass the results back to our delegate using our existing protocol.

Note All achievements have a percentageComplete regardless of whether they allow a percentage to be completed at a time. If your achievement can only be completely earned or unearned, then you will want to pass 100 for earned.

Achievement Protocol

The last thing that we need to do in this section is implement our protocol method in
`UFOGameViewController`. Add the following method to the implementation of that file; all we will worry
about right now is printing the error and success information to the console.

```
- (void)achievementSubmitted:(GKAchievement *)achievement error:(NSError *)error;
{
    if (error)
     {
         NSLog(@"There was an error in reporting the achievement: %@", [error↵
            localizedDescription]);
    }
     else
      {
         NSLog(@"achievement submitted");
    }
}
```

Resetting Achievements

There are circumstances when you might want to reset user achievements. Not only is doing so
extremely helpful in debugging; you might find it also useful to provide users with an option to
reset. You might want to add a prestige mode or give the users a chance to start your game over
from the beginning. The following code snippet will completely reset all achievements in your app
for the local user.

```
- (void)resetAchievements
{
    [self setEarnedAchievementCache:NULL];

    [GKAchievement resetAchievementsWithCompletionHandler:^(NSError *error) {
            if (error == NULL)
             {
                 NSLog(@"Achievements have been reset");
            }
             else
             {
                 NSLog(@"There was an error in resetting the achievements: %@", [error↵
            localizedDescription]);
            }
    }];
}
```

Important   Don't forget to remove the cached information you have stored on the achievements, or you will
not be able to progress the reset achievements until the app is restarted.

Adding Achievement Hooks

The biggest challenge in implementing achievements into your app is adding the hooks to activate and progress those achievements into your normal routines. I have found that adding these hooks when the program is almost finished is easier than trying to add them in as you go.

In this section, I will provide a number of examples of how to tie in achievements; your own app may differ significantly, but you should be able to adapt the examples easily to suit the specific needs of the achievements.

To make it easier to retrieve achievement progress details, we first add a few convenience methods to our GameCenterManager class. This is the first method we will use to populate the local achievement cache.

```
- (void)populateAchievementCache
{
    if ([self earnedAchievementCache] == NULL)
    {
        [GKAchievement loadAchievementsWithCompletionHandler:^(NSArray *achievements, ↵
        NSError *error) {
            if (error == NULL)
            {
                NSMutableDictionary* tempCache= [NSMutableDictionary ↵
                dictionaryWithCapacity: [achievements count]];

                for (GKAchievement *achievement in achievements)
                {
                            [tempCache setObject:achievement forKey:[achievement
                            identifier]];
                }

                [self setEarnedAchievementCache:tempCache];
            }
            else
            {
                NSLog(@"An error occurred while loading achievements: %@", ↵
                [error localizedDescription]);
            }
        }];
    }
}
```

This method functions very similarly to the cache population code in the submit achievement progress method previewed in the previous section. We will need to populate the local cache in order to work with the other two convenience methods. We will want to call the populateAchievementCache as soon as we can after authenticating; in our demo app, I have added a call to it from the local player did authenticate method in GameCenterManager. Add the following method as well.

```
- (double)percentageCompleteOfAchievementWithIdentifier:(NSString*)identifier
{
    if ([self earnedAchievementCache] == NULL)
    {
        NSLog(@"Unable to determine achievement progress, local cache is empty");
    }
    else
    {
        GKAchievement *achievement= [[self earnedAchievementCache]
        objectForKey:identifier];

        if (achievement != NULL)
        {
            return [achievement percentComplete];
        }
        else
        {
            return 0;
        }
    }
    return -1;
}
```

This method returns a double for the percent complete for the achievement with the identifier passed to it. If it cannot find a copy of the achievement in the local cache, we can assume the percent complete is 0. The next method uses this method to return either YES or NO on whether an achievement has been completed.

```
- (BOOL)achievementWithIdentifierIsComplete: (NSString*)identifier
{
    if ([self percentageCompleteOfAchievementWithIdentifier:identifier] >= 100)
      {
        return YES;
    }
      else
      {
        return NO;
    }
}
```

> **Note** Do not forget to call populateAchievementCache as soon as possible after authentication. Otherwise, these convenience methods will not return the correct achievement data.

Adding Hooks in UFOs

Now that we have some helper methods in place, we can begin to hook up the achievement hooks for UFOs. We have three achievements we need to tie in. The first two both have to do with the number of cows that we have abducted, so let's start there. Modify the finishAbducting method of UFOGameViewController to match the following.

```
- (void)finishAbducting
{
    if (!currentAbductee || !tractorBeamOn) return;

    [cowArray removeObjectIdenticalTo:currentAbductee];

    [tractorBeamImageView removeFromSuperview];

   tractorBeamOn = NO;

    score++;
    [scoreLabel setText:[NSString stringWithFormat:@"SCORE %05.0f", score]];

    [[currentAbductee layer] removeAllAnimations];
   [currentAbductee removeFromSuperview];

    currentAbductee = nil;

      [self spawnCow];

    if (![[self gcManager] achievementWithIdentifierIsComplete:⏎
     @"com.dragonforged.ufo.aduct1"])
       {
            [[self gcManager] submitAchievement:@"com.dragonforged.ufo.aduct1"⏎
         percentComplete:100];
    }
}
```

We are concerned with only the last few lines of this method at this time. First, we call our convenience method achievementWithIdentifierIsComplete on our identifier string for a single abduction. Because this is an earned or unearned achievement, we don't need to worry about current percentage complete. To mark the achievement as complete, we set its percent complete to 100.

> **Note**   Don't forget to change the identifier string from the example to the one that you used (if different) in iTunes Connect for a single abduction.

The next achievement is hooked up in a similar fashion; the only difference is that we use incremental progress. Add the following code snippet to the end of the finishAbducting method.

```
if (![[self gcManager] achievementWithIdentifierIsComplete:⏎
@"com.dragonforged.ufo.abduct25"])
{
    double percentComplete = [[self gcManager]⏎
      percentageCompleteOfAchievementWithIdentifier: @"com.dragonforged.ufo.abduct25"];
```

```
percentComplete += 4;
[[self gcManager] submitAchievement:@"com.dragonforged.ufo.abduct25"↩
    percentComplete:percentComplete];

}
```

In this code snippet, we use the same methodology that we did for submitting a complete achievement, but with one main difference. We first need to determine the current progress on the achievement. We then add 4 to it, since 4 percent of 25 is one. To increment by a single abduction out of 25, we need to add 4 percent.

> **Tip** Do not forget about the `resetAchievement` method that we added to `GameCenterManager`. It is very useful in debugging the submit code. It is helpful to keep a call to this in the `didAuthenticate` section to always put the app back to a clean state during debugging.

Go ahead and run the game and abduct a few cows. When you are done, you will notice that the achievement screen now shows progress similar to that shown in Figure 4-8. If you abducted at least one cow, you should have a complete achievement. If you abducted fewer than 25 cows, you should have one progressed achievement. Notice that the user is not informed when they complete an achievement; we will discuss a method of notification in the later section "Providing Feedback on Completing an Achievement."

Figure 4-8. View progressing achievements using the Apple-provided interface

A Time-Based Achievement Hook

The last hook we add for this project handles the player for the five-minute achievement. Your first instinct is probably to keep track of time played, and submit it as progress when your user exits the game. This might not be the best approach. We want to inform the user when they complete an achievement. You don't want them to have to wait until they finish a game to see which achievements they have earned. There are many approaches to this problem. For this example, we will fire an NSTimer every three seconds (which is one percent of five minutes) and update the achievement progress. Add the following code to UFOGameViewController.

```
- (void)tickThreeSeconds
{
        if ([[self gcManager]achievementWithIdentifierIsComplete:↩
        @"com.dragonforged.ufo.play5"]) return;

        double percentComplete = [[self gcManager]↩
          percentageCompleteOfAchievementWithIdentifier:@"com.dragonforged.ufo.play5"];

        percentComplete++;
        [[self gcManager] submitAchievement:@"com.dragonforged.ufo.play5"↩
      percentComplete:percentComplete];
}
```

Here we start a three-second timer. Every time the timer fires, we call tickThreeSeconds. This gives us our current progress of the achievement, to which we add one percent, and then submits it back to the server. In the event that the achievement is already complete, the method simply returns. In addition, modify the viewDidAppear and viewWillDisappear methods to match the following:

```
-(void)viewDidAppear:(BOOL)animated
{
        [super viewDidAppear: animated];

      timer = [NSTimer scheduledTimerWithTimeInterval:3.0 target:self↩
      selector:@selector(tickThreeSeconds) userInfo:nil repeats:YES];
}

- (void)viewWillDisappear:(BOOL)animated
{
        [super viewWillDisappear: animated];
        [timer invalidate];
      timer = nil;
}
```

Another Convenience Method

There might be occasions where you would like to get GKAchievement but all you have available is an achievement identifier. The following method will return a GKAchievement when passed an achievement identifier.

```
- (GKAchievement*)achievementForIdentifier:(NSString*)identifier
{
    GKAchievement *achievement = [[self earnedAchievementCache] objectForKey:identifier];

    if (achievement == nil)
    {
        achievement = [[[GKAchievement alloc] initWithIdentifier:identifier] autorelease];
        [[self earnedAchievementCache] setObject:achievement forKey:[achievement
    identifier]];
    }

    return achievement;
}
```

Providing Feedback on Completing an Achievement

It is important to let users know when they have completed an achievement. However, you don't want to just present a UIAlertView, as that would be very distracting, considering that most achievements are going to be completed in the middle of an action, such as completing 20 laps in a racing game. You wouldn't want to take the user away from any interaction, so we need a better system. I have always been a fan of the small view that slides in from the bottom or top to inform the user of the accomplishment—very similar to the way you get feedback logging in to Game Center. Since iOS 5, Apple has provided a built in achievement banner; see the section "Achievement Completion Banners" later in this chapter for its use.

The first thing we need to do in order to implement a feedback system is add a new protocol method to GameCenterManager. We will use this to inform the delegate that an achievement has been completed for the first time. Add the following method to the header file, as an optional protocol:

```
-(void)achievementEarned:(GKAchievementDescription*)achievement;
```

In addition, we need to modify our existing submitAchievement:percentComplete: method. Take a look at the last if statement block of that method. We want to modify it as shown next. Begin by adding an if statement to determine whether we have a percentageComplete over 100, which will call our new protocol. Also notice that we are using GKAchievementDescription instead of GKAchievement. We will discuss this method further in the later section, "Retrieving Achievement Data."

```
if (achievement != NULL)
{
    [achievement reportAchievementWithCompletionHandler:^(NSError *error) {
        if (percentComplete< 100)
        {
            [self callDelegateOnMainThread:↵
            @selector(achievementSubmitted:error:)↵
             withArg:achievement error:error];

            return;
        }
```

```
            [GKAchievementDescription↵
            loadAchievementDescriptionsWithCompletionHandler:↵
            ^(NSArray *descriptions, NSError *error) {
                for (GKAchievementDescription *achievementDescription in descriptions)
                {
                        if (![[achievement identifier] isEqualToString:↵
                        [achievementDescription identifier]]) continue;

                        [self callDelegateOnMainThread:@selector↵
                        (achievementEarned:)↵
                withArg:achievementDescription error:nil];
                }
        }];

        [self callDelegateOnMainThread:@selector(achievementSubmitted:error:)↵
    withArg:achievement error:error];
    }];
}
```

This completes the modifications that we need to make to the GameCenterManager class. Now we need to hook up the visual feedback for the user. Move back into UFOGameViewController.m and add our new protocol method, achievementEarned:. You could add any type of feedback here, including a standard UIAlertView, but we will be exploring something a little more user-friendly in this section.

We need to create some new IBOutlets as part of our UFOGameViewController. Make a new view and set its dimensions to 480 × 25. Then set the background of the view to black with 70% opacity. We also create a new label, place it in the center of this view, and set the text alignment to center. Your view should look similar to that shown in Figure 4-9.

Figure 4-9. Achievement earned view and label

Hook up both the view and the label to IBOutlets. The sample code names them achievementCompletionView and achievementCompletionLabel, respectively. We then modify our achievementEarned: method, as well as add an additional method to handle the animations.

```
- (void)achievementEarned:(GKAchievementDescription *)achievement;
{
        [achievementCompletionView setFrame:CGRectMake(0, 320, 480, 25)];
        [[self view] addSubview:achievementCompletionView];
    [achievementcompletionLabel setText:[achievement achievedDescription]];

        [UIView beginAnimations:@"SlideInAchievement" context:nil];
        [UIView setAnimationDuration:0.5];
        [UIView setAnimationDelegate:self];
        [UIView setAnimationDidStopSelector:@selector(achievementEarnedAnimationDone)];
```

```
        [achievementCompletionView setFrame:CGRectMake(0, 295, 480, 25)];
        [UIView commitAnimations];
}

-(void)achievementEarnedAnimationDone
{
        [UIView beginAnimations:@"SlideInAchievement" context:nil];
        [UIView setAnimationDelay:5.0];
        [UIView setAnimationDuration:1.0];
        [achievementCompletionView setFrame:CGRectMake(0, 320, 480, 25)];
        [UIView commitAnimations];
}
```

Both of these methods are fairly straightforward. When the app gets a delegate callback from completing the achievement, we add our achievementCompletionView to our game view. Then, we animate it into the bottom of the view. After a five-second delay, we animate it back off the view. You also have access to the images used in GKAchievementDescription. We will examine these properties further in the next section.

> **Tip**   You might need to reset your achievements to see any completion progress. I find it helpful to create a new button that resets achievements for use during testing.

If you run the app now and abduct a single cow (assuming you haven't yet accomplished that achievement), you should see output very similar to that shown in Figure 4-10.

Figure 4-10. Displaying a customized achievement banner

Adding Achievement Completion Banners

When Game Center was first released, you as developer were responsible for creating and displaying achievement feedback for your users. After the first updates to the game center APIs, Apple added in iOS 5 a very easy-to-use property to the GKAchievement class to allow you to quickly implement this step: setting the showsCompletionBanner property as seen in the following code snippet with display a message to the user when an achievement has been completed. The default property of showsCompletionBanner is NO.

```
myAchievement.showsCompletionBanner = YES;
```

A Custom Achievement GUI

There might be times when you will want to customize the appearance of your achievement system to match the custom GUI in your app. As you saw with leaderboards in the previous chapter, we have the ability to work with the raw data and present it in whatever fashion we choose. This section focuses on adding achievements to your app using your own GUI. As we did with custom leaderboards, the first thing we need to do is add a new button to display our custom achievement progress view. Add a new button and associated action, as shown in Figure 4-11.

Figure 4-11. Adding a custom achievement button in Interface Builder

We will need to create a new class to handle processing and displaying the achievement progress information. Create a new class named UFOAchievementViewController and make it a subclass of UIViewController. Set up actions and outlets in the XIB for a table view, a navigation bar, and a Dismiss button. Don't forget to set the datasource and delegate for the table view as well. Your XIB should look like the one shown in Figure 4-12.

Figure 4-12. Custom achievement progress view, as shown for Interface Builder

We also want to create an array that will be used to hold the achievement data. Create a new NSArray object and name it achievementArray. We also want to import the GameCenterManager header and conform to its protocol. The header file for UFOAchievementViewController should now look similar to the following.

```
#import <UIKit/UIKit.h>
#import "GameCenterManager.h"

@interface UFOAchievementViewController : UIViewController <UITableViewDelegate,↵
 UITableViewDataSource, GameCenterManagerDelegate>
{
    GameCenterManager *gcManager;

    UITableView *achievementTableView;

    NSArray *achievementArray;
}

@property (nonatomic, retain) GameCenterManager *gcManager;
@property (nonatomic, retain) NSArray *achievementArray;
@property (nonatomic, retain) IBOutlet UITableView *achievementTableView;

- (IBAction)dismissAction;

@end
```

Next, hook up the action to present our new UFOAchievementViewController class. Edit the action that was created in UFOViewController to reflect the following changes:

```
- (IBAction)customAchievementButtonPressed;
{
        UFOAchievementViewController *achievementViewController =↵
          [[UFOAchievementViewController alloc] init];

        [achievementViewController setGcManager:gcManager];

        [self presentViewController:achievementViewController animated:YES completion:nil];

        [achievementViewController release];
}
```

Let's take a minute to switch over to the implementation file for UFOAchievementViewController. First, add a method to ensure that the view is properly set for landscape orientation. Add the following method:

```
-(BOOL) shouldAutorotateToInterfaceOrientation:↵
  (UIInterfaceOrientation)interfaceOrientation
{
        if (UIInterfaceOrientationIsLandscape(interfaceOrientation)) return YES;

        return NO;
}
```

We also need a dismiss action, so add that method as well:

```
- (IBAction)dismissAction
{
     [self dismissViewControllerAnimated:YES completion:nil];
}
```

If you were to run the app now, you should see a plain and boring table view, similar to the one shown in Figure 4-13. In addition, the Dismiss button should now be working.

Figure 4-13. The blank custom table that we will use for our custom achievements

Retrieving Achievement Data

Before we can go on with our `UFOAchievementViewController`, we need to move back into our `GameCenterManager` class. Add the following method as an optional protocol to the `GameCenterManagerDelegate`:

```
- (void)achievementDescriptionsLoaded:(NSArray *)descriptions error:(NSError *)error;
```

Then add the following new method to the implementation of `GameCenterManager`:

```
- (void)retrieveAchievementMetadata
{
    [GKAchievementDescription loadAchievementDescriptionsWithCompletionHandler:
     ^(NSArray *descriptions, NSError *error) {
        [self callDelegateOnMainThread:@selector
        (achievementDescriptionsLoaded:error:) withArg:descriptions error:error];
    }];
}
```

This method will return every GKAchievementDescription found on the Game Center server. We can now move back to our UFOAchievementViewController class and finish implementing the custom achievement table.

> **Important**   The retrieveAchievementMetadata method will return hidden achievements as well. If you want to hide these from the user, you will have to filter them out of the results.

Modify the viewWillAppear: method of UFOAchievementViewController to match the following:

```
- (void)viewWillAppear:(BOOL)animated
{
    [[self gcManager] setDelegate:self];

     [super viewWillAppear: YES];

    [[self gcManager] retrieveAchievementMetadata];
}
```

In addition, add the new protocol method that we created earlier. If we do not encounter any errors, we simply set the returned descriptions to our local array. When we get the new data, we will also want to refresh the table to show the data to the user. Here's the code:

```
- (void)achievementDescriptionsLoaded:(NSArray *)descriptions error:(NSError *)error;
{
    if (error == nil)
    {
        [self setAchievementArray:descriptions];
    }
    else
    {
        NSLog(@"An error occurred when retrieving the achievement descriptions: %@",
        [error localizedDescription]);
    }

    [achievementTableView reloadData];
}
```

For our numberOfRowsInSection method, we simply return the count on the achievementArray, as follows.

```
- (NSInteger)tableView:(UITableView *)tableView numberOfRowsInSection:(NSInteger)section
{
    return [[self achievementArray] count];
}
```

We also need to implement a cellForRowAtIndexPath method. Add the following method to the implementation as well. After it is added, we will look at it in more detail.

```objc
- (UITableViewCell *)tableView:(UITableView *)tableView
 cellForRowAtIndexPath:(NSIndexPath *)indexPath
{
    static NSString *CellIdentifier = @"Cell";
    UITableViewCell *cell = [tableView dequeueReusableCellWithIdentifier:CellIdentifier];

    if (cell == nil)
    {
        cell = [[[UITableViewCell alloc] initWithStyle:UITableViewCellStyleDefault
        reuseIdentifier:CellIdentifier] autorelease];
        [cell setSelectionStyle:UITableViewCellSelectionStyleNone];
    }

    GKAchievementDescription *achievementDescription = [[self achievementArray]
    objectAtIndex:[indexPath row]];
    [[cell textLabel] setText:[achievementDescription title]];

    if ([achievementDescription image] == nil)
    {
        [[cell imageView] setImage:[GKAchievementDescription
        placeholderCompletedAchievementImage]];
            [achievementDescription loadImageWithCompletionHandler:^(UIImage *image,
            NSError*error) {
                if (error == nil)
                {
                    [[cell imageView] setImage:image];
                }
            }];
    }
    else
    {
        [[cell imageView] setImage:[achievementDescription image]];
    }

    return cell;
}
```

The first half of this method is rather standard; we create a new table cell or use one from our reusable collection. We are using the default built-in table cell to save some time as well. We create a new GKAchievementDescription and populate it based on the row number from our achievementArray.

The first property we work with is the title, which we use to set the textLabel of the cell. In most circumstances, you will want to use the achievedDescription or unachievedDescription as well as the title. For the sake of simplicity once again, we use only the title here. Next, we need to set the image for the achievement. This is slightly more complex.

GKAchievementDescription has an image property associated with it, which is nil until you populate it. First, check to see whether the property is populated; we can accomplish this with a simple nil check. If it is populated, we set the cell image to the one that we have cached. If not, we need to load an image from the Game Center servers. To populate it, we call loadImageWithCompletionHandler on the GKAchievementDescription object. This returns the earned image. Notice that we used the default placeholder image, which we can access through a class method on GKAchievementDescription.

> **Tip** When setting an image in the UITableViewCellSytleDefault cell, do not set the image to nil. This will cause the cell to left align the text and remove the image view. If we then use our block to load the image, it wouldn't appear until the cell or table has been reloaded. This is the reason we set the placeholder image first.

If we were to run the app now and visit our custom achievement view, it should look similar to the one shown in Figure 4-14.

Figure 4-14. Achievement data, as displayed in a custom GUI

We are able to view only a list of achievements and associated images, but we cannot see how far the user has progressed toward unlocking the achievements. If you recall, earlier in this chapter we wrote a few convenience methods, which can be useful here. We have two methods that will return just the progress for the achievement, percentageCompleteOfAchievementWithIdentifier: and achievementWithIdentifierIsComplete. In addition, if we want access to the entire GKAchievement object, we can use achievementForIdentifier. Let's use percentageCompleteOfAchievementWithIdentifier: to display the percentage complete here. Modify the section of code in the cellForRowAtIndexPath: that sets the text label of the cell. The new code snippet should look like the following.

```
NSString *percentageCompleteString = [NSString stringWithFormat: @" %.0f%% Complete",↵
 [[self gcManager] percentageCompleteOfAchievementWithIdentifier:↵
[achievementDescription identifier]]];

[[cell textLabel] setText:[[achievementDescription title]↵
 stringByAppendingString:percentageCompleteString]];
```

If you run the game again, you will notice that the output is more helpful, as shown in Figure 4-15.

Figure 4-15. Achievements with custom GUI and completion percentage

Recovering from a Submit Failure

Developers are solely responsible for handling failures in submitting achievements. You do not want your users to lose any achievement progress. Losing an achievement is very frustrating to your users and should be avoided at all cost. To prevent this, take the same approach that we used when working with score failures. The primary difference is that there is no need to store the GKAchievement object, because it does not contain any date information or time-sensitive information. We just need to store the percentageComplete value. We will create a new method to handle this behavior for us. Add the following method to the GameCenterManager class.

```
-(void)storeAchievementToSubmitLater:(GKAchievement *)achievement
{
        NSMutableDictionary *achievementDictionary = [[NSMutableDictionary alloc]↵
        initWithArray:[[NSUserDefaults standardUserDefaults]↵
        objectForKey:@"savedAchievements"]];

        if ([achievementDictionary objectForKey:[achievement identifier]] == nil)
         {
                [achievementDictionary setObject:[NSNumber numberWithDouble:[achievement↵
            percentComplete]] forKey:[achievement identifier]];
        }
         else
         {
                double storedProgress = [[achievementDictionary objectForKey:↵
                    achievement.identifier] doubleValue];
                if ([achievement percentComplete] > storedProgress)
                  {
                        [achievementDictionary setObject:[NSNumber↵
                        numberWithDouble:[achievement percentComplete]]↵
                        forKey:[achievement identifier]];
                }
        }

        [[NSUserDefaults standardUserDefaults] setObject:achievementDictionary↵
            forKey:@"savedAchievements"];

        [achievementDictionary release];
}
```

This method will treat an achievement as an argument, and verify whether it is already stored as a reference in our achievements that have failed to properly be submitted. If it has failed, then we need to see which one is progressed further so we do not have any instances in which we delete a user's progress. Once that is done, we store it into userDefaults as a dictionary, using the identifier as the key and the percentage completed as the value. We add a call to this method from an error in the su bmitAchievement:PercentComplete: method. You can find the relevant snippet of code, as follows:

```
if (achievement!= NULL)
{
    [achievement reportAchievementWithCompletionHandler: ^(NSError *error) {
    if (error != nil)
        {
                [self storeAchievementToSubmitLater: achievement];
         }

        if (percentComplete >= 100)
        {
                [GKAchievementDescription
                loadAchievementDescriptionsWithCompletionHandler:↵
          ^(NSArray *descriptions, NSError *error) {
                        for (GKAchievementDescription *achievementDescription in descriptions)
                        {
                                if (![[achievement identifier]↵
```

```
                          isEqualToString:[achievementDescription↵
                            identifier]]) continue;

                          [self callDelegateOnMainThread:↵
                          @selector(achievementEarned:)↵
                          withArg:achievementDescription error:nil];
                    }
              }];
      }

      [self callDelegateOnMainThread: @selector(achievementSubmitted:error:)↵
      withArg: achievement error: error];
      }];
}
```

> **Tip**   It is recommended to inform your users that their achievement could not be submitted at this time but
> has been saved and will be submitted later. This lets the user know that any progress has not been lost.

We also need a new method that will check to see whether we have uncommitted achievement progress. There is no right answer for the best time to call this method. You can typically get away with calling it after a user authenticates with Game Center, but you may want to add additional methods that it is called from, such as whenever the reachability status is updated. Add the following method to your GameCenterManager class.

```
- (void)submitAllSavedAchievements
{
      NSMutableDictionary *achievementDictionary = [[NSMutableDictionary alloc]↵
      initWithArray:[[NSUserDefaults standardUserDefaults]↵
        objectForKey:@"savedAchievements"]];

      NSArray *keys = [achievementDictionary allKeys];

      for (int x = 0; x < [keys count]; x++)
        {
            [self submitAchievement:[keys objectAtIndex:x] percentComplete:↵
            [[achievementDictionary objectForKey:[keys objectAtIndex:x]] doubleValue]];

            [[NSUserDefaults standardUserDefaults] removeObjectForKey:[keys↵
            objectAtIndex:x]];
        }

      [achievementDictionary release];
}
```

This method loads a copy of our nonsubmitted progress and loops through each item, attempting to resubmit them as they go. In the event that they fail to be submitted again, they will be added back to our saved data.

Achievement Challenges

With the introduction of iOS 6, achievements can now be issued as challenges to Game Center friends. If your app is using the standard Apple-provided interface, you do not need to make any changes in order to provide your users with Achievement Challenges.

If you are working with an app that uses a custom interface for achievements, or if you would otherwise prefer to enable programmatic challenges, you can do so using the following code snippet:

```
[(GKAchievement *)achievement issueChallengeToPlayers: (NSArray *)players message:@"Think you can
earn this achievement!?"];
```

You may also want to retrieve a list of all players who can be issued a current achievement challenge. The following code will take an array of player IDs, such as your friends list, and return a list of players who can accept a challenge. This is useful if your app is preventing users from accepting Achievement Challenges for achievements they have already completed.

```
[achievement selectChallengeablePlayerIDs: arrayOfPlayersToCheck withCompletionHandler:^(NSArray
*challengeablePlayerIDs, NSError *error)
{
    if(error != nil)
    {
                    NSLog(@"An error occurred while retrieving a list of
        challengeable players: %@", [error
        localizedDescription]);
    }

    NSLog(@"The following players can be challenged: %@",        challengeablePlayerIDs);
}];
```

> **Note**   In order for users to accept challenges on achievements they have previously completed, Achievable More Than Once needs to be checked off in iTunes Connect for each achievement.

It is also possible to retrieve an array of all pending GKChallenge items for the authenticated user, using the following code snippet:

```
[GKChallenge loadReceivedChallengesWithCompletionHandler:^(NSArray *challenges, NSError *error)
{
    if (error != nil)
    {
        NSLog(@"An error occurred: %@", [error localizedDescription]);
    }
    else
    {
        NSLog(@"Challenges: %@", challenges);
    }
}];
```

Each challenge has an associated state such as completed, invalidated, declined, or pending. These can be polled in the following fashion:

```
if(challenge.state == GKChallengeStateCompleted)
    NSLog(@"Challenge Completed");
```

Finally, it is also possible to decline an incoming challenge by simply calling `decline` on it, as shown here:

```
[challenge decline];
```

Summary

You now have all the tools you need to add rich and complex achievements into your Game Center–enabled app. You know the value of adding achievements, as well as how to set up and configure them in the iTunes Connect Portal. We have discussed the pros and cons of using both Apple's default GUI for achievements and a custom GUI that you have designed. You now know how to expand our `GameCenterManager` class to include posting achievement progress, getting achievement feedback, and resetting achievement progress all together.

The most important step you've completed in this chapter is expanding the reusable `GameCenterManager` class in ways that will allow you to add achievements in future projects easily. In the next chapter, we will explore Game Center's matchmaking and invitation systems so you can add multiplayer capabilities and other networking features.

Chapter **5**

Matchmaking and Invitations

Choose your enemies carefully, 'cause they will define you'.

—U2, "Cedars Of Lebanon"

Beginning with this chapter, and through the next few chapters, we will discuss how to add networking with Game Center, and later Game Kit, into your app or game. Adding networking capability to your app is considered almost essential technology in the modern era. The process of adding networking support normally begins with finding people to connect with. Virtually all modern software has some sort of networking component associated with it today, whether it is talking to an online service to retrieve or post information, or talking directly to a peer device to exchange data.

In the following chapters we will discuss communicating with other peer devices, although not all of our networking configurations will be peer-to-peer (see Chapter 7 for details on network design).

This chapter, in particular, explores how to use Game Center to find and invite peers into your app using Game Center's invitation system.

Game Center provides an amazingly undervalued selling and distribution tool to you for very little overhead in handling invitations. When inviting nonlocal users to begin a multiplayer experience in your game or app, you have the option to invite any of your Game Center friends. If the friends that you invite do not currently have the app installed, they will be prompted to purchase the app instantly and begin playing. There are no other methods on the iPhone to send a "Buy Now" link to another user in this manner. This functionality provides a great way to grow your user base—just let your users do the selling for you.

In addition to a "Buy Now" link, Game Center also allows users to rate your app directly from within the Game Center interface, and as of iOS 6 it has provided functionality to share your app via Twitter and Facebook. These features alone make a compelling argument to add Game Center without even diving into the incredible networking abilities it provides.

Why Add Networking to Your App?

When looking at the list of the top-ten selling PC or console games for any recent year, you will find it heavily dominated by games that demonstrate a strong focus on multiplayer interaction. Let's take a quick look at the top-selling PC game for 2012, *Call of Duty: Black Ops 2*. While this game does feature a single-player mode, it is considered more of an add-on to the game than the primary selling point. The focus was obviously the multiplayer gaming, even at the sacrifice of the single-player campaign. Multiplayer iOS games have begun to find their footing from *Letterpress* to *Clash of Clans*. In recent years, the industry's focus has shifted from creating rich and in-depth single-player campaigns to putting more effort into the multiplayer. There is a perfectly reasonable answer for this new phenomenon: you get more bang for the buck with multiplayer.

Humans are, by nature, social creatures. We crave social interaction for healthy mental development. Video games and other social software are increasingly becoming an outlet for that interaction. Whether you agree with the politics of that statement is not what is important here, but the fact remains that multiplayer games are becoming more and more popular. Software users have grown increasingly fond of multiplayer interaction, whether in a massive multiplayer online role-playing game or your garden-variety first-person shooter.

Adding a multiplayer element to your game can increase user playtime by a hundredfold. If you need proof, look at *Quake 3* or *Unreal Tournament,* both of which were released in 1999 and both of which still had users logging in for many years after. If these games had focused solely on single-player, they most likely wouldn't have had such a devoted fan base. Listed here are some additional reasons why adding matchmaking and invitations through Game Center should be a simple business decision for your products:

- Adding a multiplayer component to a game is a great way to add additional polish. Depending on the type of game you are working with, it might be very minor additional work to add a multiplayer element.

- Users have come to expect multiplayer from top-notch games on the App Store.

- You can justify a higher price if you have a well-done multiplayer component.

- There is no better way to have users download your app on the fly than the auto-buy invitation system. If you can set up prospective users for a situation in which they are invited to play and can purchase immediately, you will have a much better chance of closing the sale.

- You can increase playtime or use-time in your app or game, if you are using an ad-supported system. This will result in more income. If you are selling a paid app, users will feel they have gotten more for their money.

- Humans like to compete, so encourage your users to do what they enjoy. Multiplayer might not be for everyone, but for many, it is all they are interested in when shopping for a new game.

- Multiplayer can also open the door for additional in-app purchases over time, which will increase revenue and profitability.

> **Tip** Whenever possible, also provide your users with a single-player option for your game, as there is still a noticeable user base that prefers single-player campaigns. In addition, some players may not have an Internet connection available at all times.

Common Matchmaking Scenarios

Before we begin working with matches and invitations themselves, it is important to understand some of the scenarios that you might encounter in your quest to implement multiplayer networking in your iOS app or game.

- The first, and probably most common, scenario that you might encounter would be a player who is already in your app and want to create an auto-matched game. All the players will already have the app installed and loaded, as well as be in a place where it is expected that they will want to begin a networked session with each other. The invitee player will receive a notification asking whether he or she wants to join a game with the inviter. When both agree, the matchmaking GUI is dismissed and a new match is created.

- Another common scenario that you might encounter would be if the user creates a new matchmaking event and invites other players from their Game Center friends list. The invited friends will receive a push notification informing them that they have been invited to a game. If those friends already have the game installed and accept the invitation, the game will be launched. Once all invited players have entered the match, the game will begin. If they do not yet have the game installed, they will be prompted to install it and it will automatically be launched after it has been successfully installed.

- A slightly different event path would occur if a friend is invited, and they do not yet have the app installed, and have decided to install the app. After the install process, the app will automatically launch and you can continue with the normal flow of the matchmaking event.

- A player can create a new matchmaking event from within the Game Center.app itself. In this scenario, all players are launched into the app and receive an invitation to join the match. The best part about this scenario is that if your app already supports invitations; you don't need to write any additional code to support this scenario.

- A player can also invite a friend or multiple friends and fill any remaining slots with the auto-matcher. This is a mix-and-match of the first two scenarios and, if support for both of them is added, you shouldn't have any additional programming to do for this scenario.

- The last scenario you could encounter (optionally) is to programmatically auto-match players. In this case, a request would be sent to the Game Center servers and matches would be returned for you. The player would not see any standard GUI, and you have the option to implement your own interface.

> **Note**   Matchmaking is based on the bundle ID of the app; apps without matching bundle IDs will not be able to communicate through the matchmaking system.

Creating a New Match Request

To create a new match, you first have to create a new GKMatchRequest object. This object represents the desired parameters for the new match that you will be creating. A GKMatchRequest is used both when presenting a GUI as well as when creating matches programmatically. When working with the GUI, you will pass the GKMatchRequest object to a new instance of GKMatchmakerViewControlleron the other hand, if you are handling the matchmaking programmatically, you will pass the object to an instance of GKMatchmaker. See the following sections for more details on programmatic match interaction. For the time being, let's focus on how to create a new match request in your code. Take a look at the following code snippet:

```
GKMatchRequest *request = [[GKMatchRequest alloc] init];
request.minPlayers = 2;
request.maxPlayers = 2;
```

This example is the simplest demonstration of how to create a new match. You must specify the maximum number of players as well as the minimum. In this example, we are creating a new request that will require exactly two players.

A GKMatchRequest also has a property titled playersToInvite, in which you can use an array of GKPlayer identifiers to automatically populate into a new match. This can be very helpful when playing multiple games that are chained back to back and you want to keep the same groups of players together. This property is also prepopulated when your app is launched from the Game Center.app with the players that invited you into the app.

> **Note**   When accepting an invite to a match with a friend, the event is handled from the Game Center.app, and the playersToInvite property will be populated.

GKMatchRequest also has an additional two properties, playerAttributes and playerGroup, which you will be working with in later sections of this chapter. These two properties are discussed at length in the sections that share their names.

> **Note**   If you are using Game Center as your server for hosting games, you are limited to a maximum of four players. However, if you implement your own server as discussed in the "Using Your Own Server" section of this chapter, you can invite up to 16 players.

Presenting a Match GUI

We begin by first working with the standard matchmaking GUI provided by Apple. Start by first adding a new button to handle presenting the view on the main screen of our test game. I have also gone ahead and renamed the old Play button to Single Player, and created a new button called Multiplayer (see Figure 5-1). We will use the UFOViewController to act as the delegate for our matchmaking behavior, so set the view controller to conform to GKMatchmakerViewControllerDelegate. Additionally, modify the action method of the multiplayer button we just added to match the following code:

```
- (IBAction)multiplayerButtonPressed;
{
    GKMatchRequest *request = [[GKMatchRequest alloc] init];
    request.minPlayers = 2;
    request.maxPlayers = 2;

    GKMatchmakerViewController *mmvc = [[GKMatchmakerViewController alloc]
initWithMatchRequest:request];
    mmvc.matchmakerDelegate = self;
    [request release];

    [self presentModalViewController:mmvc animated:YES];
    [mmvc release];
}
```

Figure 5-1. Adding a new button for multiplayer in the UFOViewController.xib

We create a new instance of GKMatchRequest, as we did in the previous section. Our demo game will consist of exactly two players, so we set the max and the min both to two.

In the next part of the code snippet, we create a new instance of GKMatchViewController and allocate and initialize it with the GKMatchRequest we just created. We also set the delegate to our UFOViewController class. When that is done, we present it as we present any other modal view. You should have output that looks similar to Figure 5-2.

Figure 5-2. MatchmakerViewController creating a new match GUI with two players

If you haven't already done so, now would be a good time to populate your friends list on your sandboxed Game Center account. It is helpful to have several unused email addresses available for this process, as you don't want to use any email addresses that have previously been used with iTunes Connect or with Game Center. Once you have populated a friend or two, you can go ahead and tap on the Invite Friend button shown in Figure 5-2. You'll be provided with auto-match functionality automatically, assuming you have followed the previous steps.

> **Reminder**   Do not use any email addresses you have previously used in iTunes Connect or Game Center when creating sandboxed accounts, as it can cause strange and unexpected behavior.

You should now see a list of your friends and have the ability to invite them into your app, as shown in Figure 5-3.

iOS Simulator – iPhone (Retina 3.5-inch) / iOS 7.0 (11A4372q)

❮ Multiplayer Game **Invite up to 3 players**   Next

Friends | Recent | Nearby

Friends Who Play This Game

○ KR kyle2 richter
Last played: Mar 23, 2013

Playing
○ Cory Bohon
Last played: Jan 22, 2013

○ TD Tyler Durden
Last played: Mar 7, 2011

Figure 5-3. Inviting a friend from your Game Center friends list

Before we can continue, we need to implement the required delegate methods for the GKMatchmakerViewController. Specifically, we need to implement the following three methods before we can continue working with matchmaking:

```
- (void)matchmakerViewControllerWasCancelled:(GKMatchmakerViewController
 *)viewController
{
      [self dismissViewControllerAnimated:YES completion:NULL];
}

- (void)matchmakerViewController:(GKMatchmakerViewController *)viewController
 didFailWithError:(NSError *)error
{
      [self dismissViewControllerAnimated:YES completion:NULL];

      if (error != nil)
      {
              NSString *message = [NSString stringWithFormat:@"An error occurred:
%@", [error localizedDescription]];
```

```
                UIAlertView *alert = [[UIAlertView alloc] initWithTitle:@""
                                                 message:message
                                                 delegate:nil
                                                 cancelButtonTitle:@"Dismiss"
                                                 otherButtonTitles:nil];

                [alert show];
                [alert release];
        }
}

- (void)matchmakerViewController:(GKMatchmakerViewController
*)viewController didFindMatch:(GKMatch *)match
{
        [self dismissViewControllerAnimated:YES completion:NULL];
}
```

The first two methods handle user cancellations and failures,: while the third handles the successes. The last method will return a GKMatch object upon success; we will use this object in the following chapters to begin a new match.

When working with a variable number of players allowed per match, the user will have the option of adding and removing player slots from the matchmaker view controller as shown in Figure 5-4.

Figure 5-4. *A matchmaker screen with a variable number of players*

When inviting friends into a Game Center match, you will have the option of supplying a short message to be displayed with the invitation, as shown in Figure 5-5.

Figure 5-5. Sending an invitation method to a friend asking them to begin a match with you. This message will be sent as a push notification and displayed as an incoming text message on the invitee's device, as shown later in Figure 5-6

Handling Incoming Invitations

When implementing matchmaking into your app, you must also implement a system to handle invitations from friends. The invitee's device will receive a push notification informing them that one of their friends has invited them to play a game. Assuming they have the game installed and accept the invitation, you will be required to handle connecting the two players together via a new match. If the invitee does not have the game or app installed, they will be instructed to download it. After the download is finished, the normal invitation process is followed.

> **Note** You will also need to process invitations from new matches created within Game Center.app. You most likely won't need to write any additional code; however, you do want to test this interaction path thoroughly.

We will process invitations using an invitation handler (special thanks to Apple for the naming). The invitation handler accepts two parameters; only one of these parameters will be non-nil, depending on the type of invitation you are handling.

- The acceptInvite parameter is non-nil when the app receives an invitation from a Game Center friend. The player who invited you has already created the match request, so your app will not need to create its own when accepting the invitation.

■ The playersToInvite parameter, which we discussed earlier in this chapter, is non-nil when Game Center.app launches your app. The property contains an array of player identifiers for the player to invite with a new GKMatchRequest. When the playersToInvite property is non-nil, you will be required to create a new GKMatchRequest and populate it with the players that you received here.

> **Important**   When working with the sandboxed mode and invitations, there can be some quirkiness. If you find yourself never getting the invited push notification, open up the app on both devices and invite the other player on both devices. After this has been done once, it restores the ability to test invitations from the Springboard.

Now that we know what kind of parameters we will be working with, as well as the scenarios that we will encounter, we can begin to write a new invitation handler. GKMatchmaker has a singleton method called sharedMatchmaker, which accepts a property for inviteHandler. We use a block here to set up and handle the invitations as they are received. To keep things clean and simple, we wrap our invitation handler in its own method in our GameCenterManager class. Add the following new method to GameCenterManager:

```
- (void)setupInvitationHandler:(id)inivationHandler;
{
    [GKMatchmaker sharedMatchmaker].inviteHandler = ^(GKInvite *acceptedInvite,↵
NSArray *playersToInvite)
    {
        GKMatchmakerViewController *mmvc = nil;
        if (acceptedInvite) {
            mmvc = [[GKMatchmakerViewController alloc] initWithInvite:acceptedInvite];
        } else if (playersToInvite) {
            GKMatchRequest *request = [[GKMatchRequest alloc] init];
            request.minPlayers = 2;
            request.maxPlayers = 2;
            request.playersToInvite = playersToInvite;
            mmvc = [[GKMatchmakerViewController alloc] initWithMatchRequest:request];
            [request release];
        }
        mmvc.matchmakerDelegate = inivationHandler;
        [inivationHandler presentViewController:mmvc animated:YES completion:NULL];
        [mmvc release];
    };
}
```

Let's break down this method to see exactly what is happening at each step of the process. The first thing we do is set a block to the inviteHandler property on the shareMatchmaker singleton. When this block is executed, which will happen when a user accepts an invitation, we have two possible outcomes.

The first is that `acceptedInvite` is not nil. In this scenario, we create a new instance of `GKMatchmakerViewController` and initialize it with the invitation that was accepted. We then present the view controller to the user.

In the second scenario, `playersToInvite` is non-nil, in which case we then need to create a new instance of `GKMatchRequest`. In our example game, we only ever allow two players, but you will set this to the total maximum players that can be played against here. We set the `playersToInvite` property of the request to the array of player IDs that was passed in from the block. After we have created the new request object, we can create a `GKMatchmakerViewController` to present the information to our user. They will see the standard matchmaker view with the players prepopulated for them.

> **Important**   You cannot accept or otherwise process the invitation formally until you have authenticated a local user with Game Center. It is, therefore, important to register an invitation handler as soon after a successful authentication as possible.

Because we want this to be called as soon as possible after authenticating with Game Center, we add a call to the new `setupInvitationHandler:` method after we have successfully authenticated. Modify the `processGameCenterAuthentication` method of `UFOViewController` to match the following code:

```
- (void)processGameCenterAuthentication:(NSError*)error;
{
        if (error != nil) {
                NSLog(@"An error occured during authentication: %@",↵
 [error localizedDescription]);
        } else {
                [gcManager setupInvitationHandler:self];
        }
}
```

> **Tip**   If you don't have two devices to test invitations on, you can use the simulator as one of the devices. Don't forget to sign in to the simulator and your device from two different Game Center accounts, or you won't be able to invite each other.

We will use `self` (that is, `UFOViewController`) as the delegate for our invitation handler. If you completed the required delegate calls in the previous section, "Presenting a Match GUI," you will not need to make any additional changes to this class.

Congratulations! You can now handle incoming invitations to your app (see Figure 5-6). In the next section, we will explore how to configure auto-matching to populate invitees for you.

Figure 5-6. *Receiving an invitation outside of your App. The name of your app is automatically populated into the alert view. While inviting, you have the option of specifying a message, as shown previously in Figure 5-5*

Note   The buy-now feature of invitations cannot be tested in the sandboxed environment; it can be used only in live apps. The app must be installed on every device being used in order to test invitations while in sandbox.

Auto-Matching

Auto-matching is a great feature provided to you for no extra effort when working with Game Center. Game Center keeps an online queue of people who are waiting to join a multiplayer game in your app. If you do not fill up a new match request with all invited friends, the auto-matching feature will automatically populate the remaining spots with other unmatched players online.

You can filter down the auto-matched results using player groups and player attributes, both of which will be discussed later in this chapter. In addition, you can query the activity of any live player group to see what the average wait time is to be paired up with a new match; this is also discussed more in a later section.

Matching Programmatically

It is also possible for your app to find matches programmatically, without using the matchmaker interface. You could use this methodology to implement your own custom GUI for matchmaking or create an "instant match" type action, in which users are automatically paired and a game begins with no additional user interaction. We will not be using this style of matchmaking in our demo app, but the following method will allow you to implement a match programmatically:

```
- (void)findProgrammaticMatch
{
        GKMatchRequest *request = [[GKMatchRequest alloc] init];
        request.minPlayers = 2;
        request.maxPlayers = 4;

        [[GKMatchmaker sharedMatchmaker] findMatchForRequest:request
withCompletionHandler:^(GKMatch *match, NSError *error) {

                if (error) {
                        NSLog(@"An error occurrred during finding a match: %@", [error
localizedDescription]);
                } else if (match != nil) {
                        NSLog(@"A match has been found: %@", match);
                }
        }];
        [request release];
}
```

The preceding code is fairly straightforward. We create a new GKMatchRequest and set the minimum players to two and the maximum players to four. We then call a new method, findMatchesForRequest. This will call our block when a match is found, so it might be a good idea to provide an activity indicator if a match isn't returned quickly. After you have a GKMatch, you can begin a new multiplayer game, as discussed in the following chapters.

When working with programmatically added matches, it is important to allow users a way to cancel the match request if it is taking too long or if they have changed their minds. That action can be accomplished with the following line of code:

```
[[GKMatchmaker sharedMatchmaker] cancel];
```

Adding a Player to a Match

There might be occasions in which you will want to add a new player to a match after it has already been created. For example, maybe you have a player drop out of a game and want to replace him without starting the game over, or a player fails to connect after a game starts and you want to substitute in a replacement. The following method will automatically add a new player to the match using the auto-matching behavior:

```
- (void)addPlayerToMatch:(GKMatch *)match withRequest:(GKMatchRequest *)request
{
        [[GKMatchmaker sharedMatchmaker] addPlayersToMatch:match matchRequest:request
completionHandler:^(NSError *error) {
                if (error) {
                        NSLog(@"An error occurrred during adding a player to match: %@",
[error localizedDescription]);
                } else if (match != nil) {
                        NSLog(@"A player has been added to the match");
                }
        }];
}
```

After a player has been added to a match, you will need to sync that player up with the current match. Adding a player will now allow the player to receive and send data, but they will not have any access to data that has already been sent through the match.

Reinviting Players

With the release of iOS 5.0, Apple added the ability to automatically try to reinivite a disconnected player. This method is only supported in two-person Game Center matches. The following method is called when a player is disconnected; Game Center will automatically try to reconnect to that player. If successful, you will receive an additional call to `match:player:didChangeState:`.

```
-(BOOL)match:(GKMatch *)match shouldReinvitePlayer:(NSString *)playerID
{
    return YES;
}
```

Player Groups

Player groups allow you to specify different classifications for each player. Game Center, by default, auto-matches everyone into the same group. With player groups, you can specify that certain players are looking for groups that contain only other players of that group.

For example, players who want to play at a certain level of a dungeon or a specific racetrack will be grouped together so they are paired up with other people who want to play at that same level. Player groups can be used to segregate players into many different types of groupings, such as these:

- Players who wish to play the same level of a map (such as a racecourse), area in an RPG, map in a first-person shooter, or level in an action game.

- Separate players based on skill level. Either have players choose the skill level that they wish to play at, or automatically determine their skill level based on past performance.

- Type of game that is being played. For example, players can be broken down into who wants to play Capture the Flag, Team Deathmatch, Domination, or Last Man Standing.

- Players of the same clan, guild, team, or network who want to play together.

- Players who have purchased additional in-app content and can no longer be paired up with those who have not.

A player group isn't restricted to these items and can be used to group players together in whatever fashion meets the needs of your app. A player group is represented by the playerGroup property on a GKMatchRequest. The only restriction placed on this property is that an NSUInteger must be used to represent it. Specifying a playerGroup is rather straightforward, as you can see in the following example.

```
#define kMyForestMap 123456789
GKMatchRequest *request = [[GKMatchRequest alloc] init];
request.minPlayers = 2;
request.maxPlayers = 4;
request.playerGroup = kMyForestMap;
```

Under most circumstances, you will want to let your users select the playerGroup that they belong to; however, there might be instances in which this is not true, such as automatically determining a player's skill level.

> **Caution**   After you set playerGroup to any nonzero value, players will be matched only with other players of that group.

Player Attributes

Similar to player groups, player attributes are used during matchmaking to narrow down the possible available games to the user. Player attributes, which generally function in the same way as player groups, do handle some things differently. Some of the many uses for player attributes include the following:

- Often, in role-playing games, characters pick a class. It is common to require a group of multiple classes—such as a healer, a fighter, and a mage—in order to complete a quest.

- Sports games often have various positions on a team, such as goalkeeper, fullback, midfielder, and forward. A team will require a mix of all of these to be able to play.

- In a submarine simulator game, you could also have various players, such as a captain, sonar operator, pilot, and weapons systems.

- In a first-person shooter game, you could need players in roles such as close-quarter combat specialist, sniper, medic, and platoon leader.

Understanding Player Attribute Limitations

Player attributes can be used to assign these values to each player so that you can balance a team that contains the required players. However, as of iOS 7.0, there are a number of limitations when using player attributes; it is important that you understand them before you begin working with player attributes.

- Only a single player may fill a role. For example, you cannot require three midfielders in a soccer game.

- All roles must be filled before the game is considered ready to start. For example, you can't have a first-person shooter without a sniper (based on the preceding example).

- Each player can fill only one role at a time; players cannot offer to join a game in a position that would fill more than one role. For example, you couldn't have a player in a first-person shooter willing to play either a sniper or a medic; they will need to pick one before the match request is finalized.

- Player attributes are used during auto-matching. If you invite a friend into a game, they are not tested to see whether they match the role that needs to be filled. Instead, they will automatically be assigned a random role. In short, friends do not get to pick their player attributes.

- Roles are not displayed anywhere in the standard matchmaking graphical user interface. You will need to implement your own system prior to entering this view to allow users to select their roles.

- The GKMatch object does not contain information about which players have been assigned which roles. You will need to implement your own system after the match is connected to determine who is playing which role.

- There is no system in place to determine which roles are overfilled or which are harder to find matches for. For example, everyone might want to play a mage in a role-playing game and no one might want to be a healer; therefore, it would be much harder for a mage to find an open game, while a healer can easily find one.

Working with Player Attributes

Don't let the long list of limitations scare you off from player attributes. Even with the listed limitations, they can be extremely valuable in creating a better multiplayer experience. Let's look at an example of how to build a match using player attributes.

```
#define class_SquadLeader        0xFF000000
#define class_Breacher           0x00FF0000
#define class_Grenadier          0x0000FF00
#define class_LightMachineGun     0x000000FF
```

We begin by defining a mask for each of our player attributes, which we will refer to as "classes" for the rest of this section. This example represents a standard squad in a modern military-style game. Each class is assigned a different value of a mask. Game Center uses an algorithm to match these players together, using the following rules:

- A match's mask will always begin with the mask of the inviting player.

- Game Center will ignore all players who have not set a player attribute mask if the inviting player has set a player attribute mask.

- A player will be added to a match only if their player attribute mask doesn't overlap any section of a mask from any players already invited into the match.

- After a player is added to the match, that player's attributes value is logically ORed into the match's mask.

- If a match's mask value is equal to FFFFFFFF, then the match is considered complete and can begin; if the mask does not equal FFFFFFFF, then Game Center will continue searching for a player who can fill the match.

- There is no way to query Game Center to see which player is still currently being waited for.

The following is based on the classes we just defined.

A blank match will have the player attribute mask shown in Figure 5-7.

Figure 5-7. An empty player attribute mask (0x00000000)

Player 1 begins a new match and selects Squad Leader as his class. When that player creates the match, it will now have a player attribute mask that looks like the one shown in Figure 5-8.

Figure 5-8. A player attribute mask representing the Squad Leader class (0xFF000000)

Now the creator of the match uses Game Center to auto-match for new players. The first player Game Center finds has selected a class of Grenadier. The Grenadier will have a mask that looks like Figure 5-9.

Figure 5-9. A player attribute mask representing the Grenadier class (0x0000FF00)

When we compare this to the already existing match's mask, as shown in Figure 5-10, we can see there are no overlaps, so that player can be invited into the game.

Figure 5-10. *Comparison of 0xFF000000 and 0x0000FF00*

When these masks are combined to form the new match mask, it will look like Figure 5-11.

Figure 5-11. *A new match mask, representing two players (0xFF00FF00)*

Player 3 selects Breacher as his class and searches for a game. Game Center finds the match that we have been working with and determines that there is room for a Breacher by comparing the match's mask to the Breacher's mask, as shown in Figure 5-12.

Figure 5-12. *The top is the current match's mask (0xFF00FF00), and the bottom is a Breacher's mask (0x00FF0000)*

There is no overlap between the masks, so the Breacher can be invited into the game. Player 4 selects the class of Grenadier and has Game Center look for a match. Game Center again will find our match in progress and attempt to add the new player to it.

Because the mask supplied by Player 4 overlaps a part of the match's mask (see Figure 5-13), that player is not allowed to join. If Game Center cannot find an open match for that player, it will begin looking for new players to fill in the holes on that player's match.

Figure 5-13. *The top is the current match's mask (0xFFFFFF00), and the bottom is a Grenadier mask (0x0000FF00)*

Player 5 selects Light Machine Gun as his mask and begins looking for a game to join. Game Center compares his mask to the current match's mask, as shown in Figure 5-14.

Figure 5-14. *The top is the current match's mask (0xFFFFFF00), and the bottom is a Light Machine Gun's mask (0x000000FF)*

Since there is no overlap between the two mask sets, Player 5 can join the match. This will create a complete player attribute mask for the match, as shown in Figure 5-15.

Figure 5-15. A completed match mask (0xFFFFFFFF)

If Player 5 never joined the game, and the original inviter wanted to fill the slot with a friend from Game Center, the invited friend would not have an option to select his class. The match, in that case, would have a mask that looks like that shown in Figure 5-16. The invited friend would then be assigned the mask, shown in Figure 5-17, that would complete the match's mask. This would complete the player attribute masks and allow the game to begin.

Figure 5-16. The current match's mask (0xFFFFFF00)

Figure 5-17. A Machine Gun's mask (0x000000FF), needed to complete the match's mask

Setting a player attribute is very straightforward, and is shown in the following code snippet.

```
#define class_SquadLeader        0xFF000000
#define class_Breacher           0x00FF0000
#define class_Grenadier          0x0000FF00
#define class_LightMachineGun    0x000000FF

...

GKMatchRequest *request = [[GKMatchRequest alloc] init];
request.minPlayers = 4;
request.maxPlayers = 4;
request.playerAttributes = class_SquadLeader;
```

Player Activity

Game Center provides a method to query for recent player activity. Your users will often want as much information as possible about how long a wait they may experience while looking for a multiplayer match. It is important to establish that player activity is recent activity and not current activity. There is no Apple-provided method for determining exactly how many players are waiting for a match, but Apple does provide a way to determine how many users have recently looked for a match.

Let's take a look at the required source code to get player activity. Add the following two new methods to the implementation file of your GameCenterManager class:

```
- (void)findAllActivity
{
        [[GKMatchmaker sharedMatchmaker] queryActivityWithCompletionHandler:↵
^(NSInteger activity, NSError *error) {
                [self callDelegateOnMainThread:@selector(playerActivity:error:)
withArg:[NSNumber numberWithInt: activity] error:error];
        }];
}

- (void)findActivityForPlayerGroup:(NSUInteger)playerGroup
{
        [[GKMatchmaker sharedMatchmaker] queryPlayerGroupActivity:playerGroup
withCompletionHandler:^(NSInteger activity, NSError *error) {

                NSDictionary *activityDictionary = [[NSDictionary alloc] initWithObjects:
                                [NSArray arrayWithObjects:[NSNumber numberWithInt: activity],
[NSNumber numberWithInt: playerGroup], nil] forKeys:[NSArray arrayWithObjects:@"activity",
@"group", nil]];

                [self callDelegateOnMainThread: @selector(playerActivityForGroup:error:)
withArg: activityDictionary error:error];

                [activityDictionary release];
        }];
}
```

We also need to add two new protocol methods in GameCenterManager's header file. Add the following two optional protocols.

```
- (void)playerActivity:(NSNumber *)activity error:(NSError *)error;
- (void)playerActivityForGroup:(NSDictionary *)activityDict error:(NSError *)error;
```

Implement these new protocol methods in your UFOViewController as follows:

```
- (void)playerActivity:(NSNumber *)activity error:(NSError *)error
{
        if (error != nil) {
                NSLog(@"An error occurred while querying player activity: %@",↵
 [error localizedDescription]);
        } else {
                NSLog(@"All recent player activity: %@", activity);
        }
}
```

```
- (void)playerActivityForGroup:(NSDictionary *)activityDict error:(NSError *)error
{
        if (error != nil) {
                NSLog(@"An error occurred while querying player activity: %@", [error
localizedDescription]);
        } else {
                NSLog(@"All recent player activity: %@ For Group: %@",
[activityDict objectForKey:@"activity"], [activityDict objectForKey:@"group"]);
        }
}
```

You should get output similar to the following:

```
2011-03-08 11:11:04.007 UFOs[3000:207] All recent player activity: 3 For Group: 12345
2011-03-08 11:11:04.008 UFOs[3000:207] All recent player activity: 3
```

So now that we have player activity for a specified player group, what do these numbers mean? Apple has never specified the exact meaning of these numbers, but through careful research, it appears that they represent the number of users who attempted to connect to a game using the auto-matching feature in the last one to three minutes. The numbers seem to reset at an undeterminable interval somewhere within that time frame. In addition, there appears to be a 15–30 second delay until new numbers are reflected as users attempt to join a match. This information can then be presented to a user in a variety of methods such as an average time to connect.

Even with the limitations imposed by player activity, this feature can still be a very valuable tool for determining possible wait times for your users to find a match. However, you want to make sure these numbers are used for informational purposes only, as they tend to be just unreliable enough not to depend upon.

> **Note**   You can implement your own server system to keep track of exactly how many players are waiting for a match if the Apple system does not provide specific enough information on player activity for the needs of your app. To build out a system like this, a remote server would be required to store the number of waiting players and relay it back for display.

Using Your Own Server (Hosted Matches)

Under normal circumstances, Game Center will host your match for you; however, Apple has provided a technique for implementing your own server to host a match. This approach is called a "hosted match," and it can be implemented in any app to add increased flexibility to Game Center–based multiplayer networking.

When using Game Center to host a match, every device that is connecting to that match creates an instance of GKMatch. The GKMatch class does all the legwork of connecting, handshaking, sending and receiving data, and handling errors. However, there are times when you will need to implement your own server, most notably if you want to allow more than four people to connect to a single match at a time. In this scenario, you can use Game Center to find peers for your match and use your own server to connect those peers.

> **Tip** Using a hosted match allows you to connect up to 16 users, instead of only four while using Game Center hosting.

There are several downsides to using your own server, however, most notably that you are now responsible for all the legwork that was previously given to you for free by Game Center. Specifically, you need to handle the following:

- You must design and implement all of your own networking code to connect the peers. Game Center will find the matches for you, but its involvement stops there.

- If your app is using the standard matchmaking interface, your server must inform the app when a new peer successfully connects, so that it can update the GUI.

- Voice chat is no longer provided for you free. You can still, however, use the GKVoiceChatService class to send voice data over your own networking system. See Chapter 9 for more information.

We will need to make a handful of minor changes to our code base in order to support hosted matches on the device side. We begin by modifying the multiplayer button action method that we set up earlier in this chapter.

```
- (IBAction)multiplayerButtonPressed
{
        GKMatchRequest *request = [[GKMatchRequest alloc] init];
        request.minPlayers = 2;
        request.maxPlayers = 4;

        GKMatchmakerViewController *mmvc = [[GKMatchmakerViewController alloc]
initWithMatchRequest:request];
        [request release];

        mmvc.matchmakerDelegate = self;
        mmvc.hosted = YES;

        [self presentViewController:mmvc animated:YES completion:NULL];
        [mmvc release];
}
```

As you can see, we added a new line—mmvc.hosted = YES—which tells the matchmaker GUI that this match will be hosted on our own servers. In addition to setting the matchMakerViewController to hosted, you will need to have each device connect to your server. This section does not deal with how to code the server itself, as there are dozens of languages and approaches that can be taken here. However, after a device has connected to your server, it needs to call the following with the playerID of the player who is joining.

```
[matchmakerViewController setHostedPlayerReady: playerID];
```

This will update the GUI on all the connected players' screens, informing them that a new player is ready to begin a match. After all the players are connected to your server, and have confirmed that they are ready, your delegate is called to begin the game. When working with Game Center matches, we used the delegate callback `matchmakerViewController:didFindMatch:` to begin a match. However, for a hosted game we use the following:

```
- (void)matchmakerViewController:(GKMatchmakerViewController *)viewController
didFindPlayers:(NSArray *)playerIDs
{
        [self dismissModalViewControllerAnimated:YES];

        NSLog(@"Players: %@", playerIDs);

        //Begin Hosted Game
}
```

At this point, you can begin the game with your server handling the communication between the connected players. In addition, you can begin a hosted match programmatically, as we saw with a Game Center–hosted match earlier in this chapter.

```
- (void)findProgrammaticHostedMatch
{
        GKMatchRequest *request = [[GKMatchRequest alloc] init];
        request.minPlayers = 2;
        request.maxPlayers = 16;

        [[GKMatchmaker sharedMatchmaker] findPlayersForHostedMatchRequest:request
withCompletionHandler:^(NSArray *playerIDs, NSError *error) {
                if (error) {
                        NSLog(@"An error occurred during finding a match: %@", [error
localizedDescription]);
                } else if (playerIDs != nil) {
                        NSLog(@"Players have been found for match: %@", playerIDs);
                }
        }];
        [request release];
}
```

As you can see, it is very similar to our previous method; however, instead of getting back a `GKMatch` object, we are returned an array of `playerIDs`. You will also note that we can also increase the maximum players to 16.

Summary

In this chapter you were introduced to the concepts of matchmaking and invitations. We discussed the overwhelming benefits of adding multiplayer capacity to your iOS app or game, as well as some of the hurdles you might need to jump along the way. We explored the matchmaking process from presenting the standard Apple GUI to highly customized matches using player groups and player attributes. We reviewed how to process invitations in every possible scenario, as well as how to query for player activity. Finally, we discovered how it is possible to implement your own server to remove some of the limitations placed on Game Center. We expanded our reusable `GameCenterManager` class to handle matchmaking, invitations, and the required overhead, so that you can quickly add multiplayer ability to your apps.

In this chapter, we deeply explored how to create matches and populate them with peers. In the upcoming chapters, we will not only learn how to communicate between the peers, but also explore new methods for locating peers with whom to communicate. The next chapter shows how to use Game Kit to find peers using the Peer Picker.

The Peer Picker

"I'm a great believer that any tool that enhances communication has profound effects in terms of how people can learn from each other, and how they can achieve the kind of freedoms that they're interested in."

—Bill Gates

In previous chapter, we explored how to find matches using Game Center. In this chapter, we will look at the other system iOS provides for finding peers to connect with. This system is called the Peer Picker and can be used to create a connection between two iOS devices using either Bluetooth or a local Wi-Fi network (LAN).

Before we begin working with the actual code, let's take a quick look at the history surrounding Game Kit and Game Center. When Apple released iOS 3.0, at the time called iPhone OS 3.0, it implemented a new set of API calls, collectively referred to as Game Kit. Game Kit, in the 3.0 days, handled Bluetooth, LAN networking, and voice chat services. When Game Center was added in iOS 4.0/4.1, it brought with it significant improvements to Game Kit. Game Center can really be thought of as an extension to Game Kit rather than a completely new API. Through iOS 5, iOS 6, and iOS 7, Game Kit's networking and the Peer Picker have remained largely unchanged.

In this chapter, we will look at how to establish new connections using Bluetooth and a Wi-Fi local area network. In Chapter 8 you will learn how to use shared methods to send data, regardless of whether the peer was found via Game Center or Game Kit.

Benefits of the Peer Picker

Since the introduction of iOS 4.0, Game Kit networking has been generally neglected by the developer community. This is a great injustice, as Game Kit remains an extraordinarily helpful and useful tool for iOS developers. Game Kit remains the easiest way to add peer-to-peer, two-person networking to an iOS app.

In most of the multiplayer apps that I have developed, I have implemented both systems of iOS networking. Game Center networking and Game Kit networking each have different strengths and weaknesses, and it is normally easier to provide both to your users than to be forced into a corner by the limitations of one. The following list offers some reasons for including both concurrently:

- Your users might not have access to an outside network connection, but still want to engage in multiplayer activity. Such a scenario might occur with passengers in a car or in a plane that allows Bluetooth devices to be turned on during the flight.

- You might want to allow users to connect easily to other nearby (location-based) users. Although this can be done through player groups with Game Center, it is much easier to do with Game Kit.

- You are looking for a lower-latency connection between two devices.

- You want to target users who have iPod touches or Wi-Fi iPads who might not have consistent access to Wi-Fi or might have no access to a cellular network.

- Implementing Game Kit networking is quicker and easier than a full multiplayer system done with Game Center.

As you can see, the Peer Picker approach to finding peers has some important differences from the Game Center matchmaker system. There is nothing in place to stop you from implementing both, and that approach is highly encouraged at least by me, if not by Apple as well.

In the upcoming chapters, you will learn some methods for making it easy to have both systems side by side. However, if you choose to implement only one or the other, carefully consider your options for which one will better suit the needs of your users. For example, if you have an app that sends your band's MP3 to people you meet, Game Kit would be the better approach.

Real-World Examples

Since the release of iOS 3.0, we have seen Game Kit networking used in very unexpected ways. In this section we discuss some of the notable examples of apps that use Game Kit networking to enhance user experience. Both of the apps that I show you in this section are better suited for Game Kit networking thanfor Game Center networking.

First, let's take a look at Bistromath (see Figure 6-1) from Black Pixel. The central purpose of this app is to split up a bill among multiple diners at a restaurant. This idea has been done to death on the iPhone, and there are literally dozens of apps on the App Store that provide this service. Bistromath remains hugely popular, even at a higher price than the free competition. Why is this?

Figure 6-1. Bistromath from Black Pixel, which uses Game Kit networking to split checks

Bistromath sets itself apart. Not only is it well designed and visually appealing, but it offers something that no other check splitter does: Game Kit networking. Bistromath uses Game Kit to establish a Wi-Fi or Bluetooth connection between multiple devices, allowing a user to log in to the "host" app and enter his or her meal items.

This simple feature has put Bistromath ahead of the curve in its niche. Adding in Game Kit networking removed the need for a user to pass an iPhone around the table and have everyone enter what they ordered. Small additions such as this to your app can make a major difference in its perceived value.

Handshake (see Figure 6-2) was an app that was developed by Skorpiostech in the early days of the App Store. It was the first app that allowed a user to send his or her business cards to another user. More than six months of work went into the server that powered Handshake's network connections. The server needed to support a large number of clients logging in and provide matches to other clients who were physically located within a certain distance of each other.

Figure 6-2. Handshake from Skorpiostech, which uses its own server system to share data between two local devices

Each device would determine its location and inform the server where it was and that it was looking for peers. The server would then return nearby peers and allow the app to establish a connection between them. This process could have been accomplished in days rather than months if Game Kit networking had been available at the time Handshake was being written. Handshake was never rewritten to support Game Kit; however, it was considered end-of-life when Apple introduced contact sharing alongside Game Kit in iOS 3.0.

> **Note** Game Kit and Game Center are not restricted to just games. While Apple has recently cracked down on using leaderboards and achievements in apps other than games, the argument can always be made that they add gamelike functionality to your app. Game Kit networking remains unrestricted in any app.

Working with Sessions

When working with Game Kit networking, you will be using a GKSession object (see Figure 6-3) to tie everything together. This object is used to create and manage an ad-hoc Bluetooth or local wireless network connection between devices. Copies of your app, running on multiple devices, can use these services to discover each other, connect, handshake, exchange data, and gracefully disconnect.

> **Note** Bluetooth networking is not supported on the original iPhone or the original iPod touch.

Figure 6-3. Peer-to-peer networking over Bluetooth using GKSession

A GKSession object primarily works with peers. A peer, in this context, is any iOS device made visible by creating and configuring a GKSession object of its own. Peers can only see other peers on apps that have the same bundle identifier as each other.

Each peer is represented by a peerID string, which will always be unique. Your app can use a peer's peerID to obtain a user-readable handle or name for that peer. Similarly, when your app begins a GKSession, it creates a peer to represent the local user, and this peer becomes visible to all nearby devices. Nearby devices, in this sense, would be any devices on the same local Wi-Fi network or within the range of Bluetooth, as detailed in Tables 6-1 and 6-2.

Table 6-1. Ranges of Standard Bluetooth Devices

Bluetooth Class	Milliwatts (mW)	dBm (dBmW)	Approximate Range
Class 1 (iPhone 4s/5)	100	20	~100 Meters, or ~328 Feet
Class 2 (iPhone)	2.5	4	~10 Meters, or ~32 Feet
Class 3	1	0	~1 Meter, or ~3 Feet

Table 6-2. Data Rates for Standard Bluetooth Versions

Version	Data Rate	Maximum Application Throughput
Version 1.2	1 Mbit/s	0.7 Mbit/s
Version 2.0 + EDR (iPhone)	3 Mbit/s	1.4 Mbit/s
Version 3.0 +HS	24 Mbit/s	N/A
Version 4.0 (BLE) (iPhone 4s/5)	Variable	N/A

Note Core Bluetooth was added to iDevices with iOS 5, which allows direct interaction with the bluetooth layer. If your implementation of Bluetooth is beyond the abilities of Game Kit, Core Bluetooth provides lower level functionality.

Apple has recently enabled support for Bluetooth connections between a device and the iOS Simulator. However, this support has some limitations: most notably, a device cannot find the Simulator through Bluetooth, so the Simulator will have to initiate the connection. Additionally, the iOS Simulator doesn't detect whether the Mac has Bluetooth enabled. Finally, when the device receives a connection, it appears to come from the bundle ID string and not the device name, as shown in Figure 6-10 later in this chapter.

Peers are discovered by other peers by using a unique string to identify the service that they are implementing. This unique string is the sessionID property. Sessions can be configured in one of three ways. A session can be configured to broadcast its sessionID, making it a server; or to search for other peers advertising with a sessionID, making it a client; or, finally, as both a server and a client simultaneously, referred to as a peer. In the next chapter we will explore network design on iOS in more depth.

GKSession has an associated GKSessionDelegate protocol. The delegate is called whenever a new remote peer is discovered or attempts to connect, or when the connection state of a peer has changed. In addition, you will have to set a data-received handler to specify a delegate callback when new data is received. This can be different than the main GKSessionDelegate. Chapter 8 explores exchanging data in complete detail.

> **Note**   GKSession and its associated methods are thread-safe; however, the session will always call its delegate methods on the main thread.

Presenting a Peer Picker

We will begin, as we have in the past, by adding a new button for our Peer Picker in our UFOViewController.xib, as shown in Figure 6-4. Create a new action for the button and name it localMultiplayerGameButtonPressed. In addition, you need to create two new class variables, one instance of GKPeerPickerController and another for a GKSession. Name these peerPickerController and currentSession, respectively. You also need to conform the UFOViewController to the delegate GKPeerPickerControllerDelegate.

Figure 6-4. Adding a button for a local multiplayer game

Add the following code to the action that you created for the new local button.

```
- (IBAction)localMultiplayerGameButtonPressed
{
        peerPickerController = [[GKPeerPickerController alloc] init];
         [peerPickerController setDelegate:self];

        [peerPickerController setConnectionTypesMask:GKPeerPickerConnectionTypeNearby];

        [peerPickerController show];
}
```

This code is fairly self-explanatory: we alloc and init a new instance of GKPeerPickerController, and set its delegate to self.

We do need to specify a mask for the connection type. There are two options available to us, GKPeerPickerConnectionTypeNearby and GKPeerPickerConnectionTypeOnline. In this example, we are using GKPeerPickerConnectionTypeNearby, which will allow Bluetooth connections. The GKPeerPickerConnectionTypeOnline constant will allow online connections through the local wireless network.

You can also supply both and allow the user to select. After the user selects an option, you can continue as if you had provided only one choice to the user. If you were to run the app now and select Local, you should see a new UIAlert that looks like Figure 6-5.

Figure 6-5. *The alert shown while searching for Bluetooth peers. Notice that the alert is gray instead of the blue usually seen with UIAlerts*

Go ahead and install the app on a second device, or the Simulator if you don't have a second device. When the app is ready on both devices, launch it and select the Local game option. You will, at first, see an image similar to that shown in Figure 6-5. After several seconds, the devices should find each other, and you should see an alert similar to that shown in Figure 6-6.

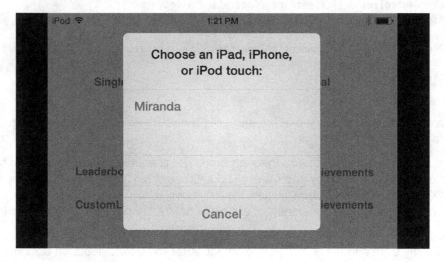

Figure 6-6. *Finding a peer with the Peer Picker*

Note   It can take up to 30 seconds for two Bluetooth devices to find each other. The farther apart the devices are, the longer it can take to establish a connection.

> **Tip**   If Bluetooth is turned off on the user's device and you begin a GKSession, the user will be prompted to enable Bluetooth, as shown in Figure 6-7.

Figure 6-7. Prompting the user to enable Bluetooth on a device. You cannot enable Bluetooth in any other manner from within your apps

If you select one of the peers from the list of available peers, you will get a waiting message, as shown in Figure 6-8. The device that was invited will see a message, as shown in Figure 6-9; or, if invited by the Simulator, the device will show a message such as that shown in Figure 6-10.

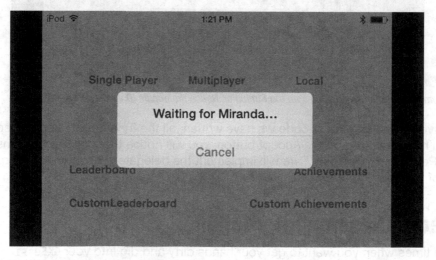

Figure 6-8. Bluetooth waiting for a connection to be established

Figure 6-9. Incoming invitation to a device from a peer device

Figure 6-10. Incoming invitation to a device from the Simulator. Notice the bundle ID as the device name

With the relatively small amount of code we have written, all the functionality is provided to us via the API. If you happen to tap on the Accept button, you will notice that nothing happens. In the section "The Peer Picker Delegate," we will implement the delegate calls required to complete the functionality of the Peer Picker.

Advanced GKSession Interaction

There may be times when you want to get your hands dirty and dig into your GKSession object a little deeper than we saw with the initial configuration. Table 6-3 lists the available properties for customization of the GKSession object.

Table 6-3. Properties Available on a GKSession Object

Property Name	Description
available	The available property is used to determine whether your peer is visible to other peers looking for a connection. This property is typically set for you through the Peer Picker, but you can set it yourself.
	After this Boolean value is set to YES, you will remain connected to any peer that you have already connected to, but you will not receive new connection requests.
delegate	The GKSession delegate property is discussed at length in the following section.
disconnectTimeout	The disconnectTimeout property is the timeout amount in seconds that your session will wait before it disconnects a non-responsive peer. Apple provides a default number for this value, which through testing, appears to be between 20 and 30 seconds. The exact number is not disclosed in the documentation.
displayName	The displayName property is a read-only NSString that represents the peer's human-readable name; this is the property that should be displayed to other users through your GUI. The displayName property is the same as the name of the device as seen in iTunes.
peerID	The peerID property is a read-only string that identifies your session peer to other devices. This value is unique. The peerID value should not be displayed directly to users.
sessionID	The sessionID property is used by sessions configured as servers to advertise themselves to other peers, and by sessions configured as clients to search for compatible servers. The sessionID should be the short name of an approved Bonjour service type.
sessionMode	The sessionMode property is the session used to find other peers. This value is read-only and is configured when you first initialize a new session. It has three possible values: GKSessionModeServer, GKSessionModeClient, and GKSessonModePeer.

The Peer Picker Delegate

In the previous sections, we saw that we get a lot for free when using a GKPeerPickerController. However, after we accepted a connection from another user, our app didn't yet know how to proceed.

In this section, we discuss the GKPeerPickerControllerDelegate. This delegate is called by the Peer Picker to create a new session object and used to handle state changes that occur throughout the course of normal networking.

The GKPeerPickerControllerDelegate has three main responsibilities that you will need to implement and respond to. It needs to create the session, respond to new connection messages, and handle the user cancelling out of the Peer Picker.

First, let's look at peerPickerController:didSelectConnectionType:. This delegate method informs us what connection type the user has selected. You may recall from earlier sections that we worked with connectionTypeMask. If you provide the user with an option for selecting whether to connect using the LAN or Bluetooth, this delegate method will return the selection. If the user selects an online connection, you should dismiss the peerPicker controller and display your own LAN connection view; see the following code snippet for an example of this behavior.

```
- (void)peerPickerController:(GKPeerPickerController*)picker
    didSelectConnectionType:(GKPeerPickerConnectionType)type
{
        if (type == GKPeerPickerConnectionTypeOnline)
        {
                [picker dismiss];
                [picker release];

                // Display your own user interface here.
        }
}
```

The GKPeerPickerControllerDelegate is also responsible for returning a GKSession. When your Peer Picker needs a session object, it will call peerPickerController:sessionForConnectionType:. If you are implementing this method, you must either create or return an existing GKSession.

> **Note**   If you are creating a new GKSession as part of peerPickerController:sessionForCon
> nectionType:, the session that you create must advertise itself as GKSessionModePeer. If you do
> not need to implement peerPickerController:sessionForConnectionType:, and the session is
> using the Bluetooth protocol, the peer controller allocates a new session with the default sessionID and
> displayName parameters. If you are creating a new LAN connection, you will need to implement peerPick
> erController:sessionForConnectionType: and return the required GKSession.

You also need to implement peerPickerControllerDidCancel:. Even though this method is optional, Game Kit expects it to be implemented. After this method is returned, the Peer Picker will automatically be dismissed, so you will not need to add code to handle this event.

The last delegate method we need to implement when working with the GKPeerPickerControllerDelegate is peerPickerController:didConnectPeer:toSession:. This method is called whenever a new peer is connected to the session.

```
- (void)peerPickerController:(GKPeerPickerController*)picker
            didConnectPeer:(NSString*)peerID
                toSession:(GKSession*)session
{
        currentSession = session;

        //hold on to session and peerID
         [self dismissModalViewControllerAnimated:YES];
}
```

When this method is called, we will want to keep a reference to the session and peerID. We will use these in the upcoming chapters when we begin to work with sending data back and forth. Once a peer has successfully connected, your app should take ownership of the session and dismiss the Peer Picker.

Figure 6-11 represents viewing a peer iPhone that has entered the connected state and set its availability flag to NO.

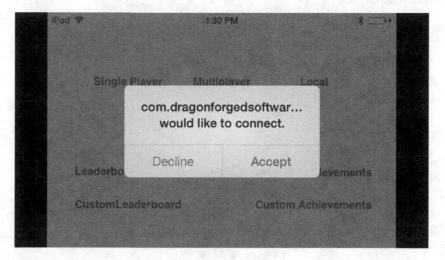

Figure 6-11. *The device named Miranda has set its availability status to false.*

> **Note** Although peerPickerController:didConnectPeer:toSession: is an optional protocol method, you will be required to implement it before you can fully enable Game Kit networking.

Summary

In this chapter you learned about using Game Kit networking to connect two devices together using either the local area network (Wi-Fi) or Bluetooth. In the previous chapter, we worked with matchmaking and invitations. Between these two technologies we have completely covered all the methods available to find and connect to peers using Game Center and Game Kit technology on the iOS platform.

We also looked at some real-world examples of iOS apps that have benefited from Game Kit networking integration, and you saw how easy it was to move your app up to the next tier of quality with only a small amount of time invested.

In addition, we explored the workings of the Peer Picker, including how to request a new session using either Bluetooth or the LAN, and how to connect peers together. We also covered the entire delegate and controller overhead required to get these systems up and running quickly in your own apps.

In the next chapter, we will discuss how to design a network for mobile devices, beginning with an overview of network types and including the do's and don'ts of mobile network design. In Chapter 8, we will tie together all the peers that we have been establishing connections with and have them begin to talk to each other.

Network Design Overview

In previous chapters, we explored how to find and establish connections to peers through a variety of methods using both Game Center and Game Kit. In this chapter, we will look at how to design a networking experience for not just an iOS game but also a game on any platform. This chapter is designed slightly differently than the previous chapters in this book. Primarily, there will be no associated source code with this chapter, and we will only briefly touch on any iOS-specific networking topics. This chapter will focus instead on the concepts of network design, as opposed to actual network implementation within an app. Long time developers may be familiar with these network types from previous development, besides iOS being inherently wireless there are no differences from textbook networking examples. In Chapter 8, you will discover how to tie everything together and have your peers begin to communicate with each other.

Plan Ahead

While it is entirely possible—and all too often done—to go ahead and just start writing networking logic, that approach will likely cause more trouble down the road. After all, you wouldn't begin writing a new app or game without first planning out how it will function. Computer networking is a complex topic, and you should approach it with a plan; otherwise, you could find yourself rewriting an entire system after putting a significant amount of time and effort into it. You don't want to find yourself up against a wall because the approach you took limited the options for future expandability. Just as with software, you shouldn't jump right into writing code on the first day. You should whiteboard things out a little and get a feel for the requirements of the project.

Take, for example, a desktop online role-playing game called Clan Lord that was written in the late 1990s for the Mac. Clan Lord has maintained a very dedicated fan base that has kept the game continuously active to the present day. However, when the game was originally written, many of the network-related issues were clearly not properly thought through.

Clan Lord uses frame-by-frame syncing for all of its network calls. This means that every frame, every element visible on the player's screen, has to be transmitted to all connected users. This approach works, and works well while you have a small game, a small user base, and limited functionality. However, when you are designing software, you cannot have a limited vision for the future. Always plan for the best, or depending on your perspective, the worst case. When designing a network, you must take into account what you will want to do six months, a year, or even ten years from now with your game or app.

Clan Lord now suffers from several long-ingrained problems. For example, its rendering engine works at 8 frames per second (fps), because you cannot sync more than eight full frames of data per second on the average home network. This could have been prevented by implementing some logic into the client when the project was first started; for example, it would have been much more efficient to inform the client where objects are and when they move, instead of fully syncing everything each frame. In addition, player movement is limited to 8 fps because actions have to be synced back to the server, making it hard to react to events. This also could have been prevented by using prediction algorithms, discussed later in this chapter, to determine where a player will end up during movement.

Clan Lord is one example of a game that was much more popular than planned, and lived a lot longer than anyone expected. Sadly, when this happens, you are limited to the vision and design that you had when the project was first started. It is much harder to undo something later than to do it initially. When designing the networking functionality of your game—your network—take time to do it carefully and intentionally, as the results can follow you around for a very long time.

Three Types of Networks

Although there are many different styles and types of network designs, there are three primary network types that you can implement when designing your game's network. Almost all specific types of network configurations will inherit from these three primary types. Picking a primary type of network is a good place to start, as it will guide you toward the next step in the design process.

We will be focusing on just three of the primary types of network design, but keep in mind that there are dozens of other well-known network configurations, some of which we will briefly touch on in this section. The three types of networks we will be discussing at length throughout this chapter are peer-to-peer, client-to-host, and ring networking.

Peer-to-Peer Network

A peer-to-peer network, shown in Figure 7-1, is the most common network that you will see on the iOS platform. No device is treated any differently than any other device, and each device is in charge of sending and receiving data to and from all the other peers it needs to communicate with.

Figure 7-1. A visual representation of a peer-to-peer network using six iOS devices

A peer-to-peer network is commonly used when dealing with Game Center networking because it is often the easiest to implement on the iOS platform. While this approach has the benefit of being extremely easy to set up, it has equally significant weaknesses and drawbacks. Primarily, it can cause a lot of redundant overhead. Each peer needs to inform every other peer about its actions. In a six-way network like the one shown in Figure 7-1, this means that each device needs to send out five messages every time it wants to update the game state. In addition, if you are implementing a system in which each peer confirms with a successful message, you will also need to receive five messages.

Another disadvantage of a peer-to-peer network is that it can become very confusing to work with a large number of peers. As you can see from Figure 7-1, things can get complicated quickly. Unlike the other primary types of networks that we will discuss in this section, the peer-to-peer approach is the only one without a clear flow. Each peer can message any other peer, by definition. This also means that you have to keep track of what every peer needs to know. Under most circumstances, this is a perfectly acceptable approach. However, when you begin to deal with more complex networks, this configuration might no longer be ideal.

In addition, no one device is in control of the state of the game. If there are artificial intelligence components, then you will need to figure out a system that will allow them to stay in sync between all the devices.

Client-to-Host Network

A client-to-host network designates one device to be the host. The host device is responsible for sending information to all the connected clients. The clients never speak to each other; they speak only to the host who then relays the required information back to the other clients. An example of what a client-to-host setup looks like is shown in Figure 7-2.

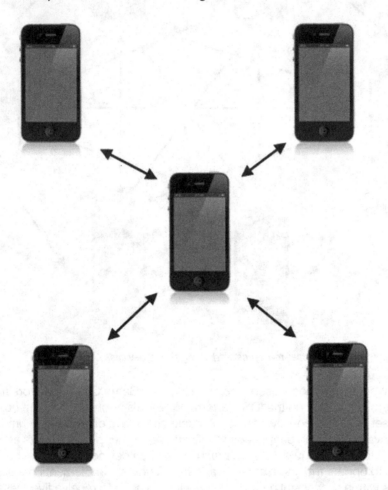

Figure 7-2. A visual representation of a client-to-host network using five iOS devices

Also known as a client-server network, this approach simplifies the flow of data. Each peer or client only needs to worry about itself and the host; they do not need to be aware of the other devices that might exist on the network. The benefit of this type of network is that one device keeps everything in sync and handles the flow of information; this makes it a very secure network (in the sense of anti-cheating). Cheating, however, is not a large concern on the iOS platform because it's a sandboxed system to begin with.

There are other benefits to this system as well, such as the fact that only one device needs to worry about the state of the network, and that sole device is in charge of the behavior of the network. This type of network simplifies events such as connections, disconnections, transmission errors, and other state changes such as computer-controlled objects like artificial intelligence. However, this same setup could be troublesome on the iOS platform; if the host device has too much information to process, that device could run slower or use more battery. Additionally, if one device needs to handle processing of all the game information, it may cause the game or app to perform poorly on that device. In typical desktop computer networking the host or server device is typically a dedicated machine or the additional duties of a host machine do not make much of an impact on available resources.

Ring Network

A ring network (see Figure 7-3) has no host and no clients. It works similarly to a peer-to-peer network, but a peer is in charge of communicating with only one designated peer and will receive information from only another separately defined peer. The information flows through a group of devices in the shape of a ring; hence the name.

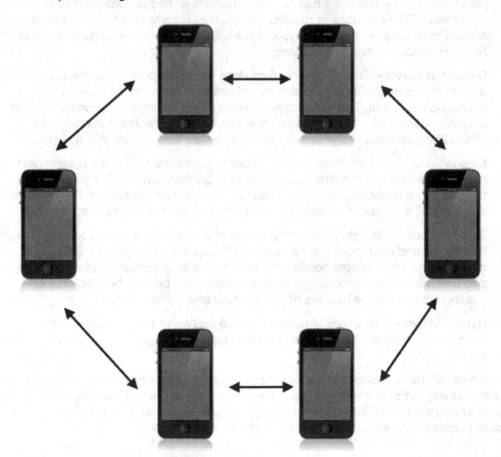

Figure 7-3. A visual representation of a ring network using six iOS devices. Notice how much simpler this diagram appears than the peer-to-peer network shown in Figure 7-1

This type of network isn't very common on the iOS platform, as there is not a lot of need for the redundancy that it typically provides for disconnected peers. Apple has done a lot of the groundwork to ensure that networks remain active and stable, without the need for the developer to spend additional design hours ensuring that there won't be instances where peers lose contact with other peers that are currently joined together. There are times, however, when you might find this type of configuration useful in designing your network on the iOS platform. While a ring network brings increased stability and connectivity, it does so with a penalty of latency and transfer speeds. On mobile devices a factor often limiting successful networking is latency, which should be kept in mind when choosing a networking approach.

Less Common Network Types

There are many additional types of network designs and styles available in computer science. Some are more practical than others and some are mostly theoretical. This section covers some of the better-known "uncommon" networks. Although some of these can be implemented on iOS devices, most will likely not have any real benefit in the average iOS project.

- Headless Client—The client has no data whatsoever, and is controlled by a host device. You can think of this type of setup as a computer terminal that is booted from a server disk. This type of setup functions very similarly to a Virtual Networking Computing (VNC) client.

- Dedicated Server—The host in this type does not participate in the game or activity and is dedicated to sending the information out from the peers and collecting new input. This is typically seen deployed by large companies creating a gaming community. While you may see this in the iOS world, it is often an offsite Ruby on Rails or Python server sending data and not another iOS device.

- Mesh/Partial Mesh Network—This is a peer-to-peer network in which each peer may not be aware of the other peers that exist on the network. The packets are tagged with a destination and every hop attempts to get the packet closer to the destination. A full-mesh network means that every peer is interconnected.

- Tree Network—This type of network consist of a tree of peers interconnected to each other and each controlled by a centralized point. The central point passes messages to other central points, and each tree branch passes messages back and forth along that branch. This type of network can be very beneficial when dealing with very large clusters of peers where latency isn't critical.

- Hybrid Network—This type of network combines two or more technologies, such as two groups of peers that are linked together through a centralized server.

This covers most of the networks you will encounter during a career in software engineering, until of course something better is invented. There is really no limit to the type of network that you can design, and every year better designs and flows become available. In the next section, we will look at the actual packets that will be sent and received on your network.

Reliable Data vs. Unreliable Data

Packet reliability is an important topic for network design. When discussing packet reliability outside of the iOS platform, we are specifically referring to the priority of the data, the ordering of the packets, and the retry determination factor. Let's look at all these attributes separately and how they relate to network design (see Table 7-1) before digging into the specifics needed for our implementation within iOS.

Table 7-1. Common Packet Attributes and How They Affect Network Behavior

Attribute	Relationship to Network Design
Priority	When you are working with low-level networking, you are dealing with packets. Each packet is a predetermined sized and contains information about the event that you want to send to another peer.
	Packets are typically sent to a queue and then sent out to the peer they are addressed for, but because networking isn't precise (especially if you are trying to get the lowest latency), packets might not always be received in the order that they are generated or even sent.
	For example, in a standard online game, you might be passing two types of information, game state changes and chat information. Obviously, your character requesting an action, such as attacking an enemy or dodging an attack, is more important to have occur in a timely manner than a chat message.
	The solution to this type of problem is to set priority for packets. The peer will cycle through all its pending messages and send the highest-priority ones first. This allows the vital messages to be retried in the event of failure first, as well as bump the important packets to the top of the queue.
Ordering	The order in which packets are received can be crucial. For example, if you are sending 10 packets, which together make up a very long chat message, then the order in which those packets are received is important to the receiving peer.
	If the packets aren't received and processed in order, your message could appear scrambled. When this happens with packets controlling a state engine, very unpredictable behavior may follow. There is a certain cost overhead involved when ensuring packets are ordered, however. If you are waiting for packet 1 of 10, then you can't do anything with the packets you might have already received. This creates a situation in which your network is only as fast as your slowest packet. If ordering isn't critical to your network functioning correctly, then you should not worry about the order.
Retry	Networks are, by nature, unreliable. Even a desktop machine hooked up to a dedicated connection will have lost packets and experience other failures. When you are dealing with network reliability on a mobile device, the only thing you can count on is failure. When you send a packet to another peer, you can handle it two ways: the first is a send-and-forget system; the second is a send-and-verify system.
	In the first approach, you send a packet and you don't really care if it gets there. Let me clarify: you do care, but if it fails, there is nothing you can do about it. A good example of this type of acceptable failure is a voice chat packet. If it fails to reach the end of the line successfully, resending it will merely bring audio out of sync with real time; it is better to accept the skip in audio and continue on streaming the data.
	In the second approach, the packet is considered vital, such as the player opening a chest, searching a slain foe for treasure, or updating their direction of movement. The peer needs this data to be sent to continue smoothly executing the commands. If you skip this packet, it will be frustrating to the user, as they will have to retry the action themselves instead of having the network retry it for them.

Now that we have covered the important issues involved in sending the data packets from one device to another, we can look at how these principles apply to the iOS platform itself.

There are two modes that data can be sent in with Game Kit: the first is GKSendDataReliable; the second is, naturally, GKSendDataUnreliable. For a look at what each of these modes does for us and how they fit in with the topics we just discussed, see Table 7-2.

Table 7-2. Packet Attributes and How They Apply to Game Center

Attribute	GKSendDataReliable	GKSendDataUnreliable
Priority	Game Kit networking doesn't factor in any type of priority when dealing with packets. Packets are sent in the order that they are fed into the system.	Game Kit networking doesn't factor in any type of priority when dealing with packets. Packets are sent in the order that they are fed into the system.
Ordering	Packets will be received in the order that they are sent.	Packets using this method may not be received in the order that they are sent.
Retry	A packet will be continuously retried until it is successfully received. The next packet will not be sent until the first one has been confirmed received.	A packet is sent and then removed from the queue. The API does not wait to receive a success notification before it sends the next packet. This is naturally faster than waiting for a response between each packet.

Sending Only What Is Needed

One of the most vital mistakes that first-timers make when designing a network is sending too much data. It is easy to just send everything. At the beginning of this chapter, we talked about a game that exhibited this very problem.

"If I had more time I would write a shorter letter."

—Blaise Pascal

Pascal could have very well been talking about network packets, in this often-misattributed quote. The size of the packet can be directly related to the speed, stability, and scalability of your network. It is important to spend the time to figure out what the absolute bare minimum is that can be sent.

Take a look at a hypothetical example that some of you might encounter while designing a game. For this example, let's say you are working on a role-playing game. You control your hero and guide him or her through a series of dungeons. In these dungeons, you can interact with items and encounter various enemies, which you will fight in real time. Well, we know we will have some static data; for example, the layout of the dungeon probably will not be changing while you are inside it, so instead of sending the map tiles to the client every frame or even periodically, we should send that data when the player first enters the zone. There might be elements that will be moving, but we can predict their behavior infinitely, such as a river flowing or a torch flickering. These items can also be loaded once with the information they need to stay in sync.

There are, of course, items that will need to be updated throughout the player's adventures in the dungeon. The player himself will need to be updated every time the user creates a new action. For example, if you are running east, you could send a packet every frame to tell the server that you are running east. However, a much more efficient way to handle this interaction is to tell the server to begin moving east at full speed. When you are done moving east, you should inform the server that you want to stop. This type of interaction drastically reduces the number of messages that need to be sent to the server to accomplish the same task. Optimizations such as these are why, when playing modern games, you sometimes see disconnected players running into walls—the server never received a stop-running command before the client disconnected.

Take the time to design carefully how you will structure your network data. You can always add more information, but it becomes very difficult to remove data as you dig deeper into your network design. Always look for a way to reduce packet size, as there is no downside to packets being too small, but a packet that is too large will cause you and your users a lot of suffering down the road.

Prediction and Extrapolation

Let's consider another example: this time, a racing game. Each player controls a car that is guided around a track. We know where each car is at the start of the race. We also know that any messages we send to the server will have an inherited latency due to the round-trip network time. Should we not update the car positions until the server tells us to? That would result in a very choppy racing game. To account for this very common issue, we use *predictive technology*.

We know that race cars will, more than likely, continue on a current course for the next handful of frames. We will assume things will continue doing what they are doing until the server tells us otherwise; if the user steers slightly to the left or right, that is a minor correction we will need to make when the server informs us of the update. The fact that an object in motion will stay in motion until acted on by an outside force is not just a law of physics; it is also the first rule of designing a predictive network.

The chances of an object completely reversing its current course are much less than of the object slightly modifying its current course. This makes it easier to account for minor changes if the server informs you that things are out of sync. In the event that a player does completely change direction or otherwise break your prediction about which actions were going to continue, you are only off the mark by as much as your current latency, which is typically only a small fraction of a second. If you have an object that is likely to continue doing what it is doing—such as a player moving, objects in a falling state, bullet trajectory, or any type of physics simulation—the best bet is to assume that those actions will continue until the server informs you that they have changed.

Using this information you can predict the information that will be coming from the server, and your network will have the appearance of being much faster than it actually is. Predictive networking technology is the reason you sometimes see players or objects jump around slightly when experiencing lag in games.

Formatting Messages

Whenever you are designing a network for a game or game-like application, you are guaranteed to be dealing with at least two types of messages. These are often referred to as *state messages* and *server messages*. A state message is a message that will directly affect your game engine, such as a player moving or opening a chest. Server messages deal with the glue that holds everything together, such as connections, disconnections, pings, and errors.

It is important to quickly sort these messages to different handlers. It is a good design pattern to keep the parsing of these messages in different places. After all, you don't want to be scanning all your chat messages in a first-person shooter for client timeout messages.

There are many different methods to handle this segregation, but I have found a simple prefix is suitable for most cases. If you prefix all of your state messages with a special character that you will not see in server messages, you can quickly check the first character in incoming messages to make sure each is delivered to the correct parser. If you are designing a more complex network, you can use a large number of possible prefixes to make sure things get to the correct place. In Chapter 8 we will look at practical examples of message formatting when we begin to send and receive data.

Preventing Cheating and Preventing Timeout-Related Disconnections

One thing that is not a big concern on the iOS platform, as of yet, is cheating through network exploits. If you are an online gamer, you are probably all too familiar with this behavior. A clever user will determine how the network behaves, and then send commands that the client itself would never send, such as increase hit points to max float or decrease respawn time to zero. Although you might need to have your server respond to things such as increase or decrease hit points, you want to make sure the server is in control. For example, instead of letting the client say "increase moment speed to fifty feet per frame," you should set up the message to something like "request increase moment speed" and then have the server return the new speed. If you put clients in charge of variables, at some point someone will take advantage of this and exploit your system.

If your client doesn't have any updates to send out to the server or its peers, it is good practice to send a message that simply states, "I'm still here don't disconnect me," which is known as a "keep alive" message. Although you don't have to worry about timeout disconnection on the iOS platform, it is still a good idea to make sure that you keep your own line of communication open between idle peers.

When you are designing message architecture, you can really think of it as designing an API; there are a lot of similarities and you have to follow the same guidelines. If you ship version one of your app with a command that lets users query for their movement speed, you can't easily pull out that command in version two, because previous clients might still be depending on it. Follow the same guidelines that API developers do: test everything thoroughly, because after it is out in the wild, it is very hard to get it back.

What to Do When All Else Fails

An issue that is bound to come up when you have been working with network design or even software development long enough what to do when the system you have designed no longer meets your needs. Let's discuss something that might be familiar to those of you who have some logic or business training. There is a syndrome known as the "Sunk Cost Fallacy," where when dealing with nonrefundable resources, such as time; those costs are weighed as equally as refundable costs. Take a look at the following equation.

$$Payoff = project\ revenue - open\ cost$$

Now let's look at the same example using some real-world data. In 1968, two researchers, Knox and Inkster, approached 141 horse bettors: 72 of the people had just finished placing a $2.00 bet within the past 30 seconds, and 69 people were about to place a $2.00 bet within the next 30 seconds. The hypothesis was that people who had just committed themselves to a course of action would reduce post-decision dissonance by believing more strongly than ever that they had picked a winner. Knox and Inkster asked the bettors to rate their horse's chances of winning on a seven-point scale. What they found was that people who were about to place a bet rated the chance that their horse would win at an average of 3.48, which corresponded to a "fair chance of winning," whereas people who had just finished betting gave an average rating of 4.81, which corresponded to a "good chance of winning." This hypothesis was confirmed: after making a $2.00 commitment, people became more confident that their bet would pay off. Knox and Inkster performed an ancillary test on the patrons of the horses themselves and managed to repeat their finding almost identically.[1]

What we are talking about is accepting when it is time to give up and start over. When you have invested time and money into a "horse," you eventually feel that it is more valuable than it actually is. Giving up is never a popular solution; our brains are wired against it. We look at the nonrefundable cost and calculate that into our favor. Once you have already made an investment, it is easier to justify that investment and try to defend it. No one wants to be the person to call it quits and throw away all the time and money already invested into a project; however, when you spend time and resources on a development project, they are spent and they cannot be recouped. You cannot justify more time simply based on time spent.

There is no right answer on when to give up and start over, and there is no wrong answer. The only thing you can do is look at the problem objectively. If you hadn't already invested in this problem, what solution would you pick?

---

[1]Knox, R. E., & Inkster, J. A. (1968). "Postdecision dissonance at post time." *Journal of Personality and Social Psychology, 8,* 319–323.

Summary

In this chapter, we looked at the design of actual networks, as opposed to the iOS-specific information that we have dealt with in the rest of this book. You could easily design a working network without the information in this chapter, through common sense and gut instinct, but keep in mind the lesson learned throughout this chapter: just because something works, doesn't mean it works well. Designing a network is easy; designing a network correctly is very difficult.

There is significantly more information on network design than can easily fit into a single chapter, or even a single book. If I can leave you with a final piece of advice: when you begin to look at how to structure your network, think through everything as you go, and never feel the need to be satisfied with your first solution.

In the next chapter, we will finally get to work with sending our messages from one device to another. Chapter 10 will also be an extension of that technology where we look into how to add voice chat services to your iOS app.

Exchanging Data

In the past few chapters, we explored how to connect to peers through a variety of methods. So far, we have not been able to do much with that connection. In this chapter, you will learn all that there is to know about exchanging data between sets of peers using Game Kit and Game Center networking. In previous chapters we have already added to our UFO game the ability to find peers using both Game Center and the Peer Picker (Game Kit). We will now add the ability to actually play a complete multiplayer match.

Because all the groundwork has already been laid out in previous chapters, there are only two items that we need to worry about for exchanging data. First, we need to send the actual data; second, we need to receive and process that data on the other side. Everything else that we need to do is already done, except some logic for disconnecting that we'll address at the end of the chapter. Let's jump right into it by modifying our source code from Chapter 6.

Modifying a Single-Player Game

There are a few modifications that we need to make to our single-player game in order to transform it into a multiplayer game.

- Once we connect to a new peer, we need to begin the game. We also need a way to inform our existing engine that the new game is multiplayer.

- One device needs to be designated the host device. We will have this one device control the movements of the cows, since both devices can't control cow movement themselves. This is an important step if we want both devices to appear in sync.

- Each peer needs to inform the other peer(s) about its actions, such as movement and tractor beam usage.

- Each peer needs to parse the other peer's device and update its own game state to keep both devices in sync with each other.

These steps are a representation of the bare minimum that is typically required to turn a single-player game into a peer-to-peer multiplayer game. Your particular game or app might be much more complex. For example, your multiplayer experience might be so different from your single-player gameplay that you cannot reuse the same class for both modes. On the other hand, your game might be even simpler. For example, a multiplayer game of Battleship wouldn't require either device to be the host, because there are no computer-controlled elements that you need to keep track of.

Setting Up Our Engine for Multiplayer

The very first thing that we need to do is let our game engine know whether the game state should be set to multiplayer or single player. There are complex ways and simple ways of doing this. Depending on your needs, you will most likely be able to get away with a simple state variable.

A state variable is the approach that we will use for our example, since our game is extremely straightforward. In `UFOGameViewController.h`, we create a new ivar to represent a BOOL, which will be set to inform the class whether we are in single-player or multiplayer mode. Add the following two lines into our already existing header file, and don't forget to synthesize gameIsMultiplayer in the implementation.

```
@interface UFOGameViewController : UIViewController <UIAccelerometerDelegate,↵
 GameCenterManagerDelegate>
{
    BOOL gameIsMultiplayer;
}

@property(nonatomic, assign) BOOL gameIsMultiplayer;
```

We will use this property throughout our code base to determine whether the game is running in multiplayer mode.

We have two existing methods that will be called when our game begins a new multiplayer match. The first method, `matchmakerViewController`, is called when Game Center finds a match, and the second, `peerPickerController`, will be used when we find a peer through our Peer Picker. We will deal with two different identifiers for our peers: Game Center returns a `GKMatch` object, and the Peer Picker returns an `NSString` to represent the peer. We will also add some new methods in our `GameCenterManager` class to handle using the same code to communicate with both of these systems at once. For now, we will simply focus on getting the game up and running in the new multiplayer state.

```
- (void)matchmakerViewController:(GKMatchmakerViewController *)viewController↵
 didFindMatch:(GKMatch *)match
{
        [self dismissModalViewControllerAnimated:YES completion: nil];
}

- (void)peerPickerController:(GKPeerPickerController *)picker didConnectPeer:(NSString↵
 *)peerID toSession:(GKSession *)session
```

```
{
        currentSession = session;
        [self dismissModalViewControllerAnimated: YES completion: nil];
}
```

Next, we add a section of code to the end of each of these methods to begin a new multiplayer game after we find a peer that we want to play against. Add the following snippet of code into each method.

```
UFOGameViewController *gameVC = [[UFOGameViewController alloc] init];
gameVC.gcManager = gcManager;
gameVC.gameIsMultiplayer = YES;
[self.navigationController pushViewController:gameVC animated:YES];
[gameVC release];
```

We also need to hold onto either the GKMatch or the NSString that represents a peer. Create two new properties in the UFOGameViewController, named peerIDString and peerMatch. Set these up in the same fashion that you did for the gameIsMultiplayer ivar. The new section of your header should look like the following abstracted snippet:

```
@interface UFOGameViewController : UIViewController <UIAccelerometerDelegate,←
  GameCenterManagerDelegate>
{
        //...

        NSString *peerIDString;
        GKMatch *peerMatch;
}

@property(nonatomic, retain) NSString *peerIDString;
@property(nonatomic, retain) GKMatch *peerMatch;
```

Now we need to add logic to set these properties in both of the methods for beginning a new multiplayer game. These methods should now look like the following code. As you can see, we nil out the unused property; we will always have one of the two properties being set to nil, because you can never have a game that is using both the Peer Picker and Game Center at the same time.

```
- (void)matchmakerViewController:(GKMatchmakerViewController *)viewController←
  didFindMatch:(GKMatch *)match
{
        [self dismissModalViewControllerAnimated:YES completion: nil];
        UFOGameViewController *gameVC = [[UFOGameViewController alloc] init];
        gameVC.gcManager = gcManager;
        gameVC.gameIsMultiplayer = YES;
        gameVC.peerIDString = nil;
        gameVC.peerMatch = match;
        [self.navigationController pushViewController:gameVC animated:YES];
        [gameVC release];
}
```

```
- (void)peerPickerController:(GKPeerPickerController *)picker didConnectPeer:↩
(NSString *)peerID toSession:(GKSession *)session
{
        currentSession = session;
        [self dismissModalViewControllerAnimated: YES completion: nil];
        UFOGameViewController *gameVC = [[UFOGameViewController alloc] init];
        gameVC.gcManager = gcManager;
        gameVC.gameIsMultiplayer = YES;
        gameVC.peerIDString = peerID;
        gameVC.peerMatch = nil;
        [self.navigationController pushViewController:gameVC animated:YES];
        [gameVC release];
}
```

When we load our game view controller, we know whether it is multiplayer or not, and we also have a reference to our peer or peers. Our GameViewController now has all the information it needs to begin a new multiplayer game.

Picking a Host

Picking which device will be the host is harder than it sounds. Both devices, when first connected together, are treated as equals. How do we then determine which device will have more control than the other?

The most straightforward and foolproof system is to have each device generate a random number. Whichever device has the largest random number becomes the host. In the very rare event that both devices generate the same random number, we simply try again. In modern desktop games the host machine is normally determined by the computer with the lowest latency or the fastest processor.

After we have determined the random number the device has picked for its chance at being the host, we need to send that data to the other device. On the receiving side, we need to process the data and have both devices come to the same conclusion about which one has been selected as the host. This section deals only with generating the host number; the following two sections handle how to send and receive this data. We now add the following generateAndSendHostNumber method to our UFOGameCenterViewController class:

```
-(void)generateAndSendHostNumber;
{
        double randomHostNumber = arc4random();
        NSString *randomNumberString = [NSString stringWithFormat: @"%d",↩
        randomHostNumber];

        [self.gcManager sendStringToAllPeers:randomNumberString reliable: YES];
}
```

For the purpose of this example, we will work with an NSString for sending the data back and forth. You could easily send this as an NSNumber as well, but whatever we send will first need to be converted to NSData, which we will cover in the next section. In addition, we want to make sure this method is called whenever we are dealing with a multiplayer game. To do so, we need to add the following to the end of our `viewDidLoad` method. We also need to modify slightly our logic to spawn cows. If it is a multiplayer game, only the host is responsible for spawning and updating cow paths.

> **Tip** When you begin to deal with more complex networking, it is often beneficial to switch to a data type that can easily store more data with less parsing, such as a dictionary or an array.

```
-(void)viewDidLoad
{
        //...

        [self generateAndSendHostNumber];

        if (self.gameIsMultiplayer == NO)
        {
                for (int x = 0; x < 5; x++)
                        {
                                [self spawnCow];
                        }

                        [self updateCowPaths];
        }
}
```

Sending Data

We will work with two primary methods to send data to the connected peer(s). One will handle sending data to every peer we are connected to, and the other will send data only to specified peers, such as teammates or other groups of players. First, add the following two methods to our GameCenterManager class. The following methods will work for both Game Center and Game Kit networking.

```
-(void)sendStringToAllPeers:(NSString *)dataString reliable:(BOOL)reliable;
-(void)sendString:(NSString *)dataString toPeers:(id)peers reliable:(BOOL)reliable;
```

We will use these methods to send strings back and forth, but you can add additional methods to accept any type of input you want. Keep in mind that everything will need to be converted to NSData along the way. You might also notice that the first method is the same method we called previously from our generateAndSendHostNumber.

> **Tip** It is a good idea to implement methods to handle arrays and dictionaries. These are both very common data types when working with networking messages.

Before we can really begin to send data back and forth, we need to know either the GKSession or the GKMatch that was created for our multiplayer game. To do this, we create a new ivar in the GameCenterManager class. We name it matchOrSession and set it to an ID type. We need to set this property before we begin a new multiplayer game, after we have been returned either a new GKSession or GKMatch. Let's first take a look at sending data to all peers. This new sendStringToAllPeers method is printed here for your convenience. After you have examined it, we will discuss it in further detail.

```
-(void)sendStringToAllPeers:(NSString *)dataString reliable:(BOOL)reliable
{

        if (self.matchOrSession == nil)
        {
                NSLog(@"Game Center Manager matchOrSession ivar was not set, this↵
                needs to be set with  the GKMatch or GKSession before sending or receiving data");

                return;
        }

        NSData *dataToSend = [dataString dataUsingEncoding:NSUTF8StringEncoding];
        GKSendDataMode mode;

        if (reliable)
        {
                mode = GKSendDataReliable;
        }
        else
        {
                mode = GKSendDataUnreliable;
        }

        NSError *error = nil;
        if ([self.matchOrSession isKindOfClass: [GKSession class]])
        {
                [self.matchOrSession sendDataToAllPeers:dataToSend withDataMode:↵
                mode error:&error];
        }

        else if ([self.matchOrSession isKindOfClass: [GKMatch class]])
        {
                [self.matchOrSession sendDataToAllPlayers:dataToSend withDataMode:↵
                mode error:&error];
        }

        else
        {
                NSLog(@"Game Center Manager matchOrSession was not a GKMatch or↵
                a GKSession, we are unable to send data");
        }
```

```
        if (error != nil)
        {
                NSLog(@"An error occurred while sending data: %@", [error↵
                localizedDescription]);
        }
}
```

In the `sendStringToAllPeers` method we need to make sure that we have properly set the `matchOrSession` property. If we haven't, we will not be able to continue, as we will be using this object to send data. After we have ensured that we have the proper information to continue, we then transform our `NSString` to an `NSData` object. This encodes the string into a format that is safe for sending over the network. We also need to set a reliability mode, as discussed in Chapter 7.

Now that we have everything in place to actually send data, we first detect whether we are working with a `GKMatch` from a Game Center type connection or a `GKSession` from a Peer Picker type connection. All that is left to do is send the data using the Game Kit APIs.

Now is a good time to look at how we will selectively send data only to certain peers. We can build from the example we already have for sending data to all peers. Let's take a look at the `sendString` method in its entirety:

```
-(void)sendString:(NSString *)dataString toPeers:(id)peers reliable:(BOOL)reliable
{
        if (self.matchOrSession == nil)
        {
                NSLog(@"Game Center Manager matchOrSession ivar was not set, this↵
                needs to be set with the GKMatch or GKSession before sending or receiving data");

                return;
        }

        NSData *dataToSend = [dataString dataUsingEncoding:NSUTF8StringEncoding];
        GKSendDataMode mode;

        if (reliable)
        {
                mode = GKSendDataReliable;
        }
        else
        {
                mode = GKSendDataUnreliable;
        }

        NSError *error = nil;
        if ([self.matchOrSession isKindOfClass: [GKSession class]])
        {
                        if ([peers isKindOfClass:[NSArray class]])
                        {
                                [self.matchOrSession sendData:dataToSend toPeers:peers↵
                                withDataMode:mode error:&error];
                        }
```

```
                      else
                      {
                       NSLog(@"Game Kit requires peers be sent as an NSArray of Peer
                       ID Strings");
                      }
              }

       else if ([self.matchOrSession isKindOfClass: [GKMatch class]])
       {
                      if ([peers isKindOfClass:[NSArray class]])
                      {
                              [self.matchOrSession sendData:dataToSend toPlayers:peers
                              withDataMode:mode error:&error];
                      }
                      else
                      {
                              NSLog(@"Game Center requires peers be sent as an NSArray of
                              Peer ID Strings");
                      }

       }

       else
       {
              NSLog(@"Game Center Manager matchOrSession was not a GKMatch or
              a GKSession, we are unable to send data");
       }

       if (error != nil)
       {
              NSLog(@"An error occurred while sending data: %@", [error
              localizedDescription]);
       }
}
```

This method is very similar to the method for sending data to all peers. The main difference is that we use a new API call and feed in an array of peer IDs. You can, of course, change these methods to accept more than an NSString when sending data, but for the simplicity of our test game, a string is all we need.

This concludes everything you need to know about sending data between two or more iOS devices. In the next section, we will look at how to receive and parse the data that was received from another peer.

Receiving Data

GKSession and GKMatch each have their own systems for receiving delegate callbacks for incoming data. Both of these systems depend on a delegate. Game Center uses the same delegate that was used for the invitation handler in Chapter 5; Game Kit allows us to use a separate call, setDataReceiveHandler:withContext:, to specify the instance that will be in charge of handling incoming data from the network.

The first step in setting up our app to receive data is to set the receive data delegate for both systems to our GameCenterManager class. We will use the GameCenterManager class as a filter point for passing data back into our game. While you could easily receive data in your game controller itself, if we pipe everything through GameCenterManager, it will be much easier to plug this class into future apps, and we can direct both Game Kit and Game Center networking to the same protocols to make life easier when implementing.

Modify both matchmakerViewController and peerPickerController of UFOViewController.m to match the following:

```
- (void)matchmakerViewController:(GKMatchmakerViewController *)viewController↵
 didFindMatch:(GKMatch *)match
{
        [self dismissModalViewControllerAnimated:YES completion: nil];
        gcManager.matchOrSession = match;
        //Set a new received data handler
        [gcManager setupInvitationHandler: gcManager];
        UFOGameViewController *gameVC = [[UFOGameViewController alloc] init];
        gameVC.gameIsMultiplayer = YES;
        gameVC.peerIDString = nil;
        gameVC.peerMatch = match;
        [self.navigationController pushViewController:gameVC animated:YES];
        [gameVC release];
}


- (void)peerPickerController:(GKPeerPickerController *)picker didConnectPeer:↵
(NSString *)peerID toSession:(GKSession *)session
{
        [picker dismiss];
        currentSession = session;
        gcManager.matchOrSession = session;

        //Set a new received data handler
        [session setDataReceiveHandler: gcManager  withContext: nil];
        UFOGameViewController *gameVC = [[UFOGameViewController alloc] init];
        gameVC.gameIsMultiplayer = YES;
        gameVC.peerIDString = peerID;
        gameVC.peerMatch = nil;
        [self.navigationController pushViewController:gameVC animated:YES];
        [gameVC release];
}
```

The important change to focus on in the two preceding methods is setting the delegate to handle the incoming data request to our GameCenterManager class. This allows us to handle all incoming data in one centralized place; from there, we can relay it out to the relevant sections and classes of the app.

Next, you need to add the following two methods to your GameCenterManager class. The first handles incoming data from Game Kit and the second handles incoming data from Game Center. Both of these methods assume we will be working with only incoming strings, because that is the design we have chosen when dealing with sending data in our game. You can easily adapt these methods to handle receiving other types of objects. In addition, we need to add a new protocol method to handle sending the data back to our game classes. You can also further adapt this setup to use a more complex and intelligent system of data parsing, but it will be more than suitable for the needs of our UFOs.

```
- (void)receiveData:(NSData *)data fromPeer:(NSString *)peer inSession: (GKSession↩
 *)session context:(void *)context;
{

        NSString *dataString = [[NSString alloc] initWithData:data↩
        encoding:NSUTF8StringEncoding];

        NSDictionary *dataDictionary = [NSDictionary dictionaryWithObjects:↩
        [NSArray arrayWithObjects:dataString, peer, session, nil] forKeys:↩
        [NSArray arrayWithObjects:@"data", @"peer", @"session, nil]];

        [dataString release];

        [self callDelegateOnMainThread: @selector(receivedData:) withArg:↩
        dataDictionary error: nil];
}

- (void)match:(GKMatch *)match didReceiveData:(NSData *)data fromPlayer:↩
(NSString *)playerID
{

        NSString *dataString = [[NSString alloc] initWithData:data↩
        encoding:NSUTF8StringEncoding];

        NSDictionary *dataDictionary = [NSDictionary dictionaryWithObjects:↩
        [NSArray arrayWithObjects:dataString, playerID, match, nil] forKeys:↩
        [NSArray arrayWithObjects:@"data", @"peer", @"session", nil]];

        [dataString release];

        [self callDelegateOnMainThread: @selector(receivedData:) withArg:↩
        dataDictionary error: nil];
}
```

> **Tip**   You can use the context property to pass any additional data to the received delegate method.

The new protocol method is named receivedData, and you can see how it fits into our existing list of available protocols, as follows:

```
@protocol GameCenterManagerDelegate <NSObject>
@optional
- (void)processGameCenterAuthentication:(NSError*)error;
- (void)friendsFinishedLoading:(NSArray *)friends error:(NSError *)error;
```

```
- (void)playerDataLoaded:(NSArray *)players error:(NSError *)error;
- (void)scoreReported: (NSError*) error;
- (void)leaderboardUpdated: (NSArray *)scores error:(NSError *)error;
- (void)mappedPlayerIDToPlayer:(GKPlayer *)player error:(NSError *)error;
- (void)mappedPlayerIDsToPlayers:(NSArray *)players error:(NSError *)error;
- (void)localPlayerScore:(GKScore *)score error:(NSError *)error;
- (void)achievementSubmitted:(GKAchievement *)achievement error:(NSError *)error;
- (void)achievementEarned:(GKAchievementDescription *)achievement;
- (void)achievementDescriptionsLoaded:(NSArray *)descriptions error:(NSError *)error;
- (void)playerActivity:(NSNumber *)activity error:(NSError *)error;
- (void)playerActivityForGroup:(NSDictionary *)activityDict error:(NSError *)error;
- (void)receivedData:(NSDictionary *)dataDictionary;
@end
```

All that is left now is to implement our received data protocol method. We need to add the following method to the `UFOGameViewController` implementation file:

```
- (void)receivedData:(NSDictionary *)dataDictionary;
{
        if ([[dataDictionary objectForKey: @"data"] doubleValue] == randomHostNumber)
        {
                NSLog(@"Host numbers are equal, we need to reroll them");
                [self generateAndSendHostNumber];
        }

        else if ([[dataDictionary objectForKey: @"data"] doubleValue] > randomHostNumber)
        {
                NSLog(@"We are the host");
                isHost = YES;
        }

        else if ([[dataDictionary objectForKey: @"data"] doubleValue] < randomHostNumber)
        {
                NSLog(@"They are the host");
                isHost = NO;
        }
}
```

If you run the game on two devices now, you can see that each log reflects whether the device has been designated as a host or the other device is the host. The `receivedData` method is very flawed, though, because it only works with the host data message. In the next section, we will refine this method to accept not only the host message, but also input for player movements, cow movements, and other game actions.

You now have all the basic skills required to send data between two different iOS devices, as well as receive and parse that data and have your system react to it. If you want to experiment with working with these calls in practice, the next section will walk you through several examples of sending and receiving data in our UFO game.

Putting Everything Together

In the last section, you learned how to receive the data that has been sent to a device. In this section, we walk through the exercise of actually using received data in a useful way for our game. We add a second player, allow movement information to be sent over the network, sync state data across both devices (such as cow movement), track each player's score, and complete various other required overhead tasks associated with our game.

Selecting the Host

Let's start by improving the host selection logic that was implemented in the previous section. Right now, any data that we receive is assumed to be the host number. Because most of the data we receive will not be the host number, we need to find a way to filter that data to where it can be parsed. Modify the generateAndSendHostNumber method to match the following code block:

```
-(void)generateAndSendHostNumber;
{
        randomHostNumber = arc4random();
        NSString *randomNumberString = [NSString stringWithFormat: @"$Host:%f",↵
        randomHostNumber];

        [self.gcManager sendStringToAllPeers:randomNumberString reliable: YES];
}
```

As you can see, we now add an identifier prefix to the message that we will send. I have chosen for this example the prefix of "$Host:", but you can use whatever system you feel comfortable with. In addition, we need to modify the receivedData callback to support the new format.

```
- (void)receivedData:(NSDictionary *)dataDictionary;
{
        if ([[dataDictionary objectForKey: @"data"] hasPrefix:@"$Host:"])
        {
                    [self determineHost: dataDictionary];
        }
        else
        {
                    NSLog(@"Unable to determine type of message: %@", dataDictionary);
        }
}
```

If we determine that the message is a host message, we send it to a new helper method called determineHost to determine which device is the host. If we are unable to determine the type of message, we print a warning message to the console, which will help debugging as the system grows more complex. We need to move the old code from receivedData into determineHost. In addition to moving the code, we need to strip off the prefix. Although stripping off the prefix has a lot of overhead with stringByReplacingOccurrencesOfString:, it is the easiest way to accomplish this task. In more complex apps, you might need to design a more robust and efficient message system.

```
-(void)determineHost:(NSDictionary *)dataDictionary
{
        NSString *dataString = [[dataDictionary objectForKey: @"data"]↵
        stringByReplacingOccurrencesOfString:@"$Host:" withString:@""];

        if ([dataString doubleValue] == randomHostNumber)
        {
                NSLog(@"Host numbers are equal, we need to reroll them");
                [self generateAndSendHostNumber];
        }

        else if ([dataString doubleValue] > randomHostNumber)
        {
                NSLog(@"We are the host");
                isHost = YES;
        }

        else if ([dataString doubleValue] < randomHostNumber)
        {
                NSLog(@"They are the host");
                isHost = NO;
        }
}
```

Now we can still determine who the host is, but we have opened the door to processing more than only this type of data.

The next step will be transmitting and displaying our peer's UFO into our game. In the source files for this chapter, I have added two new images to the project, EnemySaucer1.png and EnemySaucer2.png. These are the same as the originals, but with a different color scheme applied to them. We will use this new artwork to display and distinguish the opponent's spacecraft.

Displaying the Enemy UFO

The first thing we need to do is detect whether this is a multiplayer game, and if so, we need to draw the enemy UFO in the viewDidLoad method of UFOGameViewController. You will notice that this is exactly the same code we use for drawing the player in single-player mode, except that we use a different graphic asset:

```
-(void)viewDidLoad
{
        if (self.gameIsMultiplayer)
        {
                CGRect otherPlayerFrame = CGRectMake(100, 70, 80, 34);
                otherPlayerImageView = [[UIImageView alloc] initWithFrame:↵
                otherPlayerFrame];
```

```
                    otherPlayerImageView.animationDuration = 0.75;
                    otherPlayerImageView.animationRepeatCount = 99999;

                    NSArray *imageArray = [NSArray arrayWithObjects: [UIImage imageNamed:↵
                    @"EnemySaucer1.png"], [UIImage imageNamed: @"EnemySaucer2.png"], nil];

                    otherPlayerImageView.animationImages = imageArray;
                    [otherPlayerImageView startAnimating];
                    [self.view addSubview: otherPlayerImageView];
            }
    }
```

If we were to run the game on two devices and begin a new multiplayer game, we would now see a red enemy UFO that just sits in the sky. The next step is to send our movement data to our peer so that they can update where the enemy player is. To do so, we add a new code snippet to the end of our movePlayer method:

```
-(void) movePlayer:(float)vertical :(float)horizontal;
{

        //... (Existing Move Player Code)

        if (self.gameIsMultiplayer)
        {
                NSString *positionString = [NSString stringWithFormat:↵
                @"$PlayerPosition: %f %f", playerFrame.origin.x, playerFrame.origin.y];
                [self.gcManager sendStringToAllPeers:positionString reliable:↵
                NO];
        }
}
```

This code sends your player's x and y coordinates to the peer every time you move. The data will be sent as unreliable, since if we fail, we can just use the next packet; the data will always be updating while the player is moving. This would be a great place to use predictive technology, as discussed in Chapter 7, but for simplicity's sake, we will be syncing every frame. In addition, there are better ways to send the x and y coordinates to another device, such as a dictionary or custom data format. However, encoding them into a string is the easiest to understand. As you develop your game or app, you can design this type of function to be more streamlined with less overhead.

Tip Using `stringWithFormat` carries with it a lot of overhead. In practice, you should use methods such as `stringByAppendingString` to further optimize this type of code.

We also need to update our receivedData method to handle the new type of data we are expecting. Modify that method to match the new one as follows. In addition, we add a new method to parse the incoming data. Also add a new method called drawEnemyShipWithData, as follows:

```
- (void)receivedData:(NSDictionary *)dataDictionary;
{
        if ([[dataDictionary objectForKey: @"data"] hasPrefix:@"$Host:"])
        {
                [self determineHost: dataDictionary];
        }

        else if ([[dataDictionary objectForKey: @"data"] hasPrefix:@"$PlayerPosition:"])
        {
                [self drawEnemyShipWithData: dataDictionary];
        }

        else
        {
                NSLog(@"Unable to determine type of message: %@", dataDictionary);
         }
}

-(void)drawEnemyShipWithData:(NSDictionary *)dataDictionary
{
        NSArray *dataArray = [[dataDictionary objectForKey: @"data"]↵
        componentsSeparatedByString:@" "];

        float x = [[dataArray objectAtIndex: 1] floatValue];
        float y = [[dataArray objectAtIndex: 2] floatValue];
        otherPlayerImageView.frame = CGRectMake(x, y, 80, 34);
}
```

The updated receivedData: method parses the incoming data from the network. We pull the x and y coordinates out of the string that we received and update the enemy player's frame with the new position using the drawEnemyShipWithData: method. This approach syncs the two devices frame by frame and is very inefficient. Given more time, this method should be updated to use predictive technology to determine where the player is heading, and only update the feed if the player goes against the prediction. However, for the purposes of this demo, it suits our needs. For more information on predictive networking see Chapter 7.

If you were to run the game now and begin a new multiplayer game, you would see that each device reflects the movement of its partnered device. We still need to spawn the cows, add the tractor beam, and update the scores, but we have a functional (albeit dull, for the time being) multiplayer game, as shown in Figure 8-1.

Figure 8-1. *Adding a second player to UFOs. Each player can move around independently and is kept in sync through the network*

Spawning Cows

Because we want the cow movement to be synced between each device, we need to dedicate one device to handling the cow spawning and movement paths. We have already picked a host device, so we will let the host determine where the cows will be placed. We begin by modifying the determineHost method. As you can see in the following code, if we are the host, we begin our normal spawn cow process:

```
-(void)determineHost:(NSDictionary *)dataDictionary
{
        NSString *dataString = [[dataDictionary objectForKey: @"data"]↵
        stringByReplacingOccurrencesOfString:@"$Host:" withString:@""];

        if ([dataString doubleValue] == randomHostNumber)
        {
             NSLog(@"Host numbers are equal, we need to reroll them");
            [self generateAndSendHostNumber];
        }

        else if ([dataString doubleValue] > randomHostNumber)
        {
                isHost = YES;
                for(int x = 0; x < 5; x++)
                {
                        [self spawnCow];
                }

                [self updateCowPaths];
        }
```

```
        else if ([dataString doubleValue] < randomHostNumber)
        {
                        isHost = NO;
        }
}
```

We also need to modify our spawnCow method to support the new networking behavior. All we are doing here is determining whether we are a network game and whether we are the host, and then sending the data to our network handlers:

```
-(void)spawnCow;
{
        int x = arc4random()%480;
        UIImageView *cowImageView = [[UIImageView alloc] initWithFrame:CGRectMake(x,↵
        260, 64, 42)];

        cowImageView.image = [UIImage imageNamed: @"Cow1.png"];
        [self.view addSubview: cowImageView];
        [cowArray addObject: cowImageView];
        [cowImageView release];

        if (isHost && self.gameIsMultiplayer)
        {
                [gcManager sendStringToAllPeers:[NSString stringWithFormat:↵
                @"$spawnCow:%i", x] reliable:YES];
        }
}
```

Modify the receivedData method to support the new $spawnCow message type. We also want to extract the x-axis origin from the message and pass it to a new method that will handle spawning a cow from the network. Both of these methods are shown next.

```
else if ([[dataDictionary objectForKey: @"data"] hasPrefix:@"$spawnCow:"])
{
        int x = [[[dataDictionary objectForKey: @"data"]↵
        stringByReplacingOccurrencesOfString:@"$spawnCow:" withString:@""] intValue];

        [self spawnCowFromNetwork: x];
}

-(void)spawnCowFromNetwork:(int)x
{
        UIImageView *cowImageView = [[UIImageView alloc] initWithFrame:CGRectMake(x,↵
        260, 64, 42)];

        cowImageView.image = [UIImage imageNamed: @"Cow1.png"];
        [self.view addSubview: cowImageView];
        [cowArray addObject: cowImageView];
        [cowImageView release];
}
```

> **Tip**   Our host doesn't need to pass the y-axis coordinate for the cows because they are always spawned on the same y-axis. If you can eliminate data from a packet, it is always beneficial.

If you were to run the game now, you would see that both devices spawn cows in the exact same location, but the host device is the only device that animates the cow movements.

The next step is to add the logic to share the animation control for the cows. Modify the existing updateCowPaths method to send the newX and array position of the cow we want to update. The following new code should be added to the end of the for loop.

```
if (self.gameIsMultiplayer)
{
        NSString *dataString = [NSString stringWithFormat:@"$cowMove:%i:%f", x, newX];
        [gcManager sendStringToAllPeers:dataString reliable:YES];
}
```

> **Note**   Because we set the data for the spawn cow call to reliable, it is guaranteed to be received in the order that it was sent. This means that we can be assured that the objects in our cowArray on both devices will be in the same order.

We also need to add a new data handler to our receivedData method. To do that, we pass the entire dictionary to our new updateCowPathsFromNetwork method:

```
else if ([[dataDictionary objectForKey: @"data"] hasPrefix:@"$cowMove:"])
{
        [self updateCowPathsFromNetwork: dataDictionary];
}

-(void)updateCowPathsFromNetwork:(NSDictionary *)dataDictionary;
{
        NSArray *dataArray = [[dataDictionary objectForKey: @"data"]↵
        componentsSeparatedByString:@":"];

        int placeInArray = [[dataArray objectAtIndex: 1] intValue];
        UIImageView *tempCow = [cowArray objectAtIndex: placeInArray];
        float currentX = tempCow.frame.origin.x;
        [UIView beginAnimations:@"cowWalk" context:nil];
        [UIView setAnimationDuration: 3.0];
        [UIView setAnimationCurve:UIViewAnimationCurveLinear];
        float newX = [[dataArray objectAtIndex: 2] intValue];

        if (tempCow != currentAbductee)
        {
                tempCow.frame = CGRectMake(newX, 260, 64, 42);
        }
```

```
[UIView commitAnimations];
tempCow.animationDuration = 0.75;
tempCow.animationRepeatCount = 99999;

//flip cow
if (newX < currentX)
{
        NSArray *flippedCowImageArray = [NSArray arrayWithObjects: [UIImage↵
        imageNamed: @"Cow1Reversed.png"], [UIImage imageNamed: @"Cow2Reversed.png"],↵
        [UIImage imageNamed: @"Cow3Reversed.png"], nil];

        tempCow.animationImages = flippedCowImageArray;
}

else
{
        NSArray *cowImageArray = [NSArray arrayWithObjects: [UIImage↵
        imageNamed: @"Cow1.png"], [UIImage imageNamed: @"Cow2.png"], [UIImage imageNamed:↵
        @"Cow3.png"], nil];

        tempCow.animationImages = cowImageArray;
}

[tempCow startAnimating];
}
```

This method is very similar to our existing method for updating cow paths. The two differences are that we get our place in the array from the network, and we don't randomly generate a newX position. If you were to run the game again, you would see that both sets of cows are now in sync with each other. When a cow changes position, the result is exactly the same on both devices. Figure 8-2 shows the current state of the game.

Figure 8-2. Syncing up the cow movements over the network between two iOS devices

Each player can now abduct cows and increment their score. There are, however, still two remaining issues that need to be addressed. The first is that we don't share scores between devices, and the second is that we don't show the other player's tractor beams or animate the cows into the UFO during the abduction. Let's start off by adding in support for the score.

Sharing Scores

When we increment the score, we send that data to our peers. Add the following snippet of code to our finishAbducting method, right after we increment the score.

```
if (self.gameIsMultiplayer)
{
        [gcManager sendStringToAllPeers:[NSString stringWithFormat:@"$score:%f",↵
        score] reliable:YES];
}
```

We, again, need to modify our receivedData method to support the new $score message. I have chosen to increment the enemy score within the receivedData method. You can, of course, write a new method to handle this functionality. In addition, we need to add a new label for the enemy score. It will be placed directly below the local player's score. Figure 8-3 shows the scores in place.

```
else if ([[dataDictionary objectForKey: @"data"] hasPrefix:@"$score:"])
{
        float enemyScore = [[[dataDictionary objectForKey: @"data"]↵
        stringByReplacingOccurrencesOfString:@"$score:" withString:@""] floatValue];

        enemyScoreLabel.text = [NSString stringWithFormat: @"ENEMY %05.0f",↵
        enemyScore];
}
```

Figure 8-3. Adding the score for the networked player

> **Tip** Technically, you don't need to pass the score value in with the network call, because scores are always incremented by one; we can assume a new score message is an instruction to increment the value by one.
>
> It would be very easy to add logic to declare a winner of the game when either player reaches a score of ten. On your own, you can add this logic to the game as a final exercise for this chapter.

Adding Network Abduction Code

The last thing that we need to handle is tying in network support for the abduction code. We need to properly remove and respawn cows as they are abducted, as well as show the enemy UFO using their tractor beam and animating a cow into the ship.

Let's begin by showing and hiding the tractor beam on each device. Because we start a tractor beam every time a user touches the screen, and end it when the user releases that touch, we can begin there. We have no values that need to be transmitted; the only thing we need to be aware of is starting and stopping the animation itself. Modify the touchesBegan and touchesEnd methods to send a message to the peer, as follows:

```
- (void)touchesBegan:(NSSet *)touches withEvent:(UIEvent *)event
{
        currentAbductee = nil;
        tractorBeamOn = YES;
        if (self.gameIsMultiplayer)
        {
                [gcManager sendStringToAllPeers:@"$beginTractorBeam" reliable:YES];
        }

        tractorBeamImageView.frame = CGRectMake(myPlayerImageView.frame.origin.x+25,↵
        myPlayerImageView.frame.origin.y+10, 28, 318);

        tractorBeamImageView.animationDuration = 0.5;
        tractorBeamImageView.animationRepeatCount = 99999;

        NSArray *imageArray = [NSArray arrayWithObjects: [UIImage imageNamed:↵
        @"Tractor1.png"], [UIImage imageNamed: @"Tractor2.png"], nil];

        tractorBeamImageView.animationImages = imageArray;
        [tractorBeamImageView startAnimating];
        [self.view insertSubview:tractorBeamImageView atIndex:4];
        UIImageView *cowImageView = [self hitTest];
```

```
        if (cowImageView)
        {
                currentAbductee = cowImageView;
                [self abductCow: cowImageView];
        }

}


-(void)endTractorFromNetwork
{
        [otherPlayerTractorBeamImageView removeFromSuperview];
}

- (void)touchesEnded:(NSSet *)touches withEvent:(UIEvent *)event
{
        tractorBeamOn = NO;
        if (self.gameIsMultiplayer)
        {
                        [gcManager sendStringToAllPeers:@"$endTractorBeam" reliable:YES];
        }

        [tractorBeamImageView removeFromSuperview];
        if (currentAbductee)
        {
                [UIView beginAnimations: @"dropCow" context:nil];
                [UIView setAnimationDuration: 1.0];
                [UIView setAnimationCurve:UIViewAnimationCurveEaseIn];
                [UIView setAnimationBeginsFromCurrentState: YES];
                CGRect frame = currentAbductee.frame;
                frame.origin.y = 260;
                frame.origin.x = myPlayerImageView.frame.origin.x +15;
                currentAbductee.frame = frame;
                [UIView commitAnimations];
        }

        currentAbductee = nil;
}
```

As you can see in the preceding code, we simply check to make sure that we have a network game, and then pass a message to begin or end the tractor beams. Next, we add a handler to our receivedData method to call two new methods that will display and animate the tractor beam on the peer's device. These two methods, beginTractorFromNetwork and endTractorFromNetwork, are modifications of our current tractor beam animation methods and are shown next for your convenience.

```
-(void)beginTractorFromNetwork
{
        otherPlayerTractorBeamImageView.frame =↵
CGRectMake(otherPlayerImageView.frame.origin.x+25,↵
otherPlayerImageView.frame.origin.y+10, 28, 318);
```

```
        otherPlayerTractorBeamImageView.animationDuration = 0.5;
        otherPlayerTractorBeamImageView.animationRepeatCount = 99999;

         NSArray *imageArray = [NSArray arrayWithObjects: [UIImage imageNamed:↵
        @"Tractor1.png"], [UIImage imageNamed: @"Tractor2.png"], nil];

        otherPlayerTractorBeamImageView.animationImages = imageArray;
        [otherPlayerTractorBeamImageView startAnimating];
        [self.view insertSubview:otherPlayerTractorBeamImageView atIndex:4];
}

-(void)endTractorFromNetwork
{
        [otherPlayerTractorBeamImageView removeFromSuperview];
}
```

If you were to run the game again, you would see that when either user touches the screen, the tractor beam appears on both devices. We don't need to worry about locking the movement for the UFO while the tractor beam is on, because this is handled for us in the single-player game, and movements are only transmitted to another device if they are acceptable in the single-player mode. Next, we need to add additional code to handle the hit test, so modify the hitTest method, as follows:

```
-(UIImageView *)hitTest
{
        if (!tractorBeamOn)
        {
                return nil;
        }

        for (int x = 0; x < [cowArray count]; x++)
        {
                UIImageView *tempCow = [cowArray objectAtIndex: x];
                CALayer *cowLayer= [[tempCow layer] presentationLayer];
                CGRect cowFrame = [cowLayer frame];
                if (CGRectIntersectsRect(cowFrame, tractorBeamImageView.frame))
                {
                        tempCow.frame = cowLayer.frame;
                        [tempCow.layer removeAllAnimations];
                            if (self.gameIsMultiplayer)
                            {
                                    [gcManager sendStringToAllPeers:[NSString↵
                                    stringWithFormat: @"$abductCowAtIndex:%i", x]
reliable:YES];
                            }

                        return tempCow;
                }
        }

        return nil;
}
```

Here we are using the same trick that we used earlier when we populated the cow array. Because we sent the data reliably to enter objects into our array, we know that the order of the array is always going to be the same. Because we know the order of the array, we can pass the index of the cow we want to modify. In addition to sending the data, we also need to write a new if statement to catch this message, as shown below. You can see that this method is set up a lot like the score method, in which we extract the value that we are interested in and call a new method using it.

```
else if ([[dataDictionary objectForKey: @"data"] hasPrefix:@"$abductCowAtIndex:"])
{

        int index = [[[dataDictionary objectForKey: @"data"]↵
        stringByReplacingOccurrencesOfString:@"$abductCowAtIndex:" withString:@""] intValue];

        [self abductCowFromNetworkAtIndex:index];
}
```

The following two methods, abductCowFromNetworkAtIndex and finishAbductingFromNetwork, handle the abduction animations that are received over the network. They are both very similar to the methods that we use to animate an abduction event in the single-player mode. You could even modify your existing methods to handle the network behavior by calling them with a flag to indicate that they are coming from a remote device.

```
-(void)abductCowFromNetworkAtIndex:(int)x
{
        otherPlayerCurrentAbductee = [cowArray objectAtIndex: x];

        otherPlayerCurrentAbductee.frame = otherPlayerCurrentAbductee.frame;
        [otherPlayerCurrentAbductee.layer removeAllAnimations];
        [UIView beginAnimations: @"abductNetwork" context:nil];
        [UIView setAnimationDuration: 4.0];
        [UIView setAnimationCurve:UIViewAnimationCurveEaseIn];
        [UIView setAnimationDelegate: self];
        [UIView setAnimationDidStopSelector: @selector(finishAbductingFromNetwork)];
        [UIView setAnimationBeginsFromCurrentState: YES];
        CGRect frame = otherPlayerCurrentAbductee.frame;
        frame.origin.y = otherPlayerImageView.frame.origin.y;
        otherPlayerCurrentAbductee.frame = frame;
        [UIView commitAnimations];
}

-(void)finishAbductingFromNetwork;
{
        [cowArray removeObjectIdenticalTo:otherPlayerCurrentAbductee];
        [self endTractorFromNetwork];
        [otherPlayerCurrentAbductee.layer removeAllAnimations];
        [otherPlayerCurrentAbductee removeFromSuperview];
        otherPlayerCurrentAbductee = nil;
        if (isHost)
        {
                [self spawnCow];
        }
}
```

We will also need to do some overhead to make sure we don't generate any new bugs. For example, we add a new pointer to keep track of which cow the enemy is currently abducting, if any. If you recall, in the updateCowPaths method we don't want to update the path for the cow that is being abducted because it will break the animation that is being used for the abduction. We need to modify that method to also ignore whatever cow the enemy happens to be abducting. If you were to run the game again, you would now see that we have a fully functional multiplayer game, as shown in Figure 8-4.

Figure 8-4. A fully functional multiplayer UFO game being played by two people using a Bluetooth connection

Disconnections

The last step that we need to take when working with multiplayer support is to add in logic to handle disconnections and other failures that are unrecoverable. Luckily for us, Apple's APIs handle most of the legwork. We do, however, want to add a more universal call to our GameCenterManager class to make things easier for us.

```
- (void)disconnect;
{
        if ([self.matchOrSession isKindOfClass: [GKSession class]])
        {
                [self.matchOrSession disconnectFromAllPeers];
        }

        else if ([self.matchOrSession isKindOfClass: [GKMatch class]])
        {
                [self.matchOrSession disconnect];
        }
}
```

This method should be called whenever you wish to end a multiplayer game. It will make sure that the peers are safely disconnected and prevent a number of issues that would be very hard to troubleshoot.

Summary

In this chapter, we covered a lot of information in a very condensed manner. You learned how to send and receive data between two or more iOS devices using

both Game Kit networking and Game Center networking. In addition, you learned how to handle network state changes, such as disconnections. We put the principles learned in this chapter into use in our UFO game, creating a multiplayer iOS game from the ground up in less than eight chapters. In the next chapter, we will explore Game Center's turn-based gaming APIs, which were added with the release of iOS 5.

9

Turned-Based Gaming with Game Center

As if you could kill time without injuring eternity.

—Henry David Thoreau

Apple announced iOS 5 at its own World Wide Developers Conference (WWDC) in 2011. In addition to a number of smaller enhancements that this new SDK brought to Game Center, it included one very important new feature: turned-based gaming through Game Center. With turn-based gaming, you can provide your users with asynchronous gaming. Turned-based games are simply any game in which players take turns playing, such as in tic-tac-toe, chess, card games, Battleship, and Monopoly. Apple has continued to improve Turned Based Gaming in both iOS 6 and iOS 7, making it a featured point of the Game Center improvements that have accompanied each release.

Turned-based gaming on iOS has become very popular in the past few years, starting with Words with Friends. Shown in Figure 9-1, this asynchronous word game from Zynga is similar to Scrabble. Each player receives a selection of letters that they must play, in turn, on a board to create a word. They are awarded points based on the difficulty of the word, as well as layout on the board. Turned-based gaming is traditionally done with a store-and-forward platform; the server holds on to the game data until the next client logs in and retrieves it. Asynchronous games have traditionally been casual games and don't require all players to be present and connected throughout the gameplay.

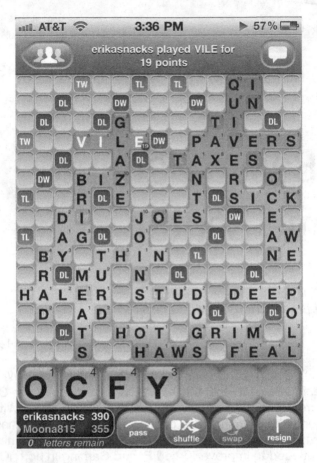

Figure 9-1. Words with Friends by Zynga

Before the introduction of iOS 5, Game Center had provided only real-time gaming, in which all the devices involved need to be active and logged in continuously throughout the multiplayer experience. Turn-based gaming adds a more casual experience, letting people run up to 20 matches at a time and only playing when it is their turn in a particular match. Prior to the new Game Center enhancements, writing this type of game would have required you to write and deploy your own server to handle the game interaction. Now, you can add the networking component of turned-based gaming and be up and running in less than a day of work. In this chapter, we explore how to write a simple tic-tac-toe game using iOS 5 and Game Center's new turned-based gaming APIs.

A New Sample Project

Unfortunately, our existing UFOs sample game is not a suitable experience for testing turned-based gaming. It wouldn't make much sense to have each player make a move and then wait for the other player to catch up. Luckily, there is another very simple type of game that we can build a project around: tic-tac-toe. This classic children's game is something almost all of us have played, and we have experience with the rules and strategy.

We begin by creating a new navigation controller-based project. There are three views that we will be working with throughout the project:

- **Main View:** This view simply contains a button that launches the `GKTurnedBasedMatchmakerViewController`.

- `GKTurnedBasedMatchmakerViewController`: This is the view provided by Apple to create and resume turned-based games. You will not need to create this view yourself.

- `Game View`: This is the class that handles user input, determining winners and ties, and populating the game board at the start of each turn.

We begin by working with the main view. These files will be created for you when you create the new project. The very first thing we need to do is make sure to import the proper Game Kit frameworks and add our reusable `GameCenterManager` class that we have been working on throughout this book; you can include the existing one from Chapter 8. We also need to create a single button in the view to start a new game, as shown in Figure 9-2.

Figure 9-2. The main view for our new tic-tac-toe game

The header file for the new base view controller class should match the following code snippet. We need to adhere to the GameCenterManagerDelegate as well as the GKTurnedBasedMatchmakerViewController. As in previous chapters, we also need to create a class instance of GameCenterManager. The last thing that needs to be added is an IBAction method to begin a new game. Make sure to hook up the Start New Game button to the IBAction in Interface Builder.

```
#import <UIKit/UIKit.h>
#import <GameKit/GameKit.h>
#import "GameCenterManager.h"

@interface tictactoeViewController : UIViewController <GameCenterManagerDelegate,
GKTurnBasedMatchmakerViewControllerDelegate>
{
    GameCenterManager *gcManager;
}

-(IBAction)beginGame:(id)sender;
@end
```

We also need to modify the viewDidLoad method to check for and then authenticate our local user with Game Center. This is the same approach that we followed in Chapter 2. If you are supporting iOS 6 or newer, you should use the new authentication methods outlined in Chapter 2.

```
- (void)viewDidLoad
{
    [super viewDidLoad];
        if ([GameCenterManager isGameCenterAvailable])
        {
                [[NSNotificationCenter defaultCenter] addObserver:self⏎
                selector:@selector(localUserAuthenticationChanged:)⏎
                name:GKPlayerAuthenticationDidChangeNotificationName object:nil];

                gcManager = [[GameCenterManager alloc] init];
                [gcManager setDelegate: self];
                [gcManager authenticateLocalUser];
        }
}
```

We also need to implement two delegate methods to monitor for successful authentication and local user changes. We are using both of these methods to print some debugging output.

```
- (void)processGameCenterAuthentication:(NSError*)error;
{
    if (error != nil)
      {
                NSLog(@"An error occured during authentication: %@", [error⏎
                localizedDescription]);
      }
}

- (void)localUserAuthenticationChanged:(NSNotification*)notif;
{
        NSLog(@"Authenication Changed: %@", notif.object);
}
```

In the next section, we will see how to call the GKTurnedBasedMatchmakerViewController and how to handle the delegate methods that are required in order to handle errors when resuming or creating new matches.

GKTurnedBasedMatchmakerViewController

Much as it does with leaderboards and achievements, Apple provides a default class to present the GUI for creating a new turn-based match. To create a match programmatically, see the later section "Programmatic Matches."

We begin by working with a new matchmaker object in the IBAction for the single button that we created in the previous section. The approach that we use here is very similar to Game Center matchmaking, as described in Chapter 5. We first allocate and initialize a copy of GKMatchRequest and set the minimum and maximum players. We then create a new GKTurnedBasedMatchmakerViewController and initialize it with the match object that we just created. Finally, we set the delegate to self and present the view modally to the user. This view will be similar to the one shown in Figure 9-3.

Figure 9-3. Starting a new turned-based match

```
- (IBAction)beginGame:(id)sender
{
    GKMatchRequest *match = [[GKMatchRequest alloc] init];
        [match setMaxPlayers:2];
        [match setMinPlayers:2];

    GKTurnBasedMatchmakerViewController *tmvc = nil;
    tmvc = [[GKTurnBasedMatchmakerViewController alloc] initWithMatchRequest:match];
    [tmvc setTurnBasedMatchmakerDelegate: self];
    self presentViewController:tmvc animated:YES completion: nil];
    [tmvc release];
    [match release];
}
```

> **Note**   A GKLocalPlayer must first authenticate with Game Center before a new turned-based game match can be created.

There are four delegate methods that need to be implemented to conform to the GKTurnedBasedMatchmakerViewControllerDelegate protocol. The first handles the user canceling in the matchmaker. The only requirement is to call dismissViewControllerAnimated:Completion:. You may add additional logic, as required, for your app.

```
- (void)turnBasedMatchmakerViewControllerWasCancelled:↵
(GKTurnBasedMatchmakerViewController*)viewController
{
    [self dismissViewControllerAnimated: YES completion: nil];
}
```

> **Important**   The list of current games may not update until you close and reopen the GKTurnedBasedMatchmakerViewController.

We also need to implement a delegate method to catch any errors that occur during this phase. The following method is called whenever an error is encountered during the matchmaking process. For debugging purposes, we are printing the error to the console; however, in practice you will want to inform the user that an error has occurred.

```
- (void)turnBasedMatchmakerViewController:
(GKTurnBasedMatchmakerViewController*)viewController didFailWithError:(NSError *)error
{
    NSLog(@"Turned Based Matchmaker Failed with Error: %@", [error localizedDescription]);
}
```

The last delegate method that is discussed in this section handles the user quitting a match from the matchmaker screen. This is accomplished by swiping across a game and selecting the Quit option.

In the following method, we call `participantQuitOutOfTurnWithOutcome` on the match object that is passed to us as part of the method. We pass in the outcome of `GKTurnBasedMatchOutcomeQuit`. If you do not call the proper method here, you will seemingly be able to quit a game, but it will reappear within a few seconds.

```
- (void)turnBasedMatchmakerViewController:(GKTurnBasedMatchmakerViewController↵
 *)viewController playerQuitForMatch:(GKTurnBasedMatch *)match
{
        [match participantQuitOutOfTurnWithOutcome:GKTurnBasedMatchOutcomeQuit↵
        withCompletionHandler:^(NSError *error) {
                            if (error)
                {
                        NSLog(@"An error occurred ending match: %@", [error↵ \
                        localizedDescription]);
                                }
                }];
}
```

The final required method, `didFindMatch`, is discussed in the next section, "Starting a New Game."

Starting a New Game

Starting a new match with turned-based gaming is a very straightforward and relatively simple process. To do so, you need to implement the following method. This new method dismisses the `GKTurnBasedMatchmakerViewController`, and then passes a copy of the match object to your game controller. The following code snippet is the procedure followed for the tic-tac-toe sample app.

```
- (void)turnBasedMatchmakerViewController:(GKTurnBasedMatchmakerViewController *)viewController
didFindMatch:(GKTurnBasedMatch *)match
{
    [self dismissViewControllerAnimated: YES completion: nil];
    tictactoeGameViewController *gameVC = [[tictactoeGameViewController alloc] init];
    gameVC.match = match;
     [[self navigationController] pushViewController:gameVC animated:YES];
     [gameVC release];
}
```

Let's now switch attention to the `tictactoeGameViewController` class. Starting with the header file, we create a new property to hold on to the match object, which we set in the previous method. We also create a new mutable dictionary to hold on to our game data, which will be discussed in more depth throughout the rest of this chapter.

```
#import <UIKit/UIKit.h>
#import <GameKit/GameKit.h>

@interface tictactoeGameViewController : UIViewController
@property(nonatomic, retain) NSMutableDictionary *gameDictionary;
@property(nonatomic, retain) GKTurnBasedMatch *match;
@end
```

> **Important**   You are strictly limited to passing only 4k of data with each new turn. If you cannot limit your game data to less than 4k, you can use a URL to point to a server holding the complete data set. Alternatively, you could pass only the delta of the game state and store the existing data locally.

We need to pause here to configure the actual game view (tictactoeGameViewController). We need nine spots for the user to move in the tic-tac-toe game, as well as a forfeit option and a label to inform the players of whose turn it is.

We use simple UIButtons to handle user input. Modify the XIB file with a layout similar to that pictured in Figure 9-4. You need to create IBOutlets for each of the buttons and the label as well as new IBAction methods for both making a move and forfeiting. Connect all the board buttons to the makeMove method that you previously created. We also need to set tags on the UIButtons to help us locate them. Begin with tag 1 in the upper-left corner and move left to right, up to down, numbering them.

Figure 9-4. A view of the game board, as seen from Interface Builder

You now have two new methods in your game view controller, as well as nine button outlets and one label outlet. Now that you have seen how to begin a new turned-based gaming match, in the next section, we look at how to make a move and pass control to the next player.

Making the First Move

The first thing we need to do in a new match-based game, before we make a move, is determine which avatar the player is representing. In our example game, there are two sides: X and O. We are going to set the first person to always be X, and the second to always be O. This means that X will always make the first move. With this setup, it becomes easy to determine who the player currently is representing using the following code snippet:

```
if (match.currentParticipant == [match.participants objectAtIndex:0])
{
    myPlayerCharacter = @"X";
    identifyTeamLabel.text = @"It is X's Turn";
}
else
{
    myPlayerCharacter = @"O";
    identifyTeamLabel.text = @"It is O's Turn";
}
```

After we have determined who the users are, then we can allow them to make a move. We will modify the code for the action to which the nine game buttons are connected. First, let's take a look at the method in its completed form. Then, we can break it down and look at each part in depth.

```
- (IBAction)makeMove:(id)sender
{
    [sender setTitle:myPlayerCharacter forState:UIControlStateNormal];
    NSString *buttonIndexString = [NSString stringWithFormat:@"%d", [sender tag]];
    [gameDictionary setObject:myPlayerCharacter forKey:buttonIndexString];
    NSData *data = [NSPropertyListSerialization dataFromPropertyList:gameDictionary
format:NSPropertyListXMLFormat_v1_0 errorDescription:nil];

    GKTurnBasedParticipant *nextPlayer;
    if (match.currentParticipant == [match.participants objectAtIndex:0]) {
        nextPlayer = [[match participants] lastObject];
    } else {
        nextPlayer = [[match participants] objectAtIndex:0];
    }

    if ([self checkWinner] != nil) {
        if ([[self checkWinner] isEqualToString:@"Tie"]) {
            UIAlertView *alert = [[UIAlertView alloc] initWithTitle:@"Game Over"⏎
message:@"Its a draw" delegate:nil cancelButtonTitle:@"Dimiss"⏎
otherButtonTitles: nil];
            [alert show];
            [alert release];
        } else {
            UIAlertView *alert = [[UIAlertView alloc] initWithTitle:@"Game Over" message:nil⏎
delegate:nil cancelButtonTitle:@"Dimiss" otherButtonTitles: nil];
            [alert show];
            [alert release];
        }
```

```
        [self.match participantQuitInTurnWithOutcome:GKTurnBasedMatchOutcomeWon ⏎
nextParticipant:nextPlayer turnTimeout: 32000 matchData:data completionHandler:^(NSError *error) {
            if (error) {
                NSLog(@"An error occurred ending match: %@", [error⏎
                localizedDescription]);
            }
        }];
    } else {
        [self.match endTurnWithNextParticipant:nextPlayer matchData:data completionHandler:^(NSError
*error) {
            if (error) {
                NSLog(@"An error occurred updating turn: %@", [error⏎
                localizedDescription]);
            }

            [self.navigationController popViewControllerAnimated: YES];
        }];
    }
}
```

This method might appear complex at first glance, but after we have stepped through all the details, you will see that it is fairly simplistic. The first thing we do is set the title of the sender (the game button) to our player character, which was determined with the previous code snippet.

Next, we know that we will need to hold on to our game data to persist it throughout each turn, so we store the player's character into a dictionary using the button's tag for our key. This allows us to later iterate over the dictionary and repopulate previous moves (you'll learn more about this in the next section, "Continuing a Game in Progress").

We now need to prepare and send our game data to the next player. This requires several steps. Because we need to send our game data as NSData, we convert our existing game NSDictionary to NSData. We do this with the NSPropertyListSerialization methods. We can then send and later retrieve this data.

The next step is to determine who the next player will be. In a two-person game, this is simple: we look at the array of our participants and determine which one isn't us, and then we set that one to the next player. When dealing with more players, you need to simply determine your current index in the match's participant array and call the next player; or, in the case that you are the last player, call the first.

Note   The size and order of the participant's array is determined when the match first begins, and will be the same throughout the match and on each device.

Tip   You might see that there are nil objects in the participant array; these are placeholders for unmatched players. Game Center will only match new players when it is their turn to move. This means that every time you are auto-matched, it will be your turn.

The next section of code checks to see whether there is a winner of the match. We'll go over this in more detail in the "Ending a Match" section of this chapter.

The last thing that we will do at the end of each move is send the new game data to the next player. This player will, in turn, update the game state and send it to the next player (which happens to be the first player again). To do this, we call endTurnWithNextParticipant on our match object. We need to pass in the next player that we determined earlier in the method.

Continuing a Game in Progress

When you resume a game on your next turn, assuming it is not the first turn of a match, you will need to first restore the game state to its current position. To do this, we begin by modifying our viewDidLoad method to get the current match data. We need to call loadMatchDataWithCompletionHandler on the match object. This returns the data that we sent to the next player in the previous method. We then convert the NSData back into an NSDictionary and then add it to the gameDictionary. Here's the code:

```
- (void)viewDidLoad
{
    //Existing viewDidLoad code...
    [self.match loadMatchDataWithCompletionHandler:^(NSData *matchData, NSError *error) {
        NSDictionary *myDict = nil;
        myDict = [NSPropertyListSerialization propertyListFromData:match.matchData
                                        mutabilityOption:NSPropertyListImmutable
                                                  format:nil
                                        errorDescription:nil];

        [gameDictionary addEntriesFromDictionary:myDict];
        [self populateExistingGameBoard];
        if (error) {
            NSLog(@"loadMatchData - %@", [error localizedDescription]);
        }
    }];
}
```

> **Tip** If you persist the game state locally, you will only need to update the turns that have occurred since your last move. This approach will help you keep packet sizes under the 4k limit.

After populating the game data dictionary, we need to call a new convenience method to populate our game GUI from that dictionary. This method will loop through all the keys in our dictionary and populate the relevant game buttons with the player's character. We also set the enabled state of the button to NO, which prevents the player from moving on top of their opponent's location.

```objc
- (void)populateExistingGameBoard
{
    NSArray *dataArray = [gameDictionary allKeys];
    for (NSString *key in dataArray) {
        UIButton *button = (UIButton*)[self.view viewWithTag: [key intValue]];
        [button setTitle:[gameDictionary objectForKey:key] forState:UIControlStateNormal];.

        [button setEnabled: NO];
    }
}
```

With the code in place, you can now play through a complete round of tic-tac-toe using two Game Center accounts; however, the game will never detect a winner or a draw. In the next section, we look at the logic required to detect an end-of-game event. Figure 9-5 shows an example of a populated game.

Figure 9-5. Populating the game board through the match's data

Ending a Match

In the section "Making the First Move," we saw a call to a method called checkWinner. In this section, we take a closer look at that method. For tic-tac-toe, we are using a brute-force approach to see if we have a winner, by checking all the rows and columns for three repeating characters. We also need to check for a tie if there are no more places to move.

```
- (NSString*)checkWinner
{
    //top row
        if ([gameButton1.titleLabel.text isEqualToString:gameButton2.titleLabel.text] &&↵
        [gameButton2.titleLabel.text isEqualToString:gameButton3.titleLabel.text])
                return gameButton1.titleLabel.text;
        //middle row
        if ([gameButton4.titleLabel.text isEqualToString:gameButton5.titleLabel.text] &&↵
        [gameButton5.titleLabel.text isEqualToString:gameButton6.titleLabel.text])
                return gameButton4.titleLabel.text;
        //bottom row
        if ([gameButton7.titleLabel.text isEqualToString:gameButton8.titleLabel.text] &&↵
        [gameButton8.titleLabel.text isEqualToString:gameButton9.titleLabel.text])
                return gameButton7.titleLabel.text;
        //first column
        if ([gameButton1.titleLabel.text isEqualToString:gameButton4.titleLabel.text] &&↵
        [gameButton4.titleLabel.text isEqualToString:gameButton7.titleLabel.text])
                return gameButton1.titleLabel.text;
        //middle column
        if ([gameButton2.titleLabel.text isEqualToString:gameButton5.titleLabel.text] &&↵
        [gameButton5.titleLabel.text isEqualToString:gameButton8.titleLabel.text])
                return gameButton2.titleLabel.text;
        //last column
        if ([gameButton3.titleLabel.text isEqualToString:gameButton6.titleLabel.text] &&↵
        [gameButton6.titleLabel.text isEqualToString:gameButton9.titleLabel.text])
                return gameButton3.titleLabel.text;
        //diagonal
        if ([gameButton1.titleLabel.text isEqualToString:gameButton5.titleLabel.text] &&↵
        [gameButton5.titleLabel.text isEqualToString:gameButton9.titleLabel.text])
                return gameButton1.titleLabel.text;
        if ([gameButton3.titleLabel.text isEqualToString:gameButton5.titleLabel.text] &&↵
        [gameButton5.titleLabel.text isEqualToString:gameButton7.titleLabel.text])
                return gameButton3.titleLabel.text;

        if (gameButton1.titleLabel.text != nil && gameButton2.titleLabel.text != nil &&↵
        gameButton3.titleLabel.text != nil && gameButton4.titleLabel.text != nil &&↵
        gameButton5.titleLabel.text != nil && gameButton6.titleLabel.text != nil &&↵
        gameButton7.titleLabel.text != nil && gameButton8.titleLabel.text != nil &&↵
        gameButton9.titleLabel.text != nil)
                return @"Tie";

    return nil;
}
```

If you return your attention to the makeMove method from the previous section, you will see that if we determine the player has won, we make a new call. We need to call participantQuitInTurnWithOutcome to end the match. We pass in GKTurnBasedMatchOutcomeWon for the argument, but if we have a scenario in which the player has lost, we can also pass in GKTurnBasedMatchOutcomeLost.

```
[self.match participantQuitInTurnWithOutcome:GKTurnBasedMatchOutcomeWon⏎
 nextParticipant:nextPlayer turnTimeout: 32000 matchData:data completionHandler:^(NSError *error)  {
        if (error)
        {
                NSLog(@"An error occurred ending match: %@", [error localizedDescription]);
        }
}];
```

Quitting and Forfeiting

A player can quit a match at any time by swiping across it from the matchmaker view controller. However, it is recommended to add a path for your users to forfeit or quit a match from inside of your game itself. To allow a player to forfeit a match, use the following code snippet:

```
- (IBAction)forfeit:(id)sender
{
    [self.match participantQuitOutOfTurnWithOutcome:GKTurnBasedMatchOutcomeQuit
withCompletionHandler:^(NSError *error) {
        if (error) {
            NSLog(@"An error occurred ending match: %@", [error localizedDescription]);
        }
    }];
}
```

Player Timeouts

Earlier in this chapter, endTurnWithNextParticipant:matchData:completionHandler: was discussed as the method for ending a turn. As of iOS 6 this method has been deprecated and replaced with endTurnWithNextParticipants:turnTimeout:matchData:completionHandler:. If your app is targeting iOS 5 you will need to continue to use the earlier method; however, if you are targeting iOS 6 or higher you can begin to use the new method, which allows for a player timeout.

Prior to iOS 6 there was no way to specify skipping a player in the turned-based lineup; if a player failed to play their round the game would enter a state of limbo until the game was forfeited. Using endTurnWithNextParticipants:turnTimeout:matchData:completionHandler: allows an NSTimeInterval parameter. Once the time interval has passed, control is sent to the next player in line and the behavior for a player missing their turn can be handled.

Player Exchanges

Prior to iOS 7 there was no way for players who's turn it was not to send an action, iOS 7 brought the ability for Player Exchanges. Player Exchanges allow any player at anytime to initiate actions, this can be used for simultaneous turns, chats, and trading between players regardless of which player is currently waiting to move.

An exchange request requires five steps to be completed successfully.

1. The initiator of the exchange sends a request to the recipient.

2. The recipient is notified that there is a pending request.

3. The receipt acts on the exchange and the response is sent back the initiator.

4. The initiator is then notified of the response.

5. The current player is finally notified of the completed exchange and updates the match data.

Any player, if your game allows it, may initiate an exchange whether or not it is currently their turn. The initiator will need to pick one or more recipients for the exchange request. The initiator also needs to specify the type of trade, is it a chat message, a trade, request for help, or something else. The exchange also needs to have a timeout set for how long the exchange is valid for.

A new method is available in iOS 7 for sending exchanges, sendExchangeToParticipants:. This method takes several arguments, first an array of recipients that will receive the request. Followed by an NSData block that represents the details of the request. A localizable message is also attached as is a timeout in seconds:

```
[GKTurnBasedExchange sendExchangeToParticipants:recipients data:data localizableMessageKey:key
arguments:arguments timeout:timeout completionHandler:^(GKTurnBasedExchange
*exchange, NSError *error) {
    }];
```

> **Note** Exchange data is limited to 1k as opposed to the 4k limit for general turn data.

The initating player may cancel an exchange request anytime before the exchange is accepted and acted on by the receiptant. This is done by using the player:exchangeCanceled: match: method.

The receiving player will need to respond to the exchange request using the following approach:

```
[GKTurnBasedExchange replyWithLocalizableMessageKey:key arguments:arguments data:data
completionHandler:^(NSError *error) {
}
```

The match data for the current game will need to be updated, if required, to account for the exchange. It may therefore be necessary to include the current player in the exchange recipients list so that the data can be updated as part of their turn.

Player Reminders

iOS 7 also adds the ability to send reminders to players about pending actions. These reminders will appear as push notifications on their devices. The push notification will contain the referenced localizable message, and considerations for the display size of that message need to be taken into account. This allows the game to send reminders that a turn or exchange action is required.

```
[GKTurnBasedMatch sendReminderToParticipants:(NSArray *)participants
localizableMessageKey:(NSString *)key  arguments:(NSArray *)arguments
completionHandler:(void(^)(NSError *error))completionHandler]
```

Programmatic Matches

If you want to bypass the GKTurnBasedMatchmakerViewController and implement your own GUI, there is an option to do so. Using the following method will create a new match without having the user go through the matchmaker:

```
- (void)findMatch
{
    GKMatchRequest *match = [[GKMatchRequest alloc] init];
    [match setMaxPlayers:2];
    [match setMinPlayers:2];

    [GKTurnBasedMatch findMatchForRequest:match ↵
withCompletionHandler:^(GKTurnBasedMatch *match, NSError *error)  {
        if (error == nil) {
            //start new game with returned match
        } else {
            NSLog(@"An error occurred when finding a match: %@", [error localizedDescription]);
        }
    }];
}
```

In addition to creating a game, you need to be able to load a list of existing games for your local user. You can do so with the following method.

```
- (void)loadMatches
{
    [GKTurnBasedMatch loadMatchesWithCompletionHandler:^(NSArray *matches, NSError *error) {
        if (error == nil) {
            NSLog(@"Existing Matches: %@", matches);
        } else {
            NSLog(@"An error occurred while loading matches: %@", [error localizedDescription]);
        }
    }];
}
```

> **Note** Because both of these methods use background tasks in order to handle the request, code that you implement within the block needs to be thread-safe.

GKTurnBasedEventHandler

The GKTurnedBasedEventHandler is a delegate protocol that is responsible for handling important messages related to turn-based games. To set a delegate for events, use the following code.

```
[[GKTurnBasedEventHandler sharedTurnBasedEventHandler] setDelegate: self];
```

The protocol has three optional methods.

- handleInviteFromGameCenter: When your delegate receives this method, it should populate a new GKMatchRequest with the playersToInvite that are passed in through the method. You then need to begin a new match or present the matchmaker GUI. This method is called when the user accepts a match invite from a friend.

- handleTurnEventForMatch: Your delegate receives this message when the user has accepted a push notification for an in-progress match. You need to end whatever task you are performing and display the game for the match that is passed in with this method.

- handleMatchEnded: When your delegate receives this message, it should display the match's results and game-over views to the player and allow the player the option of removing the match data from Game Center.

Summary

In this chapter, you learned about the turn-based gaming functionality of Game Center. We worked with our existing GameCenterManager class and wrote an entirely new sample game to work with the turn-based technology. You should now have a firm grasp on how to create a new turn-based game, as well as retain and send turn data between peers. With the skills learned in this chapter, you should now be able to easily get the networking component of turned-based gaming up and running in a few hours.

In the next chapter, we will look at another exciting topic: voice chat. Apple has gone to tremendous lengths to make voice over IP easy to use in iOS apps, and we will explore how to get VoIP up and running quickly in your Game Center– or Game Kit–enabled apps.

Voice Chat

Great discoveries and improvements invariably involve the cooperation of many minds. I may be given credit for having blazed the trail, but when I look at the subsequent developments I feel the credit is due to others rather than to myself.

—Alexander Graham Bell

Voice chat, more than any other service provided as part of Game Kit, is a true testament to Apple engineering. Apple has turned one of the most complicated features on other platforms into one of the easiest to implement on iOS. When working with Voice over Internet Protocol (VOIP) on other platforms, it is often the most complex and daunting task of an entire project. In this chapter, we will explore how to add voice chat services to our UFOs game or to any iOS app. The brevity of this chapter is evidence of how much work Apple has put into this technology to bring it within the grasp of even the greenest of developers.

Unlike our strategy in preceding chapters, we will be dealing with Game Kit Voice Chat and Game Center Voice Chat separately, instead of writing a shared class as we did previously. While there are many similarities between the two services, they differ enough that it makes sense to handle each one separately. In addition, we will apply the topics covered in this chapter as we implement voice chat into UFOs.

Voice Chat for Game Center

We will begin by looking at voice chat for Game Center. Using a GKMatch to create a voice chat session has many advantages, such as ease of use, quickness to implement, and reduced overhead compared to using Game Kit or having to implement a custom solution. A GKMatch voice chat can have multiple channels, each with an associated list of recipients. For example, you could have one channel for teammates in a first-person shooter game, and another channel for all players. This would allow you to talk about tactics for winning the match without giving away information to the other team.

> **Note**   Voice chat using a GKMatch is only available to participants who are connected to the Internet via Wi-Fi; voice chat does not support cellular networks.

Creating an Audio Session

Before you can begin to work with voice chat itself, you first need to create a new audio session. It is important to do this before you begin any voice chat services. If you create the audio session after you create the chat session, you will not be able to send or receive voice data. In the following example, we create a new audio session that allows our app to play and record audio, and then set it to active.

> **Tip**   Your app might already use an audio session for playing sound effects; if you have already created an audio session, you are not required to make a new one. If you are reusing an existing audio session, make sure that you set it to allow both play and record functionality.

```
NSError *error = nil;
AVAudioSession *audioSession = [AVAudioSession sharedInstance];

    if(![audioSession setCategory:AVAudioSessionCategoryPlayAndRecord error:&error])
    {
        if(error)
        {
            NSLog(@"An error occurred while starting audio session: %@", [error
localizedDescription]);
        }
    }

    if(![audioSession setActive: YES error: &error])
    {
        if(error)
        {
            NSLog(@"An error occurred while starting audio session: %@", [error
localizedDescription]);
        }
    }
```

Creating New Voice Channels

You can have as many voice chat channels as you want in your app, and each peer can register to be part of as many channels as they want. Channels are created and organized by a name string. This is how we will determine what channels we want the user to join. When two or more peers join a channel with the same name, they are connected to the same chat.

The code snippet that follows shows an example of how to create three different channels. Take note that the channels are created with the GKMatch object that is returned to us when we begin a new Game Center–based networking game.

```
GKVoiceChat *allChannel = [[match voiceChatWithName:@"allPlayers"] retain];
GKVoiceChat *teamChannel = [[match voiceChatWithName:@"blueTeam"] retain];
GKVoiceChat *squadChannel = [[match voiceChatWithName:@"BlueTeamSquad2"] retain];
```

In this example, we have a channel for communicating with all players, a channel for communicating with our entire team, and a third channel that is used to talk with our squad. Just because channels have been created doesn't mean that they are automatically turned on. In the next section, we will look at how to start and stop communication on a specific channel.

Starting and Stopping Voice Chat

In the previous section, we created three new voice channels for use with Game Center–type voice chat. When you want to transmit and receive voice on those channels, you need to first tell the API that you want to begin using that channel. After you are connected to a channel, you are able to send and receive data from that channel. If you want to connect to a channel and do not want to transmit any voice audio, see the following section on muting the microphone.

To begin using a voice channel, you need to call the start method on the GKVoiceChat object that was created in the previous section.

```
[allChannel start];
[teamChannel start];
```

When you want to leave a channel, you simply call the stop method. This is a better approach than simply muting all participants in the channel because the app will not be required to receive additional network data. A stopped channel can be restarted at any time.

```
[allChannel stop];
[teamChannel stop];
```

> **Tip**   It is highly recommended that you provide both visual and audio indicators when you are transmitting voice data, such as a red light and a click sound. This reduces the chance that a user will accidentally transmit voice data when they don't intend to. Always remember that a user's microphone and transmitted voice should be treated as sensitive data.

Chat Volume and Muting

The voice chat volume is set by channel. Each channel has an associated property that can be used to lower the overall volume of that chat. You cannot raise the volume past what the user has selected as the device's current volume. For example, if the user's maximum audio is 70% and you set the volume to 100%, it will scale itself down to 70%. To modify a channel's volume, add the following line of code:

```
allChannel.volume = 0.5; //half of max volume
```

In addition, you can mute individual players in a channel by referencing their playerID. Players can be muted and unmuted using the following two lines of code:

```
[teamChannel setMute:YES forPlayer: playerID];
[teamChannel setMute:NO forPlayer:playerID];
```

There might also be circumstances in which you do not want to transmit the user's voice at all times. By default, a user starts a chat in the muted state. You will need to unmute a user before they can begin to transmit voice data.

```
squadChannel.active = YES;
```

> **Important**   A user can only transmit voice on one channel at a time; if you unmute a channel, the API will automatically mute all other channels.

This is all that is required in order to completely enable voice chat in your Game Center–based networking app. Everything else, including playback, sending, and receiving the data, is handled for you by the APIs.

Monitoring Player State

I mentioned earlier in this chapter that it is important to let the user know that they are currently transmitting data. Letting the player see who is speaking is also an important step. By monitoring player state changes, you can determine which users are currently transmitting voice and highlight them in a player list or perform some other kind of indication of which player is speaking. The following block is easy to set up when you begin your chat, and it saves you from performing polling or delegate callbacks:

```
allChannel.playerStateUpdateHandler = ^(NSString *playerID, GKVoiceChatPlayerState state)
{
        switch (state)
            {
                case GKVoiceChatPlayerSpeaking:
                    [self showSpeakingPlayer: playerID];
                    break;
```

```
                case GKVoiceChatPlayerSilent:
                        [self stopShowingSpeakingPlayer: playerID];
                        break;
        }
};
```

> **Note** Player state updates are handled per channel. You will need to configure one for each channel on which you wish to watch for changes.

Voice Chat for Game Kit

When working with Game Kit Voice Chat, we will focus on the GKVoiceChatService object. The fundamentals of Game Kit Voice Chat are very similar to Game Center Voice Chat. A good starting point for implementing this system is after you are returned a GKSession object, when you connect to another player using the Peer Picker system. It is important to note that GKVoiceChatService is designed to send data to only one peer at a time. Although this isn't a limitation yet, as Game Kit only supports two peers, it is important to keep in mind should the API ever be expanded.

> **Note** Don't forget to check [GKVoiceChatService isVoIPAllowed] to make sure you are able to support voice chat before you continue. Some devices, such as the first-generation iPod touch, are unable to support voice chat.

Creating an Audio Session

As with Game Center, we can begin to work with Game Kit Voice Chat by first creating a new AVAudioSession. It is important to make sure that you create the session prior to beginning any voice chat service calls.

```
NSError *error = nil;
AVAudioSession *audioSession = [AVAudioSession sharedInstance];

    if(![audioSession setCategory:AVAudioSessionCategoryPlayAndRecord error:&error])
    {
        if(error)
        {
            NSLog(@"An error occurred while starting audio session: %@", [error↩
localizedDescription]);
        }
    }
```

```
        if(![audioSession setActive: YES error: &error])
        {
            if(error)
            {
                NSLog(@"An error occurred while starting audio session: %@", [error↵
localizedDescription]);
            }
        }
```

Required Overhead

Unlike the Game Center approach, Game Kit requires a bit more overhead to get things up and running. The first thing you need to do is implement a few required methods. The following first method posted returns the peerID for the player that you wish to communicate with. This value is easily retrieved from your current GKSession object:

```
- (NSString *)participantID
{
    return session.peerID;
}
```

You also need to implement a method to send the voice data to the connected peer, and another that will handle receiving the data; both of these methods are available in the following code snippets. Together, these two methods will handle the sending and receiving of voice data for your app.

```
- (void)voiceChatService:(GKVoiceChatService *)voiceChatService sendData:(NSData *)data
toParticipantID:(NSString *)participantID
{
    NSError *error = nil;

    if(![self.session sendData:data toPeers:[NSArray arrayWithObject: participantID]
withDataMode:GKSendDataReliable error:&error])
    {
        NSLog(@"Unable to send data to peers: %@", [error localizedDescription]);

    }
}
    - (void) receiveData:(NSData *)data fromPeer:(NSString *)peer inSession:
    (GKSession *)session context:(void *)context;
    {
        [[GKVoiceChatService defaultVoiceChatService] receivedData:data
        fromParticipantID:peer];
    }
```

Getting Things Running

In addition to the three new methods that we implemented in the previous section, you will need to complete some additional steps to get everything up and running. First, you need to initialize a new instance of GKVoiceChatClient, which should be a custom subclass of GKVoiceChatClient that you create. For more information on this step, see the next section, "Putting It Together."

```
GKVoiceChatClient *voiceChatClient = [[GKVoiceChatClient alloc] initWithSession: session];
[GKVoiceChatService defaultVoiceChatService].client = voiceChatClient;
```

After you have created a new instance of GKVoiceChatClient, you need to connect your peer to it. The following code demonstrates how to accomplish this.

```
[[GKVoiceChatService defaultVoiceChatService] startVoiceChatWithParticipantID:↵
 [self    participantID] error: &error];
```

To end the voice chat session, you need to call a similar method, as follows.

```
[[GKVoiceChatService defaultVoiceChatService] stopVoiceChatWithParticipantID:↵
 [self    participantID]];
```

After you have established a connection to the other peer, you will begin to receive voice chat data. If you want to send data, all you need to do is unmute the microphone using the following code snippet:

```
[GKVoiceChatService defaultVoiceChatService].microphoneMuted = NO;
```

These are all the steps that are required to get Game Kit Voice Chat up and running. Although it is slightly more work than with Game Center Voice Chat, it is still significantly easier than implementing your own VOIP system.

Putting It Together

In this chapter, we modify our existing code base from Chapter 8. Begin there by creating a new audio session for your voice chat service. Add the following block of code to the UFOGameViewController.m viewDidLoad: method. In addition, you need to add the AVFoundation.framework to your project. Modify the relevant section of the viewDidLoad method to match the following.

```
if (self.gameIsMultiplayer == NO)
{
    for (int x = 0; x < 5; x++)
    {
        [self spawnCow];
    }

    [self updateCowPaths];
}

else
    {

        [self generateAndSendHostNumber];

        NSError *error = nil;
        AudioSessionInitialize(NULL, NULL, NULL, self);
```

```
        AVAudioSession *audioSession = [AVAudioSession sharedInstance];

        if(![audioSession setCategory:AVAudioSessionCategoryPlayAndRecord error:&error])
        {
            if(error)
            {
                NSLog(@"An error occurred while starting audio session: %@", [error
localizedDescription]);
            }
        }

        if(![audioSession setActive: YES error: &error])
        {
            if(error)
            {
                NSLog(@"An error occurred while starting audio session: %@", [error
localizedDescription]);
            }
        }

        [self setupVoiceChat];
    }
```

> **Caution**   Make sure the device you are building for has both a speaker and a microphone available for use.

You also need to add a new method called setupVoiceChat. This method will handle the basic configuration for both Game Center and Game Kit.

```
-(void)setupVoiceChat
{
    //GameKit
    if (self.peerIDString)
    {
        NSError *error = nil;
        UFOVoiceChatClient *voiceChatClient = [[UFOVoiceChatClient alloc] init];
        voiceChatClient.session = self.gcManager.matchOrSession;
         [GKVoiceChatService defaultVoiceChatService].client = voiceChatClient;
         [[GKVoiceChatService defaultVoiceChatService]
         startVoiceChatWithParticipantID:self.peerIDString error:&error];

        [GKVoiceChatService defaultVoiceChatService].microphoneMuted = YES;
        if (error)
        {
                NSLog(@"An error occurred when setting up voice chat: %@",
                [error localizedDescription]);

        }
    }
```

```
    //Game Center
    else
    {
        mainChannel = [[self.peerMatch voiceChatWithName:@"main"] retain];
        [mainChannel start];
        mainChannel.volume = 1.0;
        mainChannel.active = NO;
    }
}
```

You might have noticed that in this code we have a new class type called UFOVoiceChatClient. This is the class that we will use to handle the incoming and outgoing data for voice, as well as other methods used to watch status and errors. The implementation for that class follows.

```
@implementation UFOVoiceChatClient
@synthesize session;
-(NSString *)participantID
{
    return self.session.peerID;
}

- (void)voiceChatService:(GKVoiceChatService *)voiceChatService sendData:(NSData *)data↵
toParticipantID:(NSString *)participantID
{
    NSError *error = nil;

    if(![self.session sendData:data toPeers:[NSArray arrayWithObject: participantID]
withDataMode:GKSendDataReliable error:&error])
    {
        NSLog(@"Unable to send data to peers: %@", [error localizedDescription]);

    }
}
- (void)receivedData:(NSData *)arbitraryData fromParticipantID:(NSString *)participantID
{
    [[GKVoiceChatService defaultVoiceChatService] receivedData:arbitraryData↵
 fromParticipantID:participantID];
}

- (void)voiceChatService:(GKVoiceChatService *)voiceChatService↵
 didReceiveInvitationFromParticipantID:(NSString *)participantID↵
 callID:(NSInteger)callID
{
    NSLog(@"Did Recieve Invitation");
}

- (void)voiceChatService:(GKVoiceChatService *)voiceChatService↵
 didNotStartWithParticipantID:(NSString *)participantID error:↵
(NSError *)error
{
    NSLog(@"Did Not Start Invitation");
}
```

```
- (void)voiceChatService:(GKVoiceChatService *)voiceChatService
 didStartWithParticipantID:(NSString *)participantID
{
    NSLog(@"Did Start Invitation");
}

@end
```

> **Note**   Make sure your voiceChatClient conforms to the GKVoiceChatClient protocol.

You also need to make some slight modifications to the GameCenterManager class to handle incoming voice data. Modify the existing receiveData:fromPeer:inSession:Context: method to match the following:

```
- (void)receiveData:(NSData *)data fromPeer:(NSString *)peer inSession: (GKSession
 *)session context:(void *)context;
{
    NSString *dataString = [[NSString alloc] initWithData:data
    encoding:NSUTF8StringEncoding];

    if (dataString == nil)
    {
        [[GKVoiceChatService defaultVoiceChatService] receivedData:data
        fromParticipantID:peer];

        [dataString release];
        return;
    }


    NSArray *objects = [NSArray arrayWithObjects:dataString, peer, session,  nil];
    NSArray *keys = [NSArray arrayWithObjects: @"data", @"peer", @"session",  nil];

    NSDictionary *dataDictionary = [NSDictionary dictionaryWithObjects:objects forKeys:keys];

    [dataString release];
    [self callDelegateOnMainThread: @selector(receivedData:) withArg: dataDictionary
    error: nil];
}
```

Notice that we added another block of code that handles passing the data to our defaultVoiceChatService client. If we cannot decode a string from the NSData, we determine whether the data is voice data. Your app may be more complex and require a prefix or other type of designator to determine whether the data is voice, but this is very suitable for a simple game like UFOs.

The last thing we need to do is hook up an action to turn our microphone on and off. I have decided to go with a simple toggle button for UFOs, but you may feel the need to implement a different approach. Add a new button, as shown in Figure 10-1, and hook up the new action posted next.

Figure 10-1. *Adding a microphone button to our UFO game demo*

```
-(IBAction)startVoice:(id)sender;
{
        micOn = !micOn;
        if (micOn)
        {
                [micButton setTitle:@"Mic On" forState:UIControlStateNormal];
                //GameKit
                if (self.peerIDString)
                {
                        [GKVoiceChatService defaultVoiceChatService].microphoneMuted =
                        NO;
                }

                //Game Center
                else
                {
                        mainChannel.active = YES;
                }
        }

        else
        {
                [micButton setTitle:@"Mic Off" forState:UIControlStateNormal];
                //GameKit
                if (self.peerIDString)
                {
                        [GKVoiceChatService defaultVoiceChatService].microphoneMuted =
                        YES;
                }
```

```
                            //Game Center
                            else
                            {
                                    mainChannel.active = NO;
                            }
                }
}
```

This method determines the current state of the microphone (on/off) and toggles it to the new state. When that happens, we update the button title and turn the microphone on or off for the type of network that we are using.

These are all the required steps to add voice chat into our UFOs example project. If you run the game on two devices, you will be able to communicate with voice back and forth.

> **Note**   Latency between speaking and receiving the voice data on the peer device may be anywhere from 500 milliseconds up to several thousand milliseconds.

Summary

In this chapter, you learned how to incorporate a traditionally very complex technology into our iOS app with very little work. We explored the differences with using voice chat on both Game Kit and Game Center, as well as implemented examples of both systems into our UFOs demo game. You now have the skills required to add full-featured VOIP technology to any iPhone or iPad app. If you have been following the book along from the beginning, you now have all the skills needed to implement all aspects of Game Kit and Game Center into your apps.

In the next chapter, we will look at another important technology when writing games or apps for iOS—StoreKit. Using StoreKit technology, we will explore how to sell additional features and add-ons to your product.

In-App Purchase with StoreKit

You don't close a sale, you open a relationship if you want to build a long-term, successful enterprise.

—Patricia Fripp

Throughout this book so far, we have been working with both Game Center and Game Kit to add rich social networking into your apps. However, there is another important feature slowly becoming more popular in modern software: in-app purchases. Allowing your users to purchase upgrades or additional content for your app, from directly within your app, opens up a potentially significant new revenue stream. Over the past few years, a new business model has emerged called freemium. Freemium is a new type of game or product that is offered to your users for free, but is monetized through selling add-ons. The 100 Top Grossing apps on the App Store consist mostly of free apps; when this chapter was written, 81 of the 100 Top Grossing apps were all free to download, seen in Figure 11-1.

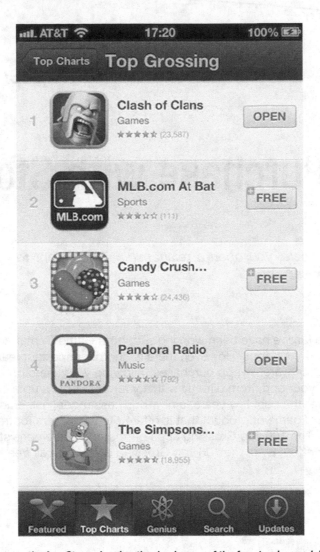

Figure 11-1. Top Grossing apps on the App Store, showing the dominance of the free-to-play model

Let's consider the popular We Rule by ngmoco:) as an example of a highly successful free-to-play game. The game is free to download and play on both iPhones and iPads. Each user is in control of a virtual kingdom, in which they are responsible for constructing buildings and growing crops. The user generates "mojo" over time and can use that in-app currency to create new structures and farms. However, some users want to construct faster than is normally allowed because of the restrictive nature of mojo, which accumulates slowly.

These power users can visit the in-app store to purchase more mojo in bulk. Shown in Figure 11-2 is We Rule's built-in store. It offers a number of purchases ranging from very affordable to shockingly expensive. It is important to cater to both types of users when working with sellable add-ons. Some of your users will be interested in spending one or two dollars occasionally, while others will be power users who want to spend one hundred dollars, or more, at a time.

Figure 11-2. The in-app purchase store, as seen in We Rule by ngmoco:)

The freemium model has become such a profitable approach that ngmoco:) has stopped working on games that do not fit into the model, going so far as to even cancel Rolando 3 in mid-development because it couldn't be adapted to a freemium-type game. The model appears to be paying off well for ngmoco:). As shown in Figure 11-3, the current highest-selling item in the We Rule store costs $9.99. This one in-app purchase is retailing for more than most stand-alone iOS games. It is able to get that sale because the customer becomes committed to the game while it is free.

Top In-App Purch...

1	Bottle of 75 Mojo	$9.99
2	Flask of 30 Mojo	$4.99
3	Carafe of 165 ...	$19.99
4	Decorative Item	$0.99
5	Decorative Item	$0.99
6	Case of 300 Mojo	$29.99
7	Decorative Item	$0.99
8	Vintage 800 Mojo	$49.99
9	Decorative Item	$1.99
10	Decorative Item	$0.99

Figure 11-3. Current listing of the best-selling in-app purchases for We Rule by ngmoco:)

Not all games or apps supported by in-app purchase need to be free. In fact, until recently, you were not allowed to implement in-app purchase in free apps. You can easily add additional features or unlocks in a paid game, such as the Mighty Eagle in Angry Birds. In-app purchase is also not only just for games. Almost any software can benefit from it, whether you are unlocking pro-level features or charging users a subscription for push notification support. Throughout this chapter we will explore how to add a full-featured in-app store to your iOS software.

Setting Up Your App in iTunes Connect

As with Game Center, the first step is a visit to iTunes Connect to configure your app for purchases.

1. Log in to iTunes Connect (`http://itunesconnect.apple.com`), as discussed in Chapter 2. You will need an existing project to work on. If you don't have a project created in iTunes Connect yet, go ahead and create one.

2. Select the project to which you want to add in-app purchase support. Then, click the button called Manage In-App Purchases, as shown in Figure 11-4.

Figure 11-4. App listing in iTunes Connect showing Manage In-App Purchases button

Important   You have 90 days from creating an app to upload a binary for review. Make sure to save the in-app purchase configuration until you are within 90 days of finishing your project.

3. Selecting the Manage In-App Purchases button will bring you to a screen for setting up a new product, as shown in Figure 11-5. Once there, click the Create New button in the upper-left corner of the window.

Figure 11-5. Setting up your first in-app purchase in iTunes Connect

There are several types of in-app purchase products that you can configure:

- Consumable: A consumable in-app purchase must be purchased every time the user downloads it. These include in-game currency, as we saw in the We Rule example in the previous section. Figure 11-6 shows the consumable purchase setup screen.

In-App Purchase Summary

Enter a reference name and a product ID for this In-App Purchase. You must also add at least one language, along with a display name and a description in that language.

Reference Name: [   ]   (?)

Product ID: [   ]   (?)

Pricing and Availability

Enter the pricing and availability details for this In-App Purchase below.

Cleared for Sale Yes ◉   No ○

Price Tier [Select   ⬍]   (?)

View Pricing Matrix

Figure 11-6. Setup screen for both consumable and non-consumable purchases in iTunes Connect

- Non-Consumables: A non-consumable purchase needs to be purchased only once by each user, and is often used for unlockable features. Examples of non-consumable purchases include additional levels, reusable power-ups, or additional content. The setup screen is the same as for consumables.

- Auto-Renewable Subscriptions: An auto-renewable subscription allows the user to purchase in-app content for a set duration of time. At the end of that time, the subscription will automatically renew and charge the customer unless they opt out. Magazines and newspapers follow this model, delivering a new issue every week or month until the user opts out. Figure 11-7 shows the auto-renewable purchase setup screen.

In–App Purchase Summary

Enter a reference name and add durations for this family of auto-renewable In-App Purchase subscriptions. A subscription duration is the length of time between automatic renewals. You must add at least one. Note that each duration can only be used once per family.

Reference Name: [   ] ⑦

Subscription Durations and Pricing

A subscription duration is the length of time between autorenewals. You must add at least one. Note that each duration can only be used once per family.

Add Duration

Duration	Product ID	Price Tier	Status	
Click Add Duration to get started.				

Figure 11-7. Setup screen for auto-renewable purchases in iTunes Connect

- Non-Renewing Subscriptions: For the most part, renewable subscriptions have eliminated the need for this model. A non-renewing subscription functions the same as an auto-renewable subscription, except that a user is required to renew it every time it is set to expire.

Note   Auto-renewable subscriptions will be sent to all devices associated with the user's Apple ID.

We will begin by adding a non-consumable purchase item to our sample UFO game.

The first item we want to add is a paid upgrade to the user's current ship; name the item com.dragonforged.ufo.newShip1. In this example the same title is used for both the product ID and the reference name. The reference name is used when searching in iTunes Connect, whereas the product ID is what will be used in your code base to identify this item.

After you have created a new item, you need to add at least one localized description and title, as shown in Figure 11-8. The last thing that you need to do is select a pricing tier for this item. You might have also noticed that there is a section for uploading a screenshot; this will be discussed in the later section "Submitting a Purchase GUI Screenshot."

Figure 11-8. Adding a localized description to a product in iTunes Connect

Adding a consumable product follows the same procedure as adding a non-consumable product. If you want to add a subscription-based product, there are a few new fields that you need to be aware of, as shown in Figure 11-9. When configuring a subscription, you need to define a duration. iTunes Connect allows any of the following: one week, one month, two months, three months, six months, or one year. You also have the option to offer a free subscription if the user agrees to a marketing campaign, such as providing you with their e-mail address.

Figure 11-9. Configuring subscription duration in iTunes Connect

You should now have at least one product configured for in-app purchase. Your screen in iTunes Connect should look similar to Figure 11-10. This completes the initial configuration that is needed in iTunes Connect to get in-app purchases working. In the next section, we begin to work with the code required to complete a purchase on a device.

3 In-App Purchases					Q Search
Reference Name ▲		Product ID ►	Type ►	Apple ID ►	Status ►
com.dragonforged.ufo.newShip1		com.dragon...rged.ufo.newShip1	Non-Consumable	458716022	◉ Waiting for Screenshot
com.dragonforged.ufo.newShip2		com.dragon...rged.ufo.newShip2	Consumable	458986484	◉ Waiting for Screenshot
com.dragonforg...cription	1 Year	com.dragon....ufo.subscription	Auto-Renewable	458720223	◉ Waiting for Screenshot

Figure 11-10. Products set up and ready for use in our app

> **Note**   Don't worry about the "Waiting for Screenshot" error yet; this will be handled later in the process. You will still be able to test your purchases while waiting to upload a screenshot.

Adding Products to Your App

Apple does not offer a predesigned GUI for in-app purchases. You, as the developer, are required to design a storefront for your user. In this section, you will learn how to get products that you have added in iTunes Connect to show up for sale in your app.

> **Note**   It can take several hours for new purchases and changes to be reflected. If you double-check everything and are still not seeing products, wait a few hours and try again.

App IDs and In-App Purchase

When working with in-app purchases, Apple requires that your App ID does not include a wildcard, such as `76P4G6KX56.*`. You are required to have a unique App ID, such as `76P4G6KX56.com.dragonforged.ufo`. If you do not have a unique App ID, you need to create one. Use the following steps to create a new unique App ID.

1. Navigate to `http://developer.apple.com/iPhone` in your web browser and select the iPhone Developer Program Portal from the list on the right.

2. Select App ID from the column on the left, and select the New App ID button in the upper right.

3. Fill in the required information about your app.

4. Click Submit.

5. Click the Configure button next to the listing, and make sure In-App Purchase is turned on (it should be on by default).

Setting Up

We will begin by requesting a list of products from our app. First, add the StoreKit framework to your project. We will be modifying our existing UFO project from the previous chapter; you can follow along in your own project if that is more convenient.

> **Important**   In-App Purchase does not work on the simulator; all testing needs to be done on a device.

Create a new class called `UFOStoreViewController`. We will use this class to display a store to the user. Set up the header to match the following:

```
#import <UIKit/UIKit.h>
#import <StoreKit/StoreKit.h>

@interface UFOStoreViewController : UIViewController <SKProductsRequestDelegate>
{
    SKProductsRequest *productsRequest
}

@end
```

As you can see, we imported the StoreKit headers. Set up the `SKProductsRequestDelegate`, and create a new object to hold the product request. We need to create a way for the user to access the store, so go ahead and add a button to the main screen and relevant code to present the new view controller (`UFOStoreViewController`).

Retrieving the Product List

Modify the `viewDidLoad` and `viewDidUnload` methods of our new store view controller to begin a new store request using the product identifiers that were set up in iTunes Connect. You may need to modify your product identifiers to match the ones that you set up in the previous section.

```
- (void)viewDidLoad
{
    [super viewDidLoad];

    NSSet *productIdentifiers = [NSSet setWithObjects:↵
@"com.dragonforged.ufo.newShip1", @"com.dragonforged.ufo.subscription", nil];
```

```
    productsRequest = [[SKProductsRequest alloc]↵
 initWithProductIdentifiers:productIdentifiers];

    productsRequest.delegate = self;
    [productsRequest start];
}

- (void)viewDidUnload
{
    productsRequest.delegate = nil;
}
```

The product request is released in the delegate callback, shown next. Right now, this method just prints your product information to the console and logs any invalid products.

```
- (void)productsRequest:(SKProductsRequest *)request↵
 didReceiveResponse:(SKProductsResponse *)response
{
    NSArray *productArray= [response products];
    for (SKProduct *product in productArray) {
    NSLog(@"Product title: %@" , product.localizedTitle);
    NSLog(@"Product description: %@" , product.localizedDescription);
    NSLog(@"Product price: %@" , product.price);
    NSLog(@"Product id: %@\n\n" , product.productIdentifier);
    }

    for (NSString *invalidProduct in response.invalidProductIdentifiers)
    {
    NSLog(@"Invalid: %@" , invalidProduct);
    }

    [request release];
}
```

> **Note** Although you can retrieve a list of invalid product identifiers using the code in this section, there are no associated errors to determine why a product is being flagged as invalid. Most often, the product ID is mistyped or not enough time has passed for the product to be distributed to the servers.

If you were to run the game now and navigate to the store, you should get output similar to the following:

```
2011-08-19 17:31:23.970 UFOs[3580:707] Product title: Ship+
2011-08-19 17:31:23.973 UFOs[3580:707] Product description: Paint your ship and show off to your friends
2011-08-19 17:31:23.975 UFOs[3580:707] Product price: 8.99
2011-08-19 17:31:23.977 UFOs[3580:707] Product id: com.dragonforged.ufo.newShip1
2011-08-19 17:31:23.979 UFOs[3580:707] Product title: Subscription
2011-08-19 17:31:23.981 UFOs[3580:707] Product description: A subscription service
2011-08-19 17:31:23.983 UFOs[3580:707] Product price: 1.99
2011-08-19 17:31:23.987 UFOs[3580:707] Product id: com.dragonforged.ufo.subscription
```

> **Note**   It can take several seconds to get a response from the product request. Best practices dictate that you should present your user with some sort of loading indicator during this loading time.

Those are all the steps required to retrieve your products from Apple's servers. In the next section we present this data to the user with a standard table view.

Presenting Your Products to the User

Begin by adding a table view to the store view controller. Don't forget to hook up the data source and delegates, as required. We also add a new property to our class to hold the products. Create a new class array named `productArray` and set the product results to it in the `productsRequest` method.

Add the two required table view delegate and data source methods to your class, as shown in the following code snippets:

```
- (NSInteger)tableView:(UITableView *)tableView numberOfRowsInSection:(NSInteger)section
{
    return [productArray count];
}

- (UITableViewCell *)tableView:(UITableView *)tableView↵
 cellForRowAtIndexPath:(NSIndexPath *)indexPath
{

    static NSString *CellIdentifier = @"Cell";
    UITableViewCell *cell = [tableView↵
dequeueReusableCellWithIdentifier:CellIdentifier];

    if (cell == nil)
    {
        cell = [[[UITableViewCell alloc] initWithStyle:↵
UITableViewCellStyleSubtitle reuseIdentifier:CellIdentifier] autorelease];

        cell.selectionStyle = UITableViewCellSelectionStyleNone;
    }
```

```
    SKProduct *product = [self.productArray objectAtIndex: [indexPath row]];
    cell.textLabel.text = [NSString stringWithFormat:@"%@ - $%@",↵
product.localizedTitle, product.price];

    cell.detailTextLabel.text = product.localizedDescription;
    return cell;
}
```

The first method simply returns the number of products that we retrieved from Apple's servers
for the number of rows in the table. When we display them as a cell, we use the built-in
UITableViewCellStyleSubtitle. We set the main label to the product title and price, and use the
detail label to display the description. All that remains is to add a reload table method to the end of
the productsRequest method. Upon running the game again, your output should look similar to that
shown in Figure 11-11.

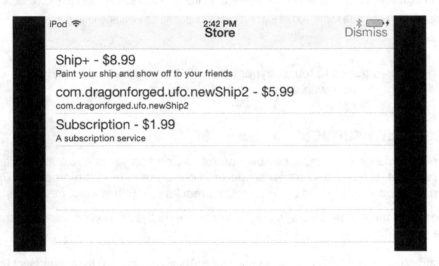

Figure 11-11. Displaying a list of products in a standard table view

---

Note   Although the API returns a localized title and description, it doesn't localize the price. You need to take
this extra step yourself in international apps.

Purchasing a Product

In the previous section, you learned how to add products to your app. Without the ability to
purchase these products, our implementation is only partially complete. In this section, we look at
how to handle purchasing products directly through your app.

Purchasing Code

The first thing that we need to do is make the UFOStoreViewController class conform to the SKPaymentTransactionObserver protocol. After that is done, we modify our existing viewDidLoad method. Add self as a new transaction observer. Additionally, we perform a test to make sure that we can make payments on this device, and if not, display a UIAlert to inform the user.

```
- (void)viewDidLoad
{
    [super viewDidLoad];
    [[SKPaymentQueue defaultQueue] addTransactionObserver:self];
    if ([SKPaymentQueue canMakePayments])
{
        NSSet *productIdentifiers = [NSSet setWithObjects:
@"com.dragonforged.ufo.newShip1", @"com.dragonforged.ufo.subscription", nil];

        productsRequest = [[SKProductsRequest alloc]
initWithProductIdentifiers:productIdentifiers];

        productsRequest.delegate = self;
        [productsRequest start];
    }

    else
{
        UIAlertView *alert = [[UIAlertView alloc] initWithTitle:nil message:
@"Unable to make purchases with this device." delegate:nil cancelButtonTitle:@"Dimiss"
 otherButtonTitles: nil];

        [alert show];
        [alert release];
    }
}
```

Next, we need to add a didSelectRowAtIndexPath method to register selection events in the table view.

```
- (void)tableView:(UITableView *)tableView didSelectRowAtIndexPath:
(NSIndexPath *)indexPath
{
    SKProduct *product = [self.productArray objectAtIndex: [indexPath row]];
    SKPayment *payment = [SKPayment paymentWithProductIdentifier:
product.productIdentifier];

    [[SKPaymentQueue defaultQueue] addPayment:payment];
}
```

If you were to run the app now and select a table row, you would get a confirmation alert, as shown in Figure 11-12. However, we have not yet written any code to process this transaction, nor have you set up a test user, so this is as far as you can currently go. We'll move on to those stages after a quick look at the code for multiple purchases of an item.

Figure 11-12. Confirming a purchase in the Sandbox

Purchasing Multiple Items

Apple has made it easy to allow your users to purchase multiple items at a time. The following code snippet can be used to bulk-purchase multiple quantities of an item at one time, such as a user purchasing five packs of 100 gold:

```
SKMutablePayment *payment = [SKMutablePayment paymentWithProductIdentifier:↵
 com.dragonforged.rpg.100gold];

payment.quantity = 5;
[[SKPaymentQueue defaultQueue] addPayment: payment];
```

Processing a Transaction

After the user has requested a purchase, there are several steps needed in order to ensure that the purchase is completed successfully. First, we implement the required method from the SKPaymentTransactionObserver. As you can see in the following code example, we test the current transaction state and then call some new methods, depending on whether the transaction succeeded, failed, or restored:

```
- (void)paymentQueue:(SKPaymentQueue *)queue updatedTransactions:(NSArray *)transactions
{
    for (SKPaymentTransaction *transaction in transactions)
    {
        if ([transaction transactionState] == SKPaymentTransactionStatePurchased)
        {
        [self transactionDidComplete:transaction];
        }
```

```
        else if ([transaction transactionState] == SKPaymentTransactionStateFailed)
        {
            [self transactionDidFail:transaction];
        }

        else if ([transaction transactionState] == SKPaymentTransactionStateRestored)
        {
            [self transactionDidRestore:transaction];
        }

        else
        {
            NSLog(@"Unhandled case: %@", transaction);
        }
    }
}
```

We need to implement some convenience methods to help streamline the process. If a transaction completed successfully or is restored, we need to record the transaction event, unlock the content that the user purchased, and perform some cleanup. If the transaction failed or was cancelled, we just need to perform the cleanup and probably notify the user that something went wrong. Here's the code:

```
- (void)transactionDidComplete:(SKPaymentTransaction *)transaction
{
    [self recordTransactionData:transaction];
    [self unlockContent:[[transaction payment] productIdentifier]];
    [self finishTransaction:transaction withSuccess:YES];
}

- (void)transactionDidRestore:(SKPaymentTransaction *)transaction
{
    [self recordTransactionData:transaction.originalTransaction];
    [self unlockContent:[[[transaction originalTransaction] payment]↵
productIdentifier]];

    [self finishTransaction:transaction withSuccess:YES];
}

- (void)transactionDidFail:(SKPaymentTransaction *)transaction
{
    if ([[transaction error] code] != SKErrorPaymentCancelled)
    {
        [self finishTransaction:transaction withSuccess:NO];
    }
    //SKErrorPaymentCancelled
    else
    {
        [[SKPaymentQueue defaultQueue] finishTransaction:transaction];
    }
}
```

Now let's take a more detailed look at each of the methods that we are calling, starting with the `recordTransactionData` method. The main purpose of this method is to keep a virtual paper trail for our purchases. We are using `NSUserDefaults` to hold on to an array of all completed transactions, which allows us to check transaction data at any point in the future:

```
- (void)recordTransactionData:(SKPaymentTransaction *)transaction
{
    NSArray *transactions = [[NSUserDefaults standardUserDefaults]↵
 objectForKey:@"transactions"];

    NSMutableArray *transactionArray = [transactions mutableCopy];
    [transactionArray addObject:[transaction transactionReceipt]];

    [[NSUserDefaults standardUserDefaults] setObject:transactionArray↵
 forKey:@"transactions"];

    [transactionArray release];
}
```

Next, take a look at the unlockContent method. This is where your app might differ. In this example, we set a flag in the `NSUserDefaults` that we can check to see whether the user has purchased a feature. Depending on how your app is structured, you might want to take a different approach to unlocking content, but no matter what approach you take, remember that you need to preserve the unlocked content through app restarts. See the section "Tying Everything Together in UFOs" for a sample of how to implement this approach.

```
- (void)unlockContent:(NSString *)productId
{
    if ([productId isEqualToString:@"com.dragonforged.ufo.newShip1"])
    {
        [[NSUserDefaults standardUserDefaults] setBool:YES forKey:↵
@"shipPlusAvailable" ];

    }

    if ([productId isEqualToString:@"com.dragonforged.ufo.subscription"])
    {
        [[NSUserDefaults standardUserDefaults] setBool:YES↵
 forKey:@"subscriptionAvailable" ];

    }
}
```

The last step that is taken for both successful and unsuccessful purchases is to perform a bit of cleanup on the transaction process. The most important step in the following method is to call the finishTransaction method. We also log the results of the transaction for debugging purposes. Until you have called finishTransaction, the transaction remains open and in the system.

```
- (void)finishTransaction:(SKPaymentTransaction *)transaction withSuccess:(BOOL)success
{
    [[SKPaymentQueue defaultQueue] finishTransaction:transaction];

    NSDictionary *transactionDictionary = [NSDictionary↵
 dictionaryWithObjectsAndKeys:transaction, @"transaction" , nil];

    if (success)
    {
        NSLog(@"Transaction was successful: %@", transactionDictionary);
    }

    else
    {
        NSLog(@"Transaction was unsuccessful: %@", transactionDictionary);
    }
}
```

Restoring Previously Completed Transactions

Often, your users will need to restore purchases that they have previously made. This could happen if they have reinstalled your app or have begun using it on a different device. It is important to always add a path for your user to download all of their content again. Luckily, Apple has planned ahead for this scenario and has provided a simple method for restoring the user's purchases.

```
[[SKPaymentQueue defaultQueue] restoreCompletedTransactions];
```

This will repurchase all of your content as if the user had selected it from your store. You will receive appropriate callbacks to the paymentQueue:updatedTransactions method and can use your existing code to unlockcontent.

Test Accounts and Testing Purchases

If you were to try to purchase one of your items in the Sandbox now, you would receive an account error. You need to first create a new test account in order to be able to test purchases without being charged for them. To set up a new test user, you need to log in to iTunes Connect (http://iTunesConnect.apple.com). Select the Manage User section from the main screen of iTunes Connect; from here, select the option for a new Test User.

Test users do not need to use a real e-mail address, and you will want to select something quick to type and easy to remember, such as abc@def.com. Although you do need to enter a date of birth and other identifying information, there is no reason you cannot fabricate this data. Make sure to select the iTunes Store that is appropriate to test the app's localization against. You can make a new account for each region that you will test with.

Signing In with a Test Account

You cannot simply sign in with your test account in the Settings App. If you did, you would be forced to agree to the standard user agreement and prompted to enter a credit card number. In order to resolve this issue, you need to use the Settings App to log out of your existing iTunes account. After you are logged out of an account, you will be prompted to log in or create a new account during a purchase attempt. This is where you will enter your test account credentials.

> **Note**   If you are testing on your primary device, don't forget to revisit the Settings App to log out of your test account before making real purchases or downloading updates.

Submitting a Purchase GUI Screenshot

We talked briefly about this step earlier in this chapter. Apple requires that you submit a screenshot of your in-app purchase before it will clear it for sale. There is some confusion about what Apple is specifically looking for in this screenshot.

Apple is looking, in the simplest terms, for a screen capture proving that your in-app purchase is working as intended. For unlockable content, this would be a screenshot of the item being used, such as the user playing a purchased level or using a purchased item. However, sometimes your product might not be visible while being used. In cases such as these, Apple has accepted a screenshot of the store showing that the item has been purchased, an example of which is shown in Figure 11-13.

> **Note**   You will not be required to submit a screenshot until you have finished writing and debugging your app and are ready to submit it for review.

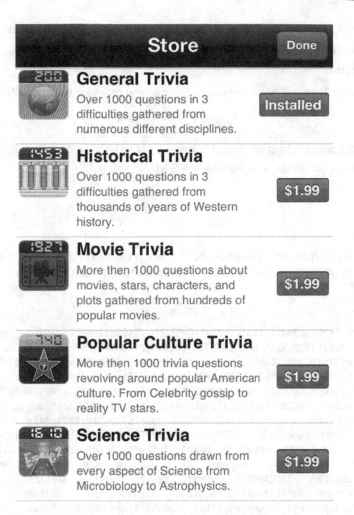

Figure 11-13. An example of an acceptable screenshot for in-app purchase when there isn't an item to capture

Note   When Apple test In App Purchase during the review process they do so using a Sandbox account. This means that apps shipped to Apple need to support both Sandbox and Production enviroments.

Developer Approval

The last step that you need to take before your in-app purchase is ready to go is developer approval. Return to iTunes Connect in your web browser and navigate to the Manage In-App Purchase section of your app review page. There will be a new green button in the upper-right corner of the screen.

You will be prompted for how to submit your product. The following two options are available.

- Submit with Binary: This option will turn on in-app purchase with your next binary upload.

- Submit Now: This will allow you to submit a new product to an existing app.

> **Note**   If you see the option Submit with a New Binary, it could be because the last version of your App was uploaded before in-app purchasing was available in iOS 3.0.

Receipts

When you successfully complete a transaction, you are provided with a receipt as part of the competed transaction object. The following is a sample receipt from one of the purchases in our UFOs demo project.

```
{
        "signature" = "AnQ+nzB60K5Lc6pI6zh8bptEO+GSGUJ+xT5DSef2p66H8gz/P/D13mBqf96ciJoLesI64
fohhZTNb9NrCEkZMVyeqkJed2t38509XpckLWeLJCDYUJqUS1t+fsoy7fwSUOv8TUBzF3Eua1h83GszxlPyylo3mRDssrG+
QcgrHwFOAAADVzCCA1MwggI7oAMCAQICCGUUkU3ZWAS1MAOGCSqGSIb3DQEBBQUAMH8xCzAJBgNVBAYTAlVTMRMwEQYDVQQKD
ApBcHBsZSBJbmMuMSYwJAYDVQQLDB1BcHBsZSBDZXJ0aWZpY2F0aW9uIEF1dGhvcml0eTEzMDEGA1UEAwwqQXBwbGUgaVR1bm
VzIFNOb3JlIENlcnRpZmljYXRpb24gQXV0aG9yaXR5MB4XDTA5MDYxNTIyMDU1NloXDTE0MDYxNDIyMDU1NlowZDEjMCEGA1UE
AwwaUHVyY2hhc2VSZWNlaXB0Q2VydGlmaWNhdGUxGzAZBgNVBAsMEkFwcGxlIGlUdW5lcyBTdG9yZTETMBEGA1UECgwKQXBwb
GUgSW5jLjELMAkGA1UEBhMCVVMwgZ8wDQYJKoZIhvcNAQEBBQADgY0AMIGJAoGBAMrRjF2ct4IrSdiTChaIOg8pwv/cmHs8p/
RwV/rt/91XKVhNl4XIBimKjQQNfgHsDs6yju++DrKJE7uKsphMddKYfFE5rGXsAdBEjBwRIxexTevx3HLEFGAt1moKx5o9
dhxtiIdDgJv2YaVs49B0uJvNdy6SMqNNLHsDLzDS9oZHAgMBAAGjcjBwMAwGA1UdEwEB/wQCMAAwHwYDVR0jBBgwFoAUNh3o4
p2COgEYtTJrDtdDC5FYQzowDgYDVR0PAQH/BAQDAgeAMBOGA1UdDgQWBBSpg4PyGUjFPhJXCBTMzaN+mV8k9TAQBgoqhkiG92
NkBgUBBAIFADANBgkqhkiG9w0BAQUFAAOCAQEAeaSbPjtmN4C/IB3QEpK32RxacCDXdVXAeVReS5FaZxc+t88pQP93BiAxv
dW/3eTSMGY5FbeAYL3etqP5gm8wrFojXOikyVRStQ+/AQOKEjtqBO7kLs9QUe8czR8UGfdM1EumV/UgvDd4NwNYxLQMg4WTQfg
kQQVy8GXZwVHgbE/UC6Y7O53pGXBk51NPM3woxhd3gSRLvXj+loHsStcTEqe9pBDpmG5+sk4tw+GK3GMeEN5/+e1QT9np/Kl1nj+
aBw7COxsy0bFnaAd1cSS6xdory/CUvM6gtKsmnOOdqTesbpObs8sn6Wqs0C9dgcxRHuOMZ2tm8npLUm7argOSzQ==";
        "purchase-info" = "ewoJImloZWOtaWQiIDOgIjQ1ODk4NjQ4NCI7Cgkib3JpZ2luYWwtdHJhbnNhY3Rpb24
taWQiIDOgIjEwMDAwMDAwMDU4NDM1MzgiOwoJInB1cmNoYXNlLWRhdGUiIDOgIjIwMTEtMDgtMjEgMjI6Mzk6NTIgRXRjRjOdNV
CI7CgkicHJvZHVjdC1pZCIgPSAiY29tLmRyYWdvbmZvcmNdlZC51Zm8ubmV3U2hpcDIiOwoJInRyYW5zYWN0aW9uLWlkIiA9ICIx
MDAwMDAwMDA1ODQzNTM4IjsKCSJxdWFudGl0eSIgPSAiMSI7Cgkib3JpZ2luYWwtcHVyY2hhc2UtZGF0ZSIgPSAiMjAxMSOw
OCoyMSAyMjozOToTo1MiBFdGMvR01UIjsKCSJiaWQiIDOgImNvbS5kcmFnb25mb25mb25sJnZWRzb2Od2FyZS5Ucml2aWFFsU2NpIjs
KCSJidnJzIiA9ICIxLjAiOwp9";
        "environment" = "Sandbox
        "pod" = "100";
        "signing-status" = "0";
}
```

Apple urges developers to check this receipt for validity. Although this step remains optional, checking adds an extra layer of security and prevents users from activating your in-app purchases without having to pay for the content. Apple provides two servers for you to validate receipts against: one for Sandbox environments, and one for shipping software, as described in Table 11-1.

Table 11-1. *Server Addresses for Verifying Receipts with Apple*

Environment	Server Address
Sandbox	sandbox.itunes.apple.com
Production	buy.itunes.apple.com

Joe D'Andrea has posted two methods to help you check for valid receipts on Stack Overflow (http://stackoverflow.com/questions/1298998). His approach is streamlined and efficient, so I have included it here for your convenience.

```
-(BOOL)verifyReceipt:(SKPaymentTransaction *)transaction
{
    NSString *jsonObjectString = [self encode:(uint8_t *)↵
transaction.transactionReceipt.bytes length:transaction.transactionReceipt.length];
    NSString *completeString = [NSString stringWithFormat:↵
@"http://url-for-your-php?receipt=%@", jsonObjectString];
    NSURL *urlForValidation = [NSURL URLWithString:completeString];
    NSMutableURLRequest *validationRequest = [[NSMutableURLRequest alloc]↵
 initWithURL:urlForValidation];
    [validationRequest setHTTPMethod:@"GET"];
    NSData *responseData = [NSURLConnection sendSynchronousRequest:↵
validationRequest returningResponse:nil error:nil];
    [validationRequest release];
    NSString *responseString = [[NSString alloc] initWithData:responseData↵
 encoding: NSUTF8StringEncoding];
    NSInteger response = [responseString integerValue];
    [responseString release];
    return (response == 0);
}

- (NSString *)encode:(const uint8_t *)input length:(NSInteger)length
{
    static char table[] =↵
 "ABCDEFGHIJKLMNOPQRSTUVWXYZabcdefghijklmnopqrstuvwxyz0123456789+/=";
    NSMutableData *data = [NSMutableData dataWithLength:((length + 2) / 3) * 4];
    uint8_t *output = (uint8_t *)data.mutableBytes;
    for (NSInteger i = 0; i < length; i += 3) {
        NSInteger value = 0;
        for (NSInteger j = i; j < (i + 3); j++) {
            value <<= 8;
            if (j < length) {
                value |= (0xFF & input[j]);
            }
        }

        NSInteger index = (i / 3) * 4;
        output[index + 0] =                     table[(value >> 18) & 0x3F];
        output[index + 1] =                     table[(value >> 12) & 0x3F];
```

```
        output[index + 2] = (i + 1) < length ? table[(value >> 6)  & 0x3F] : '=';
        output[index + 3] = (i + 2) < length ? table[(value >> 0)  & 0x3F] : '=';
    }

    return [[[NSString alloc] initWithData:data encoding:NSASCIIStringEncoding]↵
 autorelease];
}
```

After you have added these two methods to your project, you simply need to call verifyReceipt with the transaction that was returned to you, and then perform a Boolean test to see whether it is valid. This concludes all the steps that you need to take to check a receipt for authenticity.

This method of verifying receipts requires you to host an intermediate server; following is a very stripped-down PHP script to validate receipts:

```
$receipt = json_encode(array("receipt-data" => $_GET["receipt"]));
// NOTE: use "buy" vs "sandbox" in production.
$url = "https://sandbox.itunes.apple.com/verifyReceipt";
$response_json = call-your-http-post-here($url, $receipt);
$response = json_decode($response_json);
// Save the data here!
print $response->{'status'};
```

iOS 7 Local Receipt Validation

iOS 7 added the ability to verify In App Purchase receipts on the device without needing to go through a third party server. Server receipt validation is still available and may even by the more appropriate depending on the needs of your app.

Apple recommends validating local receipts within the main function of your app before the NSApplicationMain function is called. In order to verify a receipt it must first be located. NSBundle contains a convenience helper, which will locate the reciept for you. In the event that no reciept is found, verification has failed.

```
[[NSBundle mainBundle] appStoreReceiptURL];
```

Once a reciept has been located it needs to be checked to make sure it has been properly been signed by Apple. Apple provides sample code for verifying the signature of receipts as part of the Receipt Validation Programming Guide. That sample code is reprinted here for ease of access. The code will verify the signature of the receipt using OpenSSL.

```
/* The PKCS #7 container (the receipt) and the output of the verification. */
BIO *b_p7;
PKCS7 *p7;
/* The Apple root certificate, as raw data and in its OpenSSL representation. */
BIO *b_x509;
X509 *Apple;
/* The root certificate for chain-of-trust verification. */
X509_STORE *store = X509_STORE_new();
/* ... Initialize both BIO variables using BIO_new_mem_buf() with a buffer and its size ... */
```

```
/* Initialize b_out as an output BIO to hold the receipt payload extracted during
 signature verification. */
BIO *b_out = BIO_new(BIO_s_mem());
/* Capture the content of the receipt file and populate the p7 variable with the
 PKCS #7 container. */
p7 = d2i_PKCS7_bio(b_p7, NULL);
/* ... Load the Apple root certificate into b_X509 ... */
/* Initialize b_x509 as an input BIO with a value of the Apple root certificate and load it into
X509 data structure. Then add the Apple root certificate to the
 structure. */
Apple = d2i_X509_bio(b_x509, NULL);
X509_STORE_add_cert(store, Apple);
/* Verify the signature. If the verification is correct, b_out will contain the
 PKCS #7 payload and rc will be 1. */

int rc = PKCS7_verify(p7, NULL, store, NULL, b_out, 0);
/* For additional security, you may verify the fingerprint of the root certificate and verify the
OIDs of the intermediate certificate and signing certificate. The OID in the certificate policies
extension of the intermediate certificate is (1 2 840 113635 100 5 6 1), and the marker OID of the
signing certificate is (1 2 840 113635 100 6 11 1). */
```

The next code sample will parse the receipt payload using asn1c.

```
#include "Payload.h" /* This header file is generated by asn1c. */
/* The receipt payload and its size. */
void *pld = NULL;
size_t pld_sz;
/* Variables used to parse the payload. Both data types are declared in Payload.h. */
Payload_t *payload = NULL;
asn_dec_rval_t rval;
/* ... Load the payload from the receipt file into pld and set pld_sz to the payload size ... */
/* Parse the buffer using the decoder function generated by asn1c. The payload
 variable will contain the receipt attributes. */
rval = asn_DEF_Payload.ber_decoder(NULL, &asn_DEF_Payload, (void **)&payload, pld,
```

The following code sample extracts the receipt attributes

```
/* Variables used to store the receipt attributes. */
OCTET_STRING_t *bundle_id = NULL;
OCTET_STRING_t *bundle_version = NULL;
OCTET_STRING_t *opaque = NULL;
OCTET_STRING_t *hash = NULL;
/* Iterate over the receipt attributes, saving the values needed to compute the
 GUID hash. */
size_t i;
for (i = 0; i < payload->list.count; i++) {
    ReceiptAttribute_t *entry;
    entry = payload->list.array[i];
    switch (entry->type) {
        case 2:
            bundle_id = &entry->value;
            break;
```

```
        case 3:
            bundle_version = &entry->value;
            break;
        case 4:
            opaque = &entry->value;
            break;
        case 5:
            hash = &entry->value;
        break; }
}
```

Next the bundle identifier of the receipts needs to be compared to the CFBundleShortVersionStrong value found in the info.plist of the app. If these two identifiers do not match validation has failed.

Then verify that the version identifier string in the receipt also matches the hard coded value found in the CFBundleShortVersionString of the info.plist. If these values do not match verification has failed.

Finally, check the GUID of the receipt matches the GUID of the device. The GUID for the device can be obtained using the following code. Once again if these two values do not match then validation fails.

```
[[UIDevice currentDevice] identifierForVendor];
```

If the receipt is found and signed by Apple, the values for the bundle identifier, version, and GUID all match than the receipt and purchase is valid.

Tying Everything Together in UFOs

Depending on the complexity of your in-app purchase, it could be very easy or very difficult to integrate it into your code. In our UFOs app, we have a very simple product, in which paying a one-time fee unlocks a different colored ship. When the user purchases the product, we store a key in our user defaults to reflect that. To unlock this purchase in code, we simply check for that key, and then perform the required steps. To do this, we need to add some new art assets to the project. These have already been included in the Chapter 11 sample code (available at the Apress web site).

After this is done, we need to modify our viewDidLoad method to change the ship's image. The following code snippet shows those changes:

```
-(void)viewDidLoad
{
    purchasedUpgrade = [[NSUserDefaults standardUserDefaults]↩
boolForKey:@"shipPlusAvailable"];

    CGRect playerFrame = CGRectMake(100, 70, 80, 34);
    myPlayerImageView = [[UIImageView alloc] initWithFrame: playerFrame];
    myPlayerImageView.animationDuration = 0.75;
    myPlayerImageView.animationRepeatCount = 99999;
    NSArray *imageArray;
```

```
    if (purchasedUpgrade)
  {
        imageArray = [NSArray arrayWithObjects: [UIImage imageNamed:↵
@"Ship1.png"], [UIImage imageNamed: @"Ship2.png"], nil];

  }

  else
  {
        imageArray = [NSArray arrayWithObjects: [UIImage imageNamed:↵
@"Saucer1.png"], [UIImage imageNamed: @"Saucer2.png"], nil];

  }

  myPlayerImageView.animationImages = imageArray;
  [myPlayerImageView startAnimating];
  [self.view addSubview: myPlayerImageView];
}
```

Summary

In this chapter, we covered StoreKit and in-app purchases. By leveraging StoreKit, you gain a number of new ways to monetize your app, from expandable content to special upgrades for your users. You should now feel confident adding a variety of products to your own in-app store. Although StoreKit isn't directly a part of Game Center or Game Kit, you will undoubtedly find an in-app store an invaluable addition to your iOS software.

We spent some time talking about ngmoco:) and its experiments and successes with the freemium model. You should now feel confident with iTunes Connect and all the actions that are required to fully set up an in-app purchase product, as well as the required code to get that purchase to display.

We looked at how to handle failures with purchasing and also the path of a success. We also explored some of the advanced topics, such as validating receipts and multiple purchases at once. Lastly, we saw how we integrated the entire experience into our UFOs demo app.

Twitter

The qualities that make Twitter seem inane and half-baked are what makes it so powerful.

—Jonathan Zittrain, Harvard law professor

Twitter was created in March 2006 by a small team of developers in the San Francisco Bay Area. By 2012 it had more than 500 million registered users with no drop-off in sight. Twitter allows registered users to post short, 140-character messages to their timeline, where followers and the general public can browse them. Apple began making a public push into social networking with iOS 5 when they announced the addition of the Social Framework. The first supported service would be Twitter, followed by Facebook in iOS 6. While Apple has had third-party software on iOS since 2.0 with Google Maps, the integration of Twitter marked a milestone. This was the first time that a previous third-party app had become a core system component. While the Twitter app is not installed by default it can very easily be installed through Settings.app.

This chapter will walk you through the process of integrating Twitter into your apps. The primary focus will be on the built-in Twitter Composer for quick implementation. The section "Going Further with Twitter" will also provide a foundation for working with Twitter on a more direct level.

UFOs

Unlike previous chapters, this chapter will not continue to build on the existing UFOs source code. Instead, we will take the source code from Chapter 3 and add Twitter functionality into it. The primary reason behind this change of style was to cut down on the existing code base to make the project as easy to consume as possible. While previously the code has continued to build upon the lessons learned in the previous chapters, the remaining chapters all cover topics that are essentially independent of each other. The following four chapters, covering Twitter, Facebook, Airplay, and game controllers, will therefore all be based on earlier versions of the UFOs sample code.

We will use Twitter to post the user's score to their Twitter timeline once a game has been completed. This requires a single change to the behavior of the app from the Chapter 3 sample project. The exitAction: function will be updated to prompt the user to choose a Twitter posting method or an option to exit back to the main menu:

```
-(IBAction)exitAction:(id)sender
{
    UIAlertView *alert = [[UIAlertView alloc] initWithTitle:@"Tweet Score" message:@"Do you
    want to tweet your score on Twitter?" delegate:self cancelButtonTitle:@"Dismiss"
    otherButtonTitles:@"Tweet Composer", @"Custom Tweet", nil];

    [alert show];
    [alert release];
}
```

A new delegate method for the alertView is set up to handle the callbacks and determine the action required. The user is presented with three options (Figure 12-1). The two Twitter approaches will be discussed in the sections "Tweet Composer" and "Custom Tweets"; the Dismiss action will perform the previous behavior of the exitAction: method and submit the score while returning to the home screen:

```
- (void)alertView:(UIAlertView *)alertView didDismissWithButtonIndex:(NSInteger)buttonIndex
{
    //tweet composer
    if(buttonIndex == 1) {
    } else if(buttonIndex == 2) {//custom tweet

    } else if(buttonIndex == 0) {
        [[self navigationController] popViewControllerAnimated: YES];
        [self.gcManager reportScore:score forCategory:@"com.dragonforged.ufo.single"];
    }
}
```

Figure 12-1. Selecting a posting option for Twitter after the completion of a game

Twitter on iOS

Twitter has become an integral part of iOS since its introduction in 2011. Game Center added built-in functionality to share apps from within the combined Game Center view controller starting in iOS 6. Twitter accounts are configured from within the Settings.app (Figure 12-2); as of iOS 7, it is not possible to provide your users with a method of logging in via a third-party app, such as your product.

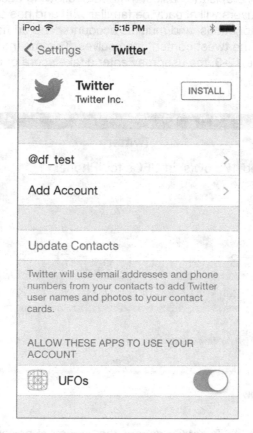

Figure 12-2. Configuration settings for Twitter on iOS 7

Twitter for iOS, through Settings.app, allows the user to configure multiple accounts, although permission is granted for all accounts at once. Each app must request permission to access the user's Twitter accounts the first time Twitter functionality is requested. A list of the apps that currently have access can be found in Settings.app under the Twitter section; here the user may also revoke Twitter access to a specific app at any time.

Social Framework provides two methods for posting items to a user's timeline. The Tweet Composer uses a built-in Graphical User Interface(GUI) that is similar to the email composer in functionality. A preset message, attachments, and URL may be set, but the user is allowed to modify the text prior to sending the tweet; this method is described in the "Tweet Composer" section. You may also use a more customized approach, allowing you to tweet from a customized user interface; this approach may send tweets without the user needing to review the information beforehand. This approach is described in the section "Custom Tweets."

Tweet Composer

The Tweet Composer (Figure 12-3) is the easiest method of allowing users to post status to Twitter. It provides an interface most users will already be familiar with and has controls and functionality to easily include images, URLs, locations, and multiple accounts. The primary drawback is that users are required to read and post the tweet content themselves. This means that when posting items like scores, as shown in Figure 12-3, the user may enter a fake score or otherwise modify the text as they see fit.

Figure 12-3. The Tweet Composer view

In order to begin working with the Tweet Composer, the user must perform a test to ensure that their device is compatible. The most common reason that isAvailableForServiceType will fail is that the user has not set up a Twitter account or is not logged into it from Settings.app:

```
[SLComposeViewController isAvailableForServiceType:SLServiceTypeTwitter]
```

Note   Don't forget to include Social.Framework and import social/Social.h before working with the Twitter Composer.

Once you have verified that Twitter is available and correctly logged in for the device, a new SLComposeViewController can be created. In this example we will be specifying SLServiceTypeTwitter, but other types are available. In Chapter 13 we will work with Facebook, and the SLComposeViewController also supports social networking with Sina Weibo, Tencent Weibo, and LinkedIn as of iOS 7.

```
SLComposeViewController *tweetController = [SLComposeViewController
composeViewControllerForServiceType:SLServiceTypeTwitter];
```

A new block is created for handling the completion of the SLComposeViewController. In the sample app under both completion circumstances the high score will be posted to Game Center and the user will be returned to the main menu.

```
SLComposeViewControllerCompletionHandler myBlock = ^(SLComposeViewControllerResult result)
{
    if (result == SLComposeViewControllerResultCancelled) {
        NSLog(@"Tweet Controller Canceled");
        [[self navigationController] popViewControllerAnimated: YES];
        [self.gcManager reportScore:score forCategory:@"com.dragonforged.ufo.single"];
    } else {
        NSLog(@"Tweet Controller Done");
        [[self navigationController] popViewControllerAnimated: YES];
        [self.gcManager reportScore:score forCategory:@"com.dragonforged.ufo.single"];
    }
    [tweetController dismissViewControllerAnimated:YES completion:nil];
};
```

The newly created block is set to the completionHandler property on the SLComposeViewController:

```
tweetController.completionHandler = myBlock;
```

Default values may now optionally be set for the Tweet Composer; these values will be prepopulated into the Composer for the user. Three values are available: setInitialText: will provide the user with the tweet text, and keep in mind there is a 140-character limit. With addImage: you can add an image; this will provide a Twitpic URL for a UIImage, which will be uploaded when the tweet is submitted. Finally, addURL: provides the ability to add a URL.

```
[tweetController setInitialText:[NSString stringWithFormat: @"I just abducted %0.0f cow(s) in UFOs
for iPhone!", score]];
```

```
[tweetController addImage:[UIImage imageNamed:@"Cow1.png"]];
[tweetController addURL:[NSURL URLWithString:@"http://bit.ly/19ak0Uv"]];
```

After the Tweet Composer has been customized, it is presented to the user like any other modal view:

```
[self presentViewController:tweetController animated:YES completion:nil];
```

When the user sends the tweet, the previous block is invoked and any callback actions specified are performed. The user is also played a brief tweet sound effect to let them know the tweet has been successfully sent. The final tweet product can be seen in Figure 12-4 as captured on the Twitter website.

Figure 12-4. A tweet sent from within UFOs visible on `Twitter.com`

Custom Tweets

There are many cases where it may be necessary to post a tweet from a customized user interface, or from no user interface at all. iOS provides this functionality as part of the Accounts Framework. While the account-based approach to Twitter posting is a bit more complex and requires the user to grant explicit permission for the app, it provides much more customization and flexibility than the previously discussed Tweet Composer.

> **Note**   Make sure to include `Accounts.framework` and import `accounts/Accounts.h` when working with custom tweets.

Unlike when working with the Tweet Composer, the first thing that needs to be done when working with accounts is to create a reference for the account from which the post will be originating. This is accomplished by creating a new `ACAccountStore` and a new `ACAccountype` as in the following code snippet:

```
ACAccountStore *account = [[[ACAccountStore alloc] init] autorelease];
ACAccountType *accountType = [account accountTypeWithAccountTypeIdentifier:
ACAccountTypeIdentifierTwitter];
```

Once the account type has been specified, the user needs to grant access for the app to interact with that account. Invoking `requestAccessToAccountsWithType:` on the newly created `ACAccountStore` performs this function:

```
[account requestAccessToAccountsWithType:accountType options:nil completion:^(BOOL granted, NSError
*error)
```

Figure 12-5. Being prompted to allow access to the device's Twitter accounts

The user will be prompted to allow the app access, as shown in Figure 12-5.

The value of the granted variable will reflect the user's decision about granting the app access to their Twitter information. This permission gives the app full access to post as well as read information from the account such as friends and timeline history.

The user may have multiple Twitter accounts set up on a device and it is important to be able to determine which account the user wishes to post from. An array of the user's accounts can be obtained with accountsWithAccountType:, for the purposes of the sample app, the last account in the array will be used by default:

```
NSArray *accounts = [account accountsWithAccountType:accountType];
```

Depending on whether the tweet has an attached image, there are two different endpoints that will need to be used. If a tweet is posted to the incorrect endpoint it will silently fail. For tweets containing image data, the endpoint is https://upload.twitter.com/1/statuses/update_with_media.json, while tweets without image data should be posted to http://api.twitter.com/1/statuses/update.json. The following example demonstrates selecting and storing the proper endpoint:

```
NSURL *requestURL = nil;
if (hasAttachment) {
    requestURL = [NSURL
    URLWithString:@"https://upload.twitter.com/1/statuses/update_with_media.json"];
} else {
    requestURL = [NSURL URLWithString:@"http://api.twitter.com/1/statuses/update.json"];
}
```

Once the proper endpoint has been established, a new SLRequest is created. An SLRequest object will do all of the legwork when working both with Social Framework and with the account-based approach. It provides a wrapper for communicating with supported third-party APIs. The service type is set to SLServiceTypeTwitter and a post method is selected. The previously determined URL is set, and finally the additional parameters are set to nil:

```
SLRequest *postRequest = [SLRequest requestForServiceType:SLServiceTypeTwitter
requestMethod:SLRequestMethodPOST URL:requestURL parameters:nil];
```

Before the SLRequest can be submitted to Twitter's servers, it must first have its metadata configured to provide information on the tweet text and any possible attachments. The specifications for the formatting of the tweet are taken from official Twitter API documentation. For specifics on API interaction, see https://dev.twitter.com/docs/api. The text of the tweet is encoded into NSData and submitted with the identifying name "status" of type "multipart/form-data".

```
NSString *text = [NSString stringWithFormat: @"I just abducted %0.0f cow(s) in UFOs for iPhone!",
score];
NSData *textData = [text dataUsingEncoding:NSUTF8StringEncoding];
[postRequest addMultipartData:textData withName:@"status" type:@"multipart/form-data" filename:nil];
```

If you want to provide an image attachment to the tweet, you may do so using the following approach. This will submit the image to Twitpic as part of the upload process:

```
NSData *imageData = UIImageJPEGRepresentation([UIImage imageNamed:@"Saucer1.png"], 1.0);
 [postRequest addMultipartData:imageData withName:@"media" type:@"image/jpg" filename:@"Image.jpg"];
```

Before the tweet can be submitted, the SLRequest needs to be informed which account the tweet will be sent to, because SLRequest supports posting to only one account at a time. This approach will also provide the user with a chance to see and modify the tweet before it is posted. We provide this information by setting the account property on the SLRequest to the Twitter account that was retrieved from the array retrieved earlier in this section:

```
postRequest.account = twitterAccount;
```

Once the account and metadata have been supplied, the tweet can be posted. The method performRequestWithHandler is called on the postRequest, and a block is provided for callbacks. In the event that the post was successfully submitted, the returning status code will be 200. Other error codes indicate an error; W3C (World Wide Web Consortium) maintains a standardized list of error codes and their meanings at http://www.w3.org/Protocols/rfc2616/rfc2616-sec10.html. Since the results are returned on a block, a convenience method is used to post the results to the user (Figure 12-6). Unlike the Composer, this method plays no sound for the user on success, nor is there any other indication that a tweet has been successfully posted.

Figure 12-6. Informing the user that a custom tweet has been posted successfully

```
[postRequest performRequestWithHandler:^(NSData *responseData, NSHTTPURLResponse *urlResponse,
NSError *error) {
    if (error != nil) {
        [self performSelectorOnMainThread:@selector(displayAlertWithString:) withObject:[NSString
stringWithFormat: @"An error occurred: %@", [error localizedDescription]] waitUntilDone:NO];
    }

    if ([urlResponse statusCode] == 200) {
        [self performSelectorOnMainThread:@selector(displayAlertWithString:) withObject:@"Tweet was
successfully posted" waitUntilDone:NO];
    }
}];
```

Going Further with Twitter

While posting to Twitter covers most of the functionality many games will need, there are times when your app may be required to pull down the user's friends list or access their timeline data. The SLRequest method provides access to these more advanced features. In this section both of these topics are briefly demonstrated.

In order to retrieve the user's last fifty posts, the following method can be implemented:

```
NSURL *requestURL = [NSURL URLWithString:@"http://api.twitter.com/1/statuses/home_timeline.json"];

NSDictionary *options = @{@"count" : @"50",@"include_entities" : @"1"};
SLRequest *postRequest = [SLRequest requestForServiceType:SLServiceTypeTwitter
requestMethod:SLRequestMethodGET URL:requestURL parameters:options];

postRequest.account = twitterAccount;
```

In order to retrieve a list of the user's friends, this method may be used:

```
NSURL *requestURL = [NSURL URLWithString:@"https://api.twitter.com/1.1/friends/list.json "];
SLRequest *postRequest = [SLRequest requestForServiceType:SLServiceTypeTwitter
requestMethod:SLRequestMethodGET URL:requestURL parameters:nil];

request.account = self.twitterAccount;
```

Working with Twitter on the API level allows complete access to the Twitter SDK. This direct access allows your app to interact with Twitter beyond just the posting of tweets. For example, the app may pull in a list of all the user's friends or download the user's avatar for use in your game.

An SLRequest is limited only by the ever-evolving third-party APIs that it interacts with. For more information on what can be done with SLRequest and Twitter, see the official Twitter API documentation at https://dev.twitter.com/docs/api.

Summary

In this chapter you learned about Social Framework as well as Accounts Framework and how they can both be leveraged to interact with the Twitter API. Posting using the built-in Tweet Composer was covered, as well as posting using a customized interface. Finally, we touched briefly on additional functionality that can be accomplished with SLRequest and the Twitter API, such as retrieving a friends list and timeline history. You should now be completely comfortable adding Twitter functionality to your next app or game. SLRequest continues to adapt to updates from the Twitter API, which means that even if a new version of iOS is not released, there may be new and exciting functionality available for social networking. In the next chapter we will explore the Facebook functionality, which expands upon the social networking knowledge you've gained in this chapter.

Facebook

"Think about what people are doing on Facebook today. They're keeping up with their friends and family, but they're also building an image and identity for themselves, which in a sense is their brand. They're connecting with the audience that they want to connect to. It's almost a disadvantage if you're not on it now."

—Mark Zuckerberg

Facebook, founded in February 2004, is the most popular social networking service in the Western world, with more than one billion active users. Facebook has become intertwined with modern society and culture, even spawning a big budget motion picture about its sordid history.

Facebook has been a fixture of mobile software since mobile began its popularity climb in 2007, beginning with a mobile version of its website and quickly transitioning into native services for every major platform. Facebook's APIs were available as early as iOS 2 and were originally called Facebook Connect. With the introduction of iOS 6, Facebook's API services became a built-in component of the iOS SDK. Facebook functionality was an expansion of the Social Framework originally introduced for iOS 5 to support Twitter.

UFOs

Starting with Chapter 12 and continuing through to the conclusion of this book, the sample code is not built upon the previous chapters. This project will be an extension of the Chapter 3 sample project; if you plan to follow along with the sample project, begin by modifying the Xcode project from that chapter.

Once the user has exited a game and achieved a final score, they will be prompted to choose whether to post that score to their Facebook wall, using either the built-in Composer or a programmatic API approach. The user will also have the option of not sharing their score and returning to the main menu view. In order to implement this change, the exitAction: method is modified to present the user with these options in the form of a UIAlert.

```
-(IBAction)exitAction:(id)sender;
{
    UIAlertView *alert = [[UIAlertView alloc]
    initWithTitle:@"Facebook Score" message:@"Do you want
    to post your score to your Facebook wall?"
    delegate:self cancelButtonTitle:@"Dismiss"
    otherButtonTitles:@"Facebook Composer", @"Custom Post",
    nil];

    [alert show];
    [alert release];
}
```

The alert view delegate is also configured to handle the callback containing the user's selection. If the user has opted not to share their score on Facebook, the score is submitted to Game Center and the user is returned to the main menu view.

```
- (void)alertView:(UIAlertView *)alertView didDismissWithButtonIndex:(NSInteger)buttonIndex
{
    //Facebook composer
    if(buttonIndex == 1)
    {

    }
    //custom post
    else if(buttonIndex == 2)
    {

    }

    else if(buttonIndex == 0)
    {
        [[self navigationController] popViewControllerAnimated: YES];
        [self.gcManager reportScore:score forCategory:@"com.dragonforged.ufo.single"];
    }
}
```

Facebook on iOS

When Twitter was announced as part of the Social Framework with iOS 5, there were a lot of raised eyebrows about why Facebook was not included as well. Apple rectified this problem with iOS 6. As in Twitter, Facebook settings are input from within Settings.app (Figure 13-1); there is no way for the user to log in directly from a third-party app. Facebook configuration also supports the syncing of Calendars and Contacts with their native equivalents on iOS. While Twitter allows a user to log into multiple accounts at once, as of iOS 7 Facebook allows only a single account to be linked at a given time.

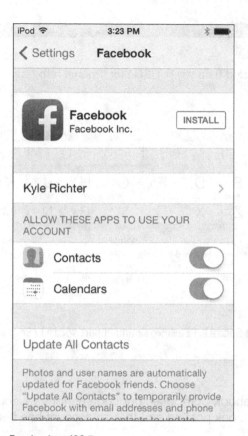

Figure 13-1. Configuration settings for Facebook on iOS 7

There are two systems in place for posting to Facebook from within your app using the Social Framework. The first is using `SLComposeViewController`, which is described in the section "Facebook Composer." This is the easiest system to implement, and the user will be presented with a standard, familiar interface. The second system involves using `SLRequest` to interact with the Facebook SDK directly; this approach is described in the sections "Facebook Permissions" and "Custom Facebook Posts." When dealing with `SLRequest` over the Composer, there are multiple layers of authentication and various pitfalls involved; on the other hand, the Composer does not need the user to supply any additional authentication or permission.

Facebook Composer

The Facebook Composer (Figure 13-2) is the easiest method of allowing a user to post information from your app to their Facebook wall. It provides options for selecting albums, setting location, attaching images, and specifying an audience with no additional configuration required. Additionally, it does not need the two extra permission requests that the `SLRequest` approach requires.

Figure 13-2. The Facebook Composer view

> **Note**   Don't forget to include `Social.Framework` and import `social/Social.h` before working with the
> Facebook Composer.

Prior to working with the Facebook Composer, our code performs a compatibility test to ensure
that the device supports Facebook posting and that an account has been properly set up and
logged into.

```
[SLComposeViewController isAvailableForServiceType:SLServiceTypeFacebook]
```

If this call returns NO, the most common reason is that the user has not set up a Facebook account
in Settings.app. Once it has been confirmed that everything is configured correctly for Facebook, a
new `SLComposeViewController` is created and its service type set to `SLServiceTypeFacebook`.

```
SLComposeViewController *facebookController = [SLComposeViewController
composeViewControllerForServiceType: SLServiceTypeFacebook];
```

A new block is created to handle the results of the Composer view. The sample project handles two
cases, cancelled and all other events. Under both cases the score is submitted to Game Center, and
the Composer view is dismissed.

```
  SLComposeViewControllerCompletionHandler myBlock = ^(SLComposeViewControllerResult result)
{
    if (result == SLComposeViewControllerResultCancelled)
    {
        NSLog(@"Facebook Controller Canceled");
    }

    else
    {
        NSLog(@"Facebook Controller Done");
    }

    [[self navigationController] popViewControllerAnimated: YES];

    [self.gcManager reportScore:score forCategory:@"com.dragonforged.ufo.single"];

    [facebookController dismissViewControllerAnimated:YES completion:nil];

};
```

The newly created block is set to the completionHandler property on the facebookController:

```
facebookController.completionHandler = myBlock;
```

There are a handful of attributes that can be supplied to appear in the Composer view, the first being the initial text that appears in the share controller. Keep in mind that the user will be able to go in and change these values before they post. An optional UIImage can also be attached to the post, which will appear as an uploaded image in Facebook. Finally, a URL can be added to the post, using the addURL: method.

```
[facebookController setInitialText:[NSString stringWithFormat: @"I just abducted %0.0f cow(s) in
UFOs for iPhone!", score]];
```

```
[facebookController addImage:[UIImage imageNamed:@"Cow1.png"]];
```

```
[facebookController addURL:[NSURL URLWithString:@"http://bit.ly/19ak0Uv"]];
```

Once the Composer view has been fully configured, it can be presented to the user with the following code snippet:

```
[self presentViewController:facebookController animated:YES completion:nil];
```

When the post has been successfully sent, it will play the standard outgoing email sound from iOS to let the user know the action has successfully completed. The result of this posting can be seen in Figure 13-3 as visible on the Facebook website.

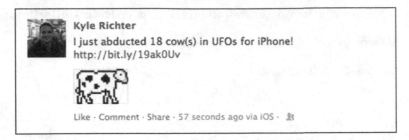

Figure 13-3. *The results of a Facebook Composer post viewed on the Facebook website*

Facebook Apps

Every app that should interact with the Facebook API needs to have an associated Facebook app. (If your app is using the previously described Facebook Composer approach, you will not need to create a dedicated Facebook app.) You create a new Facebook app through the Facebook Developer Portal (https://developers.facebook.com/apps), shown in Figure 13-4.

Figure 13-4. *Creating a new iOS app from the Facebook Developer Portal*

Once a Facebook App has been created, you will need to capture the App ID (Figure 13-5), as it will be used throughout the integration of Facebook to identify your app to the Facebook servers. Facebook will also supply an App Secret; this is not required when working with the Social Framework.

Figure 13-5. Configuring a Facebook App to work as a native iOS app, as required for the Social Framework

> **Note**   Make sure the Bundle ID under the Native iOS App section matches the Bundle ID found in the
> `info.plist` of the iOS app.

Facebook Permissions

Facebook has a stacked system of permissions for accessing and posting data. This means that in order to access high-level permissions like posting, you first need lower-level permissions such as reading.

The first set of permissions that needs to be requested are the general profile read permissions, which allow the app to read basic user profile info such as name, email, and friends list. There is an additional permission needed to read wall posts, and even more permissions are required to make a post.

To add to the complexity, basic read permissions need to be authorized before additional permissions can be requested. It is not possible to group all permissions together into a single call. The result of this is that to post to the user's timeline, two separate permissions need to be requested.

> **Note**   Throughout this sample project, the Facebook ID for UFOs (165243936994502) is used; make sure that this value is correctly changed to the Facebook ID for your app during development.

The first set of permissions that is requested is the basic profile reading access group. Requesting any of the basic attribute fields will grant access to the entire basic profile. In the following example the email property is requested. Once a user has approved reading the email property, the app will also gain access to read all basic profile info as well as the friends list.

A new ACAccountStore will need to be allocated and initialized, and a new ACAccountType with the identifier ACAccountTypeIdentifierFacebook is created. This will inform the API that you will be working with a Facebook account.

An options dictionary is created next; it will contain three key/value pairs. The first is the audience key; while the value is not crucial for this step, since we aren't posting new data, we specify ACFacebookAudienceEveryone. The next value is the App ID, which was established in the previous section by creating a new Facebook app. The final pair represents the permission name that is requested, which will be email in the example project.

```
ACAccountStore *accountStore = [[ACAccountStore alloc] init];
ACAccountType *facebookAccountType = [accountStore
accountTypeWithAccountTypeIdentifier:ACAccountTypeIdentifierFacebook];

NSDictionary *options = @{
                    ACFacebookAudienceKey : ACFacebookAudienceEveryone,
                    ACFacebookAppIdKey : @"165243936994502",
                    ACFacebookPermissionsKey : @[@"email"]};
```

Once the parameters have been configured, the call can be executed:

```
[accountStore requestAccessToAccountsWithType:facebookAccountType options:options
completion:^(BOOL granted, NSError *error){}];
```

The user will then be prompted to grant basic profile access for your app, as seen in Figure 13-6.

Figure 13-6. UFOs requesting basic profile access to a Facebook account

Since basic permissions need to first be granted before the app can request additional permissions, the request for publish-to-stream permission can be requested in response to the user granting access to the basic profile. Modify the previous block from the basic permission request to allow for publishing to the user's stream, as seen in the following code sample.

```
[accountStore requestAccessToAccountsWithType:facebookAccountType options:options
completion:^(BOOL granted, NSError *error)
{
    if (granted)
    {
        NSLog(@"Basic access granted");

        NSDictionary *secondOptions = @{
                                        ACFacebookAudienceKey :
ACFacebookAudienceEveryone,
                                        ACFacebookAppIdKey :
@"165243936994502",
                                        ACFacebookPermissionsKey :
@[@"publish_stream"]};

        [accountStore requestAccessToAccountsWithType:facebookAccountType options:secondOptions
        completion:^(BOOL granted, NSError *error)
        {
            if (granted)
            {
                NSLog(@"Extended access granted");

                NSArray *accounts = [accountStore accountsWithAccountType:facebookAccountType];
                self.facebookAccount = [accounts lastObject];

                [self performSelectorOnMainThread:@selector(postFromFacebook) withObject:nil
                waitUntilDone:NO];
            }
```

```
        else
        {
            [self performSelectorOnMainThread:@selector(displayAlertWithString:)
withObject:error
            waitUntilDone:NO];
        }
    }];

}
else
{
    NSLog(@"Basic access denied: %@", [error localizedDescription]);
}}];
```

Once basic access has been granted, a second request is created in the same way as the initial permission request, with a single change. Instead of requesting email access, we will request access to publish_stream; this will allow your app to post on behalf of the user. The remainder of the code handles failures and informs the user; remember that UIAlerts cannot be displayed from a block, so they will need to be called on the main thread. Once the user has granted access for your app the first time, they will not need to do so again unless they specifically remove permissions at a later time.

Custom Facebook Posts

Once permission has been granted to publish to the user's stream a custom post can be made. There are many circumstances where it may be necessary to post to Facebook from a custom interface.

Using the Accounts framework discussed in Chapter 12, with the user's permission you can make post on their behalf with your own interface or even with no interface at all. The Accounts approach is more complex that the Facebook Composer but allows much more freedom.

Note   Make sure to include Accounts.framework and import accounts/Accounts.h when working with custom status updates.

Because an ACAccount object was created when asking for permission, a new object does not need to be created; however, you will need a pointer to the account that was created while requesting permissions. As Twitter did in Chapter 12, Facebook requires a different feed URL depending on whether the status update contains media such as images or videos or if it contains only text. When you post status updates that do not contain an image, the URL should be set to https://graph.facebook.com/me/feed. Otherwise, the URL needs to be set to https://graph.facebook.com/me/photos. Posting to the wrong URL will result in failure.

```
BOOL attachedImage = YES;
NSURL *feedURL = nil;

if(attachedImage)
{
    feedURL = [NSURL URLWithString:
    @"https://graph.facebook.com/me/photos"];
}

else
{
    feedURL = [NSURL URLWithString:
    @"https://graph.facebook.com/me/feed"];
}
```

Once the proper URL has been determined, the text for the message can be set. This is done as part of the parameter dictionary. A new key named message is created, and its value is set to the text that will be posted:

```
NSDictionary *parameters = [NSDictionary dictionaryWithObject:[NSString stringWithFormat: @"I just
abducted %0.0f cow(s) in UFOs for iPhone!", score] forKey:@"message"];
```

A new SLRequest object is created. The SLRequest object will contain all the information required for interacting with the Facebook API and provides a networking wrapper for those calls. The service type is specified as SLServiceTypeFacebook, and the requestMethod is set to POST. The URL is set to the previously established URL, depending on whether there is a media attachment, and finally the parameters that were previously created are set:

```
SLRequest *feedRequest = [SLRequest
            requestForServiceType:SLServiceTypeFacebook
                requestMethod:SLRequestMethodPOST
                    URL:feedURL
                parameters:parameters];
```

If the status update contains an attached image file, that image file will also need to be specified. The image data is first converted to NSData in the form of a PNG representation. It is then added to the SLRequest through the addMultipartData: method. When adding an image, make sure the withName and type values appear exactly as they are in the following code snippet. The filename property can be customized to help identify the image.

```
if(attachedImage)
{
    NSData *imageData = UIImagePNGRepresentation([UIImage
    imageNamed:@"Saucer1.png"]);

    [feedRequest addMultipartData:imageData
     withName:@"source" type:@"multipart/form-data"
     filename:@"Image"];
}
```

The account property of the SLRequest needs to be set to the previously authenticated account from the section "Facebook Permissions."

```
feedRequest.account = self.facebookAccount;
```

Once the SLRequest has been completely configured, it can then be sent to Facebook's servers for processing and posting. To post to Facebook, call performRequestWithHandler on the SLRequest object. If the message is successfully handled by Facebook, it will return a status code of 200. Any other status code indicates a failure; a full list of possible HTTP response status codes can be found at http://www.w3.org/Protocols/rfc2616/rfc2616-sec10.html.

```
[feedRequest performRequestWithHandler:^(NSData *responseData,
                                         NSHTTPURLResponse *urlResponse, NSError *error)
{
    NSLog(@"Facebook post statusCode: %u", [urlResponse statusCode]);
    if([urlResponse statusCode] == 200)
    {
        [self performSelectorOnMainThread:@selector(displayAlertWithString:) withObject:@"Your
        message has been posted to Facebook" waitUntilDone:NO];
    }
    else if(error != nil)
    {
        [self performSelectorOnMainThread:@selector(displayAlertWithString:) withObject:error
        waitUntilDone:NO];
    }
}];
```

The framework does not provide any kind of user feedback upon a successful posting. The example app provides the user with a UIAlert that informs them if the post was successful or describes the error if one occurred. The result of a custom Facebook post can be seen in Figure 13-7 as it appears on the Facebook website. Note that the "posted via" line reflects the app name set in the Facebook Developers Portal, while using the Composer simply states "via iOS."

Figure 13-7. The result of a custom Facebook posting as seen from the Facebook website

Going Further with Facebook

Posting information to a user's wall will cover the use cases of most games, whether it is posting a score, sharing a link to the game, or bragging about a reward. However, Facebook is a huge social platform, which can handle many types of requests.

For example, if you wanted to retrieve the user's feed you could implement an SLRequest in the following format. The Facebook Timeline is returned as a JSON object, which is displayed in the console.

```
NSURL *feedURL = [NSURL URLWithString:@"https://graph.facebook.com/me/feed"];

SLRequest *feedRequest = [SLRequest
                          requestForServiceType:SLServiceTypeFacebook
                          requestMethod:SLRequestMethodGET
                          URL:feedURL
                          parameters:nil];

    feedRequest.account = self.facebookAccount;

    [feedRequest performRequestWithHandler:^(NSData *responseData,
                                     NSHTTPURLResponse *urlResponse, NSError *error)
     {

    NSLog(@"Facebook post statusCode: %u", [urlResponse statusCode]);

    if([urlResponse statusCode] == 200)
    {
        NSLog(@"Facebook Timeline: [[NSJSONSerialization JSONObjectWithData:responseData
        options:NSJSONReadingMutableLeaves error:&error] objectForKey:@"data"]);
    }
}];
```

There is a lot of flexibility and functionality in the Facebook API, and it is updated more frequently than the iOS SDK. SLRequest is a transparent wrapper class for interacting with the Facebook API, so any changes that Facebook makes will be immediately available to you. A full list of functions for Facebook can be found on its developer site at https://developers.facebook.com/docs/reference/api/.

Summary

This chapter introduced the Facebook functionality added in iOS 6. We began with a background in Facebook and an explanation of how it integrates into the core system, and moved into interacting with the Facebook API. We also covered the Facebook Composer, walking through the process of quickly and easily adding Facebook posting support to your app. Finally, the chapter demonstrated the process of creating a Facebook app through the developer portal and requesting the required permissions to read and post to a user's timeline.

You should now be entirely comfortable with posting status updates to Facebook using either the built-in Composer or a custom interface. You should also now have a firm understanding of using the Facebook API to implement more advanced features.

AirPlay

AirPlay, introduced as part of iOS 4.3 and greatly enhanced in iOS 5.0, allows for the sharing of audio or visual information with compatible devices. These devices are most commonly the Apple TV for video and audio and AirPlay-enabled sound systems for music playback.

This chapter will cover working with AirPlay audio as well as handling mirroring and second-screen technology. Starting with iOS 5.0, AirPlay buttons are available on any video or audio playback on your app using `MPMoviePlayerController` or `UIWebViews`.

Apple has made AirPlay one of the easiest technologies to use on the iOS platform. Under most circumstances supporting AirPlay in your apps will require no additional code, and even in the most complex circumstances AirPlay will require only a few lines of code.

AirPlay for Built-In Players

Three classes natively support AirPlay output: `AVPlayer`, `MPMoviePlayerController`, and `UIWebView`. AirPlay is on by default when playing media content; however, for copyright or other reasons it may be necessary to modify this default behavior.

An `AVPlayer` object has a property `allowsAirPlayVideo`, which accepts a Boolean value to determine whether it presents the controls for AirPlay output. Likewise, the `MPMoviePlayerController` class has a similar property, named `allowsAirPlay`. Finally, a `UIWebView` uses the property `mediaPlaybackAllowsAirPlay`. When disabling or enabling AirPlay in a `UIWebview`, be mindful of the content, which can specifically disable AirPlay.

> **Note** AirPlay does not work in the iOS Simulator; additionally, the AirPlay controls will show up only when a local AirPlay device, such as an Apple TV, is available.

MPNowPlayingInfoCenter

Many AirPlay-enabled sound systems support metadata for the currently playing item; this is often an LCD display that shows information such as song name and artist. AirPlay allows this information to be set using the `MPNowPlayingInfoCenter` class; this metadata can be set for display where applicable.

```
MPNowPlayingInfoCenter *center = [MPNowPlayingInfoCenter defaultCenter];

NSDictionary *songInfo = [NSDictionary dictionaryWithObjectsAndKeys:
@"Counting Crows", MPMediaItemPropertyArtist,
@"Rain King", MPMediaItemPropertyTitle,
@"August and Everything After", MPMediaItemPropertyAlbumTitle, nil];

center.nowPlayingInfo = songInfo;
```

The physical device handling the playback determines which items are shown on its display; however, the `MPNowPlayingInfoCenter` class provides optional values for several items, which are detailed in Table 14-1.

Table 14-1. Available Constants for `MPNowPlayingInfoCenter` When Setting Metadata

Constant	Description
MPMediaItemPropertyAlbumTitle	An NSString representing the name of the album.
MPMediaItemPropertyAlbumTrackCount	An NSNumber representing the total number of tracks.
MPMediaItemPropertyAlbumTrackNumber	An NSNumber representing the current track number.
MPMediaItemPropertyArtist	An NSString representing the name of the artist.
MPMediaItemPropertyArtwork	An instance of MPMediaItemArtwork representing the artwork for the item that is playing.
MPMediaItemPropertyComposer	An NSString representing the name of the composer.
MPMediaItemPropertyDiscCount	An NSNumber representing the total number of discs.
MPMediaItemPropertyDiscNumber	An NSNumber representing the current disc number.
MPMediaItemPropertyGenre	An NSString representing the name of the genre.
MPMediaItemPropertyPersistentID	An NSNumber which indicates the item being played. This identifier persist across launches, but may be reset when syncing.
MPMediaItemPropertyPlaybackDuration	An NSNumber representing a NSTimeInterval in seconds for the current playback duration.
MPMediaItemPropertyTitle	An NSString representing the name of the item being played, such as the filename.

Responding to Remote Events

When AirPlay is playing back media, it is very likely that the device handling output of the media can also accept user input such as changing tracks, pausing, skipping, or scanning. It is important that your app responds to and properly handles these events. Your app must first make the OS aware that it is interested in receiving these notifications; this can be done by calling beginRecievingRemoteControlEvents on the UIApplication singleton:

```
[[UIApplication sharedApplication] beginReceivingRemoteControlEvents];
```

It is also important to remember to stop receiving notifications when your app is no longer interested in them; to do this, call another method, endReceivingRemoteControlEvents, as shown here:

```
[[UIApplication sharedApplication] endReceivingRemoteControlEvents];
```

There are twelve types of events that your app can be notified about. When these events occur, a call to remoteControlReceivedWithEvent: is processed. The following example shows how to handle some of these events:

```
- (void) remoteControlReceivedWithEvent: (UIEvent *) receivedEvent
{
    if (receivedEvent.type == UIEventTypeRemoteControl)
    {
        switch (receivedEvent.subtype)
        {
            case UIEventSubtypeRemoteControlPlay:
                [self play];
                break;

            case UIEventSubtypeRemoteControlPause:
                [self pause];
                break;

            case UIEventSubtypeRemoteControlNextTrack:
                [self nextTrack];
                break;

            case UIEventSubtypeRemoteControlPreviousTrack:
                [self previousTrack];
                break;
        }
    }
}
```

Enabling AirPlay in an App

If your app is not using one of the three supported AirPlay classes, you can still present the user with AirPlay options. To show the AirPlay device picker, use the MPVolumeView class. In the following code snippet the volume slider bar is hidden to show just the device picker; however, there is no requirement to hide the volume slider. The results can be seen in Figure 14-1.

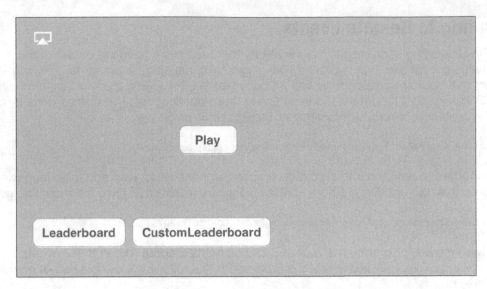

Figure 14-1. Enabling an AirPlay picker, seen in the upper left corner, by using the `MPVolumeView` *class*

```
MPVolumeView *volumeView = [[MPVolumeView alloc] initWithFrame:
CGRectMake(15, 15, 0, 0)];

[volumeView setShowsVolumeSlider:NO];
[self.view addSubview: volumeView];
[volumeView release];
```

> **Note**   To use AirPlay classes, the app must first import the required Media Player headers by using `#import`
> `<MediaPlayer/MediaPlayer.h>` as well as the MediaPlayer.Framework.
>
> System sounds such as keyboard clicks and alert noises are not sent through AirPlay speakers; if your app is
> using system sounds in a significant manner, they should be played as part of your app's normal audio to be
> sent with AirPlay.

AirPlay Mirroring

As of iOS 7, an app cannot enable AirPlay Mirroring on its own and must use the system tools in order to enable it. However, no additional development needs to be done in order to enable mirroring.

In iOS 7, bring up the control panel by swiping up from the bottom of the screen and select the AirPlay button. You will be given the option of selecting an AirPlay-enabled device. If the device supports AirPlay Mirroring (such as an Apple TV), you will be presented with a toggle switch to enable it (Figure 14-2). iOS 6 users should double-tap the Home button and swipe left in the fast app switcher to arrive on the playback controls, where another swipe to the right will bring up the AirPlay Controls, and you will be able to turn on AirPlay Mirroring.

Figure 14-2. Enabling AirPlay Mirroring on iOS 7 through the Control Center

AirPlay for a Second Screen

It may be prudent for your app to display different content on the iOS device and the AirPlay device. While the user will still need to turn on AirPlay monitoring as described in the previous section, you can display entirely different content for each screen. First a test can be performed to determine if the second screen is available.

```
if ([[UIScreen screens] count] > 1)
```

A reference to the second screen needs to be set up, and a new window must be created. Each screen needs to have a dedicated window available to it:

```
UIScreen *secondScreen = [[UIScreen screens] objectAtIndex:1];

CGRect screenBounds = secondScreen.bounds;
UIWindow * secondWindow = [[UIWindow alloc] initWithFrame:screenBounds];

secondWindow.screen = secondScreen;
```

The new window is by default hidden; to view the window on the external display we must first set its hidden property to NO:

```
secondWindow.hidden = NO;
```

If this code were run now, the AirPlay screen would show a blank, black view, because the second window doesn't have any views to display. Using UFOs as an example, we can present the game data to the second screen. Modify the existing playButtonPressed method to match the following:

```
-(IBAction)playButtonPressed
{
    if([self checkForExistingScreenAndInitializeIfPresent])
    {
        //Using second screen
    }

    else
    {
        gameViewController = [[UFOGameViewController alloc]  init];
        gameViewController.gcManager = gcManager;
        [self.navigationController pushViewController: gameViewController animated:YES];
    }
}
```

A new method will also need to be added to detect and set up the second screen; this method is titled checkForExistingScreenAndInitializeIfPresent and returns a Boolean YES if a second screen is detected. If there is no second screen, the game will continue using the single-screen approach. This method follows the approach just shown for detecting and displaying a second window. In addition, a new button is created to handle the firing of the tractor beam on the AirPlay screen; it's needed because the AirPlay screen doesn't support touch events. The tractor beam events are handled by calling the touchesBegan and touchesEnded methods of the game controller. The UFOGameViewController is also created, and its view is added to the second window.

```
- (bool)checkForExistingScreenAndInitializeIfPresent
{
    if ([[UIScreen screens] count] > 1)
    {
        UIScreen *secondScreen = [[UIScreen screens] objectAtIndex:1];

        CGRect screenBounds = secondScreen.bounds;
        UIWindow * secondWindow = [[UIWindow alloc] initWithFrame:screenBounds];
        secondWindow.screen = secondScreen;

        UIButton *button = [UIButton buttonWithType:UIButtonTypeRoundedRect];
        [button addTarget:self action:@selector(fire)
        forControlEvents:UIControlEventTouchDown];

        [button addTarget:self action:@selector(fireStop)
        forControlEvents:UIControlEventTouchUpInside | UIControlEventTouchUpOutside];
```

```
    [button setTitle:@"Fire!" forState:UIControlStateNormal];
    button.frame = CGRectMake(80.0, 180.0, 160.0, 40.0);
    [self.view addSubview:button];

    secondWindow.hidden = NO;

    gameViewController = [[UFOGameViewController alloc] init];
    gameViewController.view.frame = screenBounds;
    gameViewController.gcManager = gcManager;
    [secondWindow addSubview:gameViewController.view];


    return YES;
}

    return NO;
}
```

It is important to remember that Apple TV displays may not conform to the normal screen sizes you may expect, and app elements need to be set up to detect the bounds that they are appearing in and scale accordingly. The result of displaying UFOs to an Apple TV hooked up to a widescreen LCD TV can be seen in Figure 14-3.

Figure 14-3. UFOs running on a widescreen TV through an Apple TV using AirPlay

Responding to Screen Notifications

It may be necessary to detect the connection and disconnection of external AirPlay screens. Apple provides a set of notifications that can handle these events and inform your app for proper handling. To register for these notifications, implement the following code:

```
[[NSNotificationCenter defaultCenter] addObserver:self selector:@selector
(handleScreenDidConnectNotification:) name:UIScreenDidConnectNotification object:nil];

[[NSNotificationCenter defaultCenter] addObserver:self selector:@selector
(handleScreenDidDisconnectNotification:) name:UIScreenDidDisconnectNotification object:nil];
```

When a screen is disconnected or connected, the app should create and remove the displayed UIScreen as required. As the developer, you are solely responsible for cleaning up the second window when it is not being used.

Summary

This chapter covered all things AirPlay. Although AirPlay is a fairly simple and limited topic, this feature can add a unique element to your game. Most developers have not yet implemented custom AirPlay gaming elements into their products, and there is a definite demand for them. Apple announced in early 2013 that it had sold 13 million Apple TVs. Being one of the first developers to support and understand what AirPlay can add to a product will put you in a powerful position when Apple moves the Apple TV from a hobby into a mainstream product.

Game Controllers

I cannot trust a man to control others who cannot control himself.

—Robert E. Lee

iOS Game Controllers were announced at the Apple Worldwide Developers Conference (WWDC) 2013 as part of iOS 7, in response to one of the chief complaints that had arisen after the launch of the iPhone in 2007 and the arrival of iPhone gaming in 2008: the lack of tactile feedback. Focusing on the screen while not being able to feel where gaming controls were proved difficult. While there have been many third-party solutions, ranging from stickers placed on the iPhone screens to Bluetooth controllers, there has not, until now, been a universal method of gaming input.

The primary issue had been that every game needed to support every type of game controller, all of which used different protocols. This resulted in a cluster of devices, each of which supported only a handful of games. Apple was the only company that could implement and enforce standards, and that is exactly what it did in iOS 7. The new hardware would all conform to a universal protocol, freeing developers to focus on the software instead of device support. If your game supports one game controller, it will support them all.

This chapter and associated source code was written before any game controller had yet reached the consumer markets, although the ads for controllers were beginning to surface (Figure 15-1). While every effort has been taken to ensure that the technical material discussed is accurate, it is impossible to ensure that when faced with production hardware the game will behave as expected.

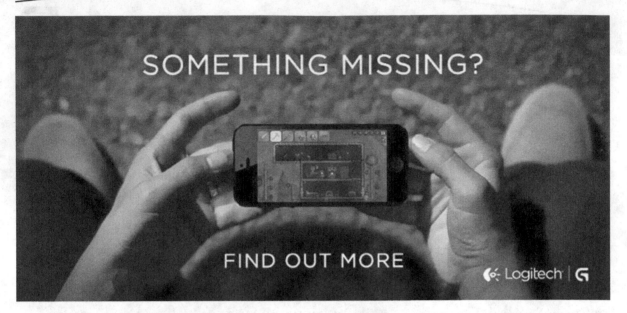

Figure 15-1. The first ad by Logitech for the new iOS 7 physical game controllers

Types of Game Controllers

There are two general types of game controllers, standard and extended. These may also be made available in wired (dock connector) or wireless (Bluetooth) models. Regardless of other physical and layout differences, all controllers will conform to the same types of input. It is important to note that extended controllers have more input controls than standard controllers.

Standard controllers feature a directional D-pad, four primary buttons (A, B, X, and Y), two shoulder buttons (left and right), and a Pause button. Extended controllers feature all the buttons found on the standard controller as well as a second set of shoulder buttons and two directional thumb sticks. Wireless controllers also feature a player indicator LED, which has four positions.

> **Note**   While a game controller can add a lot of functionality to your iOS game, it is important to remember that it must be optional. In addition to any game controller support, the game must also provide all the required functionality through the touch screen or accelerometer.

While several companies have announced iOS game controllers, as of October 2013 none had yet made it to the consumer market. During the announcement of support for game controllers in iOS 7, Apple stated that the first hardware would be making its way into the public's hands during the fall of 2013.

Connecting to Game Controllers

When a nonwireless (dock connector) controller is connected to a device, it is automatically detected. To detect a wireless controller, however, the app must specifically begin looking for one. The sample app adds a new button in the upper-left corner of the menu screen to toggle searching for a wireless controller, as shown in Figure 15-2.

Figure 15-2. Adding a button for Find Wireless Controller to the existing UFO main screen

> **Note**   Prior to making any Game Controller–specific calls, you will first need to import the
> GameController.Framework into your project and include the Game Controller/GCController.h
> header. Remember that game controllers are available only on iOS 7 and greater.

A new action is created for the Find Wireless Controller button. When the user first taps the button, the class method startWirelessControllerDiscoveryWithCompletionHandler is invoked. The second toggle will end the search process with the class method stopWirelessControllerDiscovery.

```
- (IBAction)findWirelessController:(id)sender
{
    findingWirelessController = !findingWirelessController;

    if(findingWirelessController)
    {
        [GCController startWirelessControllerDiscoveryWithCompletionHandler:^{
            NSLog(@"Wireless controller searching has finished");
        }];
    }
```

```
else
{
    [GCController stopWirelessControllerDiscovery];
    NSLog(@"Wireless controller stopped by user");
}

}
```

When a new controller is detected, whether it is wireless or physically connected, a notification is fired, GCControllerDidConnectNotification. This notification and the partner notification for a game controller being disconnected should be registered at the first chance possible. In the sample project we do this in the viewDidLoad: method of the UFOViewController class:

```
[[NSNotificationCenter defaultCenter] addObserver:self selector:@selector(setupControllers:)
name:GCControllerDidConnectNotification object:nil];

[[NSNotificationCenter defaultCenter] addObserver:self selector:@selector(setupControllers:)
name:GCControllerDidDisconnectNotification object:nil];
```

> **Note**   When a controller is disconnected, it is recommended that the game automatically pause to allow the player to either correct the issue with the controller or return to touch-based game play. Do not forget to test disconnecting controllers during game play as part of the quality assurance process.

Upon receiving either of these notifications, our code calls a new setup Controllers: method This method allows the app to keep track of which controllers are connected at any given time, as there may be more than one. The game controllers are available via the controllers method on the GCController object; this method will return an array of all the connected controllers. The value of the controller array is also saved to an array property for later use in the sample app.

```
-(void)setupControllers:(NSNotification *)notif
{
    self.gameControllerArray = [GCController controllers];

    if([gameControllerArray count] > 0)
    {
        NSLog(@"Game Controllers Found: %i",
        [gameControllerArray count]);
    }

    else
    {
        NSLog(@"No game controllers found");
    }
}
```

> **Note** It is possible for the controllers to be detected before the notification is set up, so it is important to check the contents of the controller array when the notification is added to determine if there are any currently connected controllers.

As a typical example, the user launches an app before the game controller is connected. The app has already registered for game controllers being connected, and the notifications described in this section are fired.

A counter example would be if the user already has the game controller connected before launching the app. In this case the notification is not fired, because the game controller was not connected after the notification was configured. In this case the developer should manually test for any connected game controllers.

Reading Data Through Polling

Once a controller has been connected to a device, the input from that controller needs to be read. In the UFOs sample app, accelerometer data is read every 0.05 seconds. Since not all users will have access to game controllers, this behavior will still be needed even after adding game controller support. This makes the accelerometer polling method ideal for reading data from the game controller. If your game doesn't have an existing loop that can be tied into, a simple `NSTimer` can be set up. Modify the existing `motionOccurred:` method in UFOs to add game controller functionality.

First the game must determine if the player is using a game controller. It does this by determining if the device is currently connected to any game controllers; in your own applications you may want to provide the user with an option. In the event that more than one game controller is connected, the last one in the array is used. In your own apps it may also be beneficial to allow the user to select which controller they intend to use. A new `Controller` object is created, and the last controller in the array is stored into it.

The UFOs game has two primary functions. The first begins the tractor beam action, and the second moves the ship from location to location on the screen. For the purposes of the demo, the Y button on the controller will be used to engage the tractor beam. Since the tractor beam remains on as long as the button is held down, we create a `bool` to keep track of when the button is currently pressed. The action from the button is simply passed to the `touchesBegan:` method, which is the same method that controls the tractor beam when handling touch events. The benefit of this approach is that the touch events will still work even with a controller connected. Since both standard and extended game controllers have a Y button, there is no specific code required to handle the different controllers.

With a standard controller, the D-pad will be used for movement. However, the thumb directional pads on the extended game controller make for a better experience when controlling the ship, so the app will use those when available. The property `extendedGamePad` controls this choice; if this value is non-nil, then an extended controller is hooked up.

Like the A, B, X, and Y buttons, the D-pad values can be accessed via a property on the GCController object. However, the D-pad returns a float value of 0.0 to 1.0 for the X and Y axes. This value can be used in place of the accelerometer value used when a game controller is not hooked up. The process of hooking up the values for the extended game controller's thumb stick is nearly identical, but the values are stored under extendedGamepad instead of the root gamepad property.

```
-(void)motionOccurred:(CMAccelerometerData *)accelerometerData;
{
    bool gameControllerBeingUsed = NO;
    GCController *myController = nil;

    if([parentViewController.gameControllerArray count] > 0)
    {
        gameControllerBeingUsed = YES;

        myController = [parentViewController.gameControllerArray lastObject];
    }

    if(gameControllerBeingUsed == YES)
    {
        //Testing for button press
        if(myController.gamepad.buttonY.pressed && gameControllerYHit == NO)
        {
            gameControllerYHit = YES;
            [self touchesBegan:nil withEvent:nil];
        }

        if(!myController.gamepad.buttonY.pressed && gameControllerYHit == YES)
        {
            gameControllerYHit = NO;
            [self touchesEnded:nil withEvent:nil];
        }

        //no extended gamepad
        if(myController.extendedGamepad == nil)
        {
            accel[0] = myController.gamepad.dpad.xAxis.value * accelerometerDamp +
            accel[0] * (1.0 - accelerometerDamp);
            accel[1] = myController.gamepad.dpad.yAxis.value * accelerometerDamp +
            accel[1] * (1.0 - accelerometerDamp);
        }

        //extended gamepad
        else
        {
            GCExtendedGamepad *extendedGamePadProfile = myController.extendedGamepad;

            accel[0] = extendedGamePadProfile.leftThumbstick.xAxis.value * accelerometerDamp +
            accel[0] * (1.0 - accelerometerDamp);
            accel[1] = extendedGamePadProfile.leftThumbstick.yAxis.value * accelerometerDamp +
            accel[1] * (1.0 - accelerometerDamp);
```

```
        }
    }

    else
    {
        //Use a basic low-pass filter to keep only the gravity in the accelerometer values
        accel[0] = accelerometerData.acceleration.x * accelerometerDamp + accel[0] *
        (1.0 - accelerometerDamp);
        accel[1] = accelerometerData.acceleration.y * accelerometerDamp + accel[1] *
        (1.0 - accelerometerDamp);
        accel[2] = accelerometerData.acceleration.z * accelerometerDamp + accel[2] *
        (1.0 - accelerometerDamp);

        if(!tractorBeamOn)
            [self movePlayer:accel[0] :accel[1]];
    }
}
```

> **Note**   The 0.0 value is determined when the D-pad and thumb sticks are at rest. Before the Game Controller framework, developers found it necessary to design a "dead zone" around the at-rest positions; this is no longer necessary, and any value above 0.0 should be considered intended movement.

Data Callbacks

There are many circumstances where it doesn't make sense to poll for game controller input each time the game loop cycles. Luckily, Apple has provided functionality for callbacks that can be set upon a value change on any physical button on a game controller. In the following snippet a handler is set for the right shoulder button. When the button value is changed, this method will call the rightShoulderButtonAction.

```
myController.gamepad.rightShoulder.valueChangedHandler = ^(GCControllerButtonInput *button, float
value, BOOL pressed))
    {
        if(pressed)
            [self rightShoulderButtonAction];
    };
```

In addition to setting up a callback per action, you can share the callback across multiple buttons at once. To do this, create a new block and set it up as shown in the following code snippet. Any action on the A, B, X, or Y button will then cause the log statement to be printed.

```
void(^buttonHandler)(GCControllerButtonInput *, float, BOOL) = ^(GCControllerButtonInput
*button, float value, BOOL pressed)
{
    NSLog(@"Handle action for %@ pressed: %i, with value: %f", button, pressed, value);
};
```

```
myController.gamepad.buttonA.valueChangedHandler = buttonHandler;
myController.gamepad.buttonB.valueChangedHandler = buttonHandler;
myController.gamepad.buttonX.valueChangedHandler = buttonHandler;
myController.gamepad.buttonY.valueChangedHandler = buttonHandler;
```

It is also possible to set up data callbacks for dealing with changing axis values with the D-pad or thumb sticks. To do so, use the following code snippet:

```
myController.extendedGamepad.rightThumbstick.valueChangedHandler = ^(GCControllerDirectionPad
*dpad, float xValue, float yValue)
{
    NSLog(@"Right Thumb Stick value did change: %f, %f", xValue, yValue);

};
```

Pausing

If your game supports game controllers, it must also support the Pause button that is found on all game controllers. Even if your game did not previously support Pause, doing so becomes a requirement of having a game controller connected. Working with the Pause button on a game controller is very simple and requires only a couple of extra lines of code:

```
myController.controllerPausedHandler = ^(GCController *controller)
 {
    [self togglePauseState];
 };
```

Player Indicator Lights

Wireless game controllers also feature player indicator lights, as the Game Controller framework supports connecting multiple controllers to a single device. Your game can support multiplayer functionality using a single device through additional wireless controllers. Each wireless controller will feature four LED lights, which will indicate the player number. These lights are also used to let the user know they have successfully connected a wireless controller, even in single-player mode. The following code illuminates the first light of the wireless controller, letting the player know they are successfully connected:

```
if(myController.playerIndex == GCControllerPlayerIndexUnset)
{
        myController.playerIndex = 0;
}
```

The playerIndex property can also be used to illuminate other player index values, from 0 to 3. Only one player indicator light can be toggled on at a time per controller.

Snapshotting

It may become necessary to create a snapshot of the controller input state. This can be useful not only for debugging but also for creating playback profiles or sending the controller data over a network. Snapshots are stored through an NSData representation, as shown here:

```
GCGamepadSnapshot *snapshot = [myController.gamepad saveSnapshot];
NSData *snapshotData = snapshot.snapshotData;
```

One of the benefits of a GCGamePadSnapshot is that it conforms as a subclass of GCGamePad, so reading the data from it will not require any changes to your game logic.

Summary

In this chapter you learned about the Game Controller functionality of iOS 7, from the requirements of the framework to connecting and reading data. This chapter also covered topics such as pausing, player indicator lights, and snapshotting data. While these APIs are very new and the hardware is not yet available, they open up a world of possibilities for mobile gaming. Never before has there been a standardized input method for game controllers for the iPhone and iPod. The addition of the Game Controller framework is a large validation from Apple of the continuing trend of iOS gaming and is the first step into these devices becoming the primary gaming machine of the next generation. If you happen to be a Mac developer as well, the wireless game controllers will also function for Mac-based games using the same code and practices discussed in this chapter.

Index

I, J, K

U

Get the eBook for only $10!

Now you can take the weightless companion with you anywhere, anytime. Your purchase of this book entitles you to 3 electronic versions for only $10.

This Apress title will prove so indispensible that you'll want to carry it with you everywhere, which is why we are offering the eBook in **3 formats** for only $10 if you have already purchased the print book.

Convenient and fully searchable, the PDF version enables you to easily find and copy code—or perform examples by quickly toggling between instructions and applications. The MOBI format is ideal for your Kindle, while the ePUB can be utilized on a variety of mobile devices.

Go to www.apress.com/promo/tendollars to purchase your companion eBook.

Apress®
THE EXPERT'S VOICE™